S0-AYR-674

DISCARDED BY THE LEVI
HEYWOOD MEMORIAL LIBRARY

LEVI HEYWOOD MEMORIAL LIBRARY

GARDNER, MASS.

Class B Ro.   No.

BY HOMER CROY

Fiction

WEST OF THE WATER TOWER

THEY HAD TO SEE PARIS
    (made into a motion picture with Will Rogers as star)

SIXTEEN HANDS
    (made into a motion picture under the title *I'm from Missouri*)

FAMILY HONEYMOON
    (made into a motion picture)

Fact

COUNTRY CURED
    (autobiography)

CORN COUNTRY
    (American Folkways)

JESSE JAMES WAS MY NEIGHBOR

HE HANGED THEM HIGH

OUR WILL ROGERS
    (biography)

Our Will Rogers

Our Will Rogers

by

HOMER CROY

LIBRARY DISCARD

B
R₀

Duell, Sloan and Pearce · *New York*
Little, Brown and Company · *Boston*

107766

COPYRIGHT 1953, BY HOMER CROY

ALL RIGHTS RESERVED. NO PART OF THIS BOOK IN EXCESS OF FIVE
HUNDRED WORDS MAY BE REPRODUCED IN ANY FORM WITHOUT
PERMISSION IN WRITING FROM THE PUBLISHER

LIBRARY OF CONGRESS CATALOG CARD NO. 53-10229

Published October 1953
Reprinted October 1953

DUELL, SLOAN AND PEARCE — LITTLE, BROWN
BOOKS ARE PUBLISHED BY
LITTLE, BROWN AND COMPANY
IN ASSOCIATION WITH
DUELL, SLOAN & PEARCE, INC.

Published simultaneously
in Canada by McClelland and Stewart Limited

PRINTED IN THE UNITED STATES OF AMERICA

Foreword

IT HAD BEEN in and out of my mind for some time to write the life of Will Rogers. I had known him for some years, although it was only during the last part of his life that I came in close contact with him. But could I contribute anything new?

He had been eulogized so ecstatically that I wondered if I could paint him as I saw him — mole and all. There was the vast bulwark of legend that one must go up against; did I dare set the story down as I saw it? One item of the Will Rogers saga was close to the heart of America: "I never met a man I didn't like." I knew that this quotation was mostly a happy accident and that in reality there were many men he couldn't abide. Also I knew he had a simple way of taking care of that: he just dodged them. And I knew also that he had a hot and hasty temper and that he had had two fist fights. As I began to think earnestly of this biography, I asked myself, should I write the traditional Will Rogers story, or the story that I believed to be more nearly true?

He had written very little about himself. What he did write of an autobiographical nature was as thin as the skeleton of a crow. He devoted five sentences to his school career (he attended six different schools) and three sentences to his courtship and marriage. The reason for this, as he always said, was that he was planning to write his autobiography and was saving the goodies.

As I look back on it, now that the book is finished and in the hands of the publisher, I do think I hit on one lucky expedient. I decided to get material firsthand, and so went to Oklahoma where I spent five weeks with his old cowboy friends and neighbors. Here were the very men who had ridden with him, the girls he had hopped around with, the Negroes and Indians he had played with as a boy. Here was where he had forded the crick; here was where he had chaw-beefed another boy's clothes; and here, probably, was where he had slept when he had herded cattle on the Caney; and here was where Uncle Blue Starr had scared the living daylights out of him with the set of chain harness.

I spent a week in the remarkable Memorial, at Claremore. There is a room not open to the public; it's packed with gold like a crib with yellow dent corn. I almost foundered. The number of ancient scrapbooks is surprising. People had them for years just because they loved young Will. When the end came, they sent them to the Memorial. It is a fine testimony of the feeling Oklahoma had for him. Most of the scrapbooks have been kept by women; in them, along with the items about Will, there are family souvenirs and cooking recipes. In a way they thought of him as a member of their family.

Now that my manuscript has gone into the works, I am beginning to realize how lucky I was to get out to Will's Country and interview the people who knew him, for already two of them are no more, so hasty is Time. And one person I had to interview by correspondence is no longer there. I had been careful to send carbon copies and here I was lucky again, for I had made some mistakes, but, so far as I know, all these have been remedied. I think I can say that no one has been quoted without permission and without having seen what I set down.

I wanted to talk to people who represented different phases of his life. In addition to his boyhood friends I saw people who told me of the days when he had roped a running horse on the stage, his vaudeville days (when a horse was no longer necessary), his Ziegfeld Follies days, his polo days, his silent picture days, his talking picture days, his lecture days, his aviation days, for he had more facets than anyone I ever knew. He moved in many worlds.

I was astonished to find how people disagreed on him. I found that he had many enemies, people who said bitter and acrimonious things about him; some who called him a faker and pretender; and some who found his humor not at all to their liking. Sometimes, as I went from one to another, I could hardly believe they were talking about the same person.

I must bring out another point, and this was how little, during the time I knew him, I appreciated his greatness. I knew he was unique, but I thought vaguely that this was "just his way." I saw his rough clothes, heard his high-pitched laugh and his banter, and thought of him as "carrying on." I didn't appreciate his philosophy, either. Sometimes I thought he didn't know what he was talking about, and that he wasn't being very funny today. Then, later, when I saw in the paper something I'd already heard him say, I had the sense of saying to myself, "Why, that's just the way I feel about it. He's right."

I have not quoted many of his witticisms; this is because some of them have been quoted to death. And I have not used many of the anecdotes that are always being told of Will, for the reason they do not stand up under inspection.

And now I want to say, after some detailed study and after living over old days and old scenes, that I come away realizing that he was a far greater man than I dreamed. It seems to me, in retrospect, that he represents the best in American life. His day is gone forever — the day of the old West, the day when each man depended on himself, the day when honesty and integrity were qualities that mattered very much.

In closing, I think I can say that I loved Will Rogers. Sometimes he made me as mad as hops . . . what friend doesn't? But to say that one loved him is no distinction, for millions did. In all America what man was more deserving?

HOMER CROY

Contents

Our Will Rogers

CHAPTER I

Birth of Will Rogers.
His Irish-Indian Ancestry

W ILL ROGERS was born November 4, 1879, in the Indian Territory, twelve miles from a post office. He was, in blood, more Irish than Indian, but he was such a master showman that he played up the Indian and let the Irish take care of itself. On top of this he had quite a bit of Welsh blood, and a dash of English. Oddly enough, he never knew just how much Indian he was. One reason why he didn't know was because of the casual way the Cherokee Indian Rolls were kept. When the Cherokees went to the agency, the enrolling clerk would ask them how much Indian blood they had and their answers would be set down. But the answers were not always right. In fact, in Will's own family there was a bald spot. Will turned himself in as a quarter-blood; one of his sisters said she was one-fourth Indian, another one-sixteenth. And, in later years, Will wrote in a Sunday syndicated article that his father was one-eighth Indian, when, as a matter of fact, he was a quarter-blood. It wasn't until Emmett Starr came along with his remarkable book on Cherokee blood that anything like the truth became known. Will never saw this book or made a study of the tribal rolls to turn up the facts. Will was nine-thirty-seconds Indian; that is, a trifle more than one-quarter. He always said that he was a quarter-Indian, which was close enough for all practical purposes. Nor did he know what his real name was; at least there is no evidence that he knew, for he never mentioned the Colonel part. It was Colonel William Penn Adair Rogers — quite a name to pin on a young Irish Indian.

The house where Will was born was originally log, but had been "boxed in"; that is, sawed boards had been put over the logs. The rest of the house was new, sawed lumber. His mother said she wanted him to be born in a log house, so she moved into that part and there Will put in his appearance. It happened that he was born on Election Day. In later years he made a great deal of this. But, on the other hand, he never registered and never voted in his life.

I was able to get a firsthand account of Will's birth from Clement Vann Rogers. *This* Clement Vann Rogers was not Will's father, but a colored man named for him. The interview took place just outside of Nowata, Oklahoma; he was driving a white horse and a black horse to a wagon. He was a dignified Negro, with a white mustache, and had a pleasant way of talking. He said he was seventy-eight years old; he was on relief, but added to his income by doing light hauling and small jobs such as shoeing horses.

"I reckon I'm about the only one lef' who see with their own eyes Mister Willie come into the world. I was a boy about six when this happen, livin' on Rabb's Creek which was made for my father. My daddy and my uncle Huse was owned by Mister Clem. You will recognize I'm speakin' of before war times when colored people was slaves. There wasn't ever any better person to be owned by than Mister Clem. When he said a thing he mean it, an' you didn't trifle around when he give you an order. More'n once he licked me, but it wasn't ever out of place. Sometimes I go see his grave in Chelsea; it gets me down, so real and personal he seems to me. Well, I was speakin' of Mister Willie's birth into the worl'. Perry Ross, a cowboy of my color, he come lopin' across the prairie land one afternoon, swingin' his hat and yellin' like a swarm of bumblebees was after him. When he get up to the house, he yell from his horse to my aunt, 'Come quick, Mrs. Clem want you desperate bad. There's a birth comin'.'

"Perry hepped hitch up our light spring-wagon, my mother and my cousin Aunt Babe Walker leap in, and they tell me to drive. The buggy whip had become broke off, but I laid on what there was of it and away we went, the wagon boundin' and leapin' and me layin' it on. It was six miles, like I said, and was about as wild a ride as anybody ever take. I still get a squeach up my backbone when I think of it. I reckon me bein' only come six made it seem all the more wild and excitin'.

"When we get there, my mother rush into the east room of the downstairs where the trouble was. This room at a time like this was no place for a lad of my age, so I go to the kitchen. Two or three ladies was in there with Mrs. Rogers. Finally there was a terrible screech and then a lot of little cries, like a pig under a gate. About this time Dr. Trent come. He had been sent for, but the river was up and he was delayed. He took charge. There was calls for hot water and bandages and there I was in the kitchen with the colored people doin' everything we could and prayin' to God everything would go well with the little white chile. Everybody was serious for a long time, comin' and goin' and dodgin' each other not to bump into each other in their hurry. Dr. Trent he come out and wash his hands and smile and say, 'Fine male chile. Be an honor to the fambly. Too bad his pappy wasn't here to be first to welcome him.'

"Pretty soon somebody come from the room and say, 'Come on, everybody, and see the young master,' and we colored folks go in. He is dressed now. I stare at him, I reckon my mouth was open. I knew he would be a fine man, with his pa and ma such fine people, but I never dreamed he would be famous clear across the ocean. Yes suh, I reckon I was one of the first persons to see Master Willie; anyway I reckon I'm about the only one livin' who see him not more thirty minutes after he have his clothes on. We growed up together, if you know what I mean. We played horse together. He used to put a saddle on my back and make me pretend I was a bucking horse and he would ride me, spurrin' with his bare heels. One time he gets mad with me and shoved a branding iron against my behind, but it wasn't very hot, scared me more'n anything else. He wouldn't ever do a person real damage; never got into fist fights like most boys, and he wasn't no hand to lie. When he got to be well known in the world and would come back to Oologah, Chelsea, or Claremore, he would always come to see us old-time colored folks. We would talk and laugh about the old days. People always had a good time when Mister Willie was around.

"One time Mr. Clem sent for me, said he wanted to see me. He was always real pleased my father name me after him. He gave me two cows and two calves, a horse, saddle, and bridle, and a suit of clothes. Then he put something in my hand, and when I look at it I think it was some kind of medal. Then he laugh and explain it was twenty dollars in gold and was real money and that I could spend it anyway I wanted to. Everybody honored Mister Clem, finest man in the Territory, word good as his bond, he stood up straighter'n most men, had a mustache that grayed up as the years come along. Mister Willie favored his mother more'n he did his father; she was more on the entertain' and joke side; his father was all business; wasn't a man to laugh much. Sometimes when I come around the house and Willie's mother was inside visitin' with the neighbors, I could hear them laughin'. Mister Willie wasn't work-brittle. He was always doin' things, but it would be indulgin' in exaggeration to say they was work. . . . So you wrote some of the things he acted in on the screen? Well, I'm real pleased to see somebody who worked for him. Of course, I never knowed anything about that part of his life."

After a time, Clement Vann Rogers clucked to his white horse and to his black horse and drove on down the road.

*   *   *

Among those in the busy household that day was Mrs. William Penn Adair. She was the wife of Colonel William Penn Adair, who was a fullblood Cherokee and one of the most powerful men in the Indian Territory. He was a lawyer and, in addition, assistant principal chief, an honor indeed. He had been a colonel in a Cherokee Mounted Regiment and had fought on the side of the South. His first lieutenant had been Clem Rogers. He was a member of the Cherokee Supreme Court and was, this November day, in Washington in the interest of his people.

Mrs. Adair, when the excitement was over, was surprised to find that no name had been chosen for the infant and asked if she could name him after her husband. Since it was a name that Clem Rogers might have chosen anyway, Mrs. Rogers said Yes; and so Mrs. Adair gave the child the name already mentioned. It appears on the *Authenticated Rolls of 1880, Cherokee Nation, Cooweescoowee District* as Number 2340. In addition to his name, the rolls reveal the notation "7 m." This means he was in his seventh month of age when he was entered on the rolls. But there it is, his official name, for anyone who wishes to have a look.

When Will was born, his father was the third richest man in the Cooweescoowee District. The two who were richer were both white men, married to Cherokee women (their names appear in the back of this book under "Sources"). He was a quarter Indian, the rest was Irish and Welsh.

The first of his family to arrive in this country was Major Downing, a British army officer who had been born in Ireland. He landed about 1720. His first name is not known; in fact, very little is known about him. But this much is pretty well authenticated: he went to Georgia and married a full blood of the Wolf Clan. When he met her she could not talk a word of English; but love overcomes all barriers, 'tis said, and soon they were married. They had four children: George, John, William, and

Nancy. The one important to us is Nancy. She was, as can be deduced, one-half Cherokee, one-half Irish.

When time came for Nancy to be married she chose an Irishman named McSwain. There was only one child — Margaret by name. And Margaret married another Irishman, Avery Vann. Of this union twelve bouncing children came along. The next to the youngest was Sallie, and Sallie is the one we're interested in. She was, seemingly, one-fourth Cherokee and three-fourths Irish. Sallie Vann was born January 28, 1818, and died May 28, 1882. She was Will Rogers's father's mother.

On the distaff side, John Gunter, a Welshman, came to northern Alabama from Wales in 1760. He went into salt; that is, he owned three salt mines. One day the Paint Clan of the Cherokees came to trade for salt. (The clan got its name from the liberal way they smeared themselves with paint; it seems they lived near a colored clay quarry and could decorate themselves whenever they chose.) One of the tribe who came that day was a brave's daughter with the unpronounceable name of Ghl-go-ne-li. She could not talk English. In spite of the language barrier, John Gunter found her charming and told her father he would like to take her hand in marriage. The chief, who seems to have been pretty astute, said this was all fine and dandy but that the clan must be paid for giving up its fairest daughter. An agreement was entered into by which John Gunter promised to give the clan salt "as long as grass grows and rivers run." He gave Ghl-go-ne-li the name of Catherine and they were married and all was well, for seven children came to bless their union, all half Indians. John and Catherine were Will's maternal great-grandparents.

The child we are most interested in is Elizabeth Hunt Gunter. She was born in September 1804, and died on Dog Creek, Cherokee Nation, February 14, 1877. She married Martin Matthew Schrimsher who was born in Blount County, Tennessee, in

1806. He went to California in the Gold Rush and died there about 1856 (there is a little confusion in the records). He left five children to miss him. One of these was Mary America Schrimsher, who was one-fourth Indian (Cherokee) and one-fourth Welsh, the rest German. She was born October 9, 1839. She was Will's mother. (*Note:* There are two or three ways of spelling Schrimsher, but in the old papers it appears as it does in this sentence.)

Another product of this union was Martha Lucretia Schrimsher who married Frederick William Gulager. (More of this later. Note in passing: I interviewed four of the Gulagers.)

We left Sallie Vann enjoying her numerous brothers and sisters; and now we will go to another branch of the family — to Thomas Cordery, who was as Irish as all get-out. He married a fullblood Cherokee of the Blind Savannah Clan whose name was Soniovie, which, understandably, he changed to Sussannah. (The name had been given the clan because in it were so many blind.) There was only one child — Lucy Cordery who was half-Irish, half-Cherokee. She married Robert Rogers, an Irishman. Five children came to bless their happy home. The youngest (James) married Catherine Vann who was Sallie Vann's sister.

There was a son named Robert Rogers who married Sallie Vann. Now we are getting somewhere, for these two were the father and mother of Clement Vann Rogers, Will's father. The name Clement had come down for two generations; Vann was, of course, his mother's maiden name. He was five-sixteenths Cherokee and, possibly, one-half Irish.

When it came time to wed, in 1859, Clement Vann Rogers chose Mary America Schrimsher who will be found in the last paragraph of the part about the Schrimshers. (I'm sure that by now the reader is delightfully confused. If you are you need not feel sensitive, for Will Rogers himself never knew much about his family, or how much Indian, Welsh, and Irish they were.) The thing worth remembering that comes out of all this family tracing is that Will Rogers was Irish, Indian, and Welsh, with a touch of German.

Clem himself was born in the northeastern part of the Indian Territory, near Bread Town. This was a settlement where food and provisions were given to immigrants and settlers. Later the name was changed to Baptist Mission. There was no post office and very little town. It takes sharp eyes today to see where these settlements were. He was born in the Going Snake district, not so far from the present town of Westville in Adair County. The date: January 11, 1839.

The Cherokees were having trouble among themselves — an intratribal dispute which is too complicated to go into here. Clem's father was on the losing side and was killed by one of John Ross's men when little Clem was a year old. Sallie Vann was now a widow. In 1844 she married William Alexander Musgrove, who seems to have been good enough a man, but little Clem took a dislike to him. The wedding was performed in the house; the five-year-old would not come in, for he looked on this stranger as taking his mother away from him. During the wedding ceremony he hid behind the house; when the happy couple came out to get into the carriage which was to take them away on their honeymoon, he ran with a hatful of rocks and began to throw them at his stepfather. The stepfather got out and tried to pacify the child, but little Clem ran into the orchard and would not come back. And there he remained until the carriage drove away.

Clem would not acknowledge the man as his father and would not call him father. In 1851 Clem was sent away to school at the Male Seminary at Tahlequah, Indian Territory. One day he came home from school and, while still on the horse he was riding, got into an argument with his stepfather. He rode toward him, intending to bump his stepfather with the horse. Young Clem was carrying a pistol and, wishing to scare his stepfather, pulled it out and fired over the man's head. This enraged Musgrove who rushed into the house, got his own gun, and came hurrying out. He cocked it as he ran, but so hastily that he snapped the mainspring. Then, in anger, he threw the gun down. Clem rode on, feeling he had got the better of the situation. The situation in the Rogers-Musgrove family grew increasingly difficult.

After his run-in with his stepfather, young Clem wanted to get away from home; it would mean giving up the Male Seminary, but that was all right; school was a nuisance; real boys didn't bother with it. He looked around and came upon Joel M. Bryan, an important cattleman, who was planning to drive a herd of cattle to St. Louis. Young Clem asked if Mr. Bryan would hire him and was delighted when Bryan said he would. Four men were engaged and on May 15, 1855, the long, long drive to St. Louis was begun. There were four hundred head of stock to be taken care of day and night on the drive. (This was before Hollywood discovered that taking care of cattle is a delightful experience.) The trip took four months, but at last the men arrived in the exciting city of St. Louis; their eyes must have been as big as saddle horns, for they saw steamboats, fashionable hotels, and fashionable people who would no more have driven a herd of steers than they would have thrown themselves under a paddle wheel. Joel Bryan paid his men off and there they were with their money, and there were the Mississippi River gamblers waiting to be friendly. Some of the men tried their luck, with the success you think. But young Clem clung to his money like a sandbur to a horse blanket. He put it in a money-belt and started across a country where people disappeared and were heard of never again. The trip home took nine days, but the boy arrived safely, with never a penny missing. And now, with this money in his pockets, he thought of himself as a young businessman; and well he might, for he was always a businessman. C. V.

Rogers knew how to make money and how to keep it. He told his mother he wanted to start a store. His mother and his stepfather were prosperous and agreed to help. (Clem still disliked his stepfather who, it would seem, was a fair-minded man.) The two gave him four horses and about a hundred head of cattle. Young Clem inherited from his father two slaves — Rabb and Houston. The latter was called "Huse," a twisting of Houston. These two became important in Clem's life and in Will's, too.

Clem and his caravan started west and came, at last, to a district called Cooweescoowee; the word was more impressive than its meaning, for all it signified was "big." At last they came to a trading post run by the hated Osages. There Clem and his two slaves camped. Clem was a driving, ambitious man and he had two slaves to back him up. It was not long before Clem was boss of the store and the Osages were outside looking in. A year or two later, Rabb made a significant remark. "We just took it over," he said. But this was the way things were done in the Indian Territory. The ousted traders were Osages, and no Cherokee, or part-Cherokee, wanted any traffic with an Osage. Lest a reader think harshly of the young Clem, it should be explained that the taking over of a store was not considered anything to be squeamish about. Also Rabb, later, made another significant comment: "After we git the store, them Osages come around and steal everything loose."

Clem now began trucking supplies to his store from Fort Smith, Arkansas. The store began to prosper; and now Clem wanted land. There it was for the asking, if you were a Cherokee; so Clem settled on a ranch not far from the store, and the land became his without any more formality.

Now that he was prospering, the young ranchman-storekeeper began to think about a girl he had met while he was attending the Cherokee Male Seminary at Tahlequah. She was Mary America Schrimsher, daughter — the close reader will remember —

of Matthew Martin Schrimsher; and she herself had been a student at the Cherokee National Female Seminary, same town. It can be pointed out that geographical names ran in the Schrimsher family, for Mary America had a sister named Elizabeth Alabama. Mary was living with her father in a settlement between Tahlequah and Fort Gibson called Eureka Springs. Clem began going there; he could get a good home-cooked meal and court Mary. It was pleasant. Clem batched, he and his two colored boys. Rabb and Huse took turns about cooking. Clem stood up under this for three and a half years. But oftener and oftener he went to see Mary Schrimsher. She was also one-fourth Indian, but she was an entirely different kind of person. Clem was gruff, domineering and demanding. Mary Schrimsher was lighthearted, with an extraordinary sense of humor. In addition, she had another trait which was almost as deep as her capacity for fun, and this was her religious outlook. She could, so the neighbors said, change from grave to gay almost in a twinkling. On top of this she had great human sympathy. Everybody liked her and she liked everybody. Her family were Methodists and she attended the Methodist church. Two young people basically as different as Mary and Clem would be hard to find.

But he prospered, and they were married at "Grandma" Schrimsher's, near Fort Gibson, Indian Territory, in 1859, and he took her off to the log house on Caney River for what, they hoped, would be a lifetime of happiness.

Suddenly, in no time at all it seemed, Clem was involved in the Civil War. A factor that made it bad was that even the Cherokees were divided on the soon-to-be bloody conflict. Some joined the North; Clem was entirely and completely Southern and, when the time came, joined the South under the Cherokee General Stand Watie, as remarkable a character as the Indian Territory ever produced. One small matter among many: as soon as Clem joined the South, the Northerners marched upon him and stole every steer he had. Clem was a plain-speaking man and he spoke plenty.

There was a touching scene between Clem and Rabb and Huse. He said, in effect, "You two can do as you wish, join whichever side you wish. If my side wins, I will come back, after the war is over, and you will be my slaves again. If the North wins you will be free men and I will have no control over you." Even the two brothers were divided on the deep and far-reaching issue of slavery, for Rabb joined the North and Huse joined the South.

Clem gathered up Mary and took her to Bonham, Texas, whence Matthew Martin Schrimsher had fled; and there Clem left Mary with her father and mother, and returned to Cooweescoowee for good or bad. It was mostly bad. He was put in Company G, first regiment, of the Mounted Cherokee Volunteers and soon was chosen lieutenant under Captain James Leon Butler. There were promotions and soon Clem was a captain, himself. The Indian Brigade marched as many miles, had as many engagements, and captured as many wagon trains as any brigade west of the Mississippi.

The forces of the North were overwhelming, and Lee surrendered on April 9, 1865. But tough General Stand Watie would have none of this. He held out until June 23, and thus became the last Southern general to surrender. When the war was over, Clem was Captain Rogers, twenty-six years old, and the world was before him, or so he thought.

He went to Bonham, Texas, where things had been happening, not of death and destruction but of life and living, for he found that he was the father of a daughter — Sallie Clementine Rogers, born December 16, 1863. (There had been an earlier child — Elizabeth Rogers — who had died when she was three.) Clem picked up his wife and Sallie Clementine and came back to Cooweescoowee to find that his log house had been burned and that he had lost everything. He had to go to work at Fort Gibson on a salary as a hauler of freight. His wife again went to live with her parents, this time at Eureka Springs where they had moved. Clem hauled freight — horses, mules, and wagons — even as far away as St. Joseph, Missouri. These were hard days for Captain Rogers. But he was tough and he meant to win.

He wasn't gone so completely that he didn't get back, now and then, to Eureka Springs, and a boy was born April 15, 1866. They named him Robert Martin Rogers. Clem's father and his grandfather had both been named Robert Rogers; so he tried to pass the name down. Next, at Fort Gibson, a fourth child was born, November 28, 1869; she was named Maude Rogers.

Clem hauled freight five years, not a pleasant job. But it wasn't all bad, for he was thriftily saving his money. He and money were always on friendly terms. He was buying cattle. At last he had enough to try his luck again, and now, after eight years of fighting and freighting, he returned to Cooweescoowee, not as well off as when he had left to go to war.

This time he did not go to the "old place," but to a new location on the Verdigris River. He didn't have to pay anything for the land; among the Cherokees whoever got there first was owner. He sent word to Rabb and Huse to come to see him and said about as follows, "Well, Rabb's side won. My side lost. I would like for you to work for me. I will pay you wages."

The two were delighted; they both liked Captain Rogers. He was a man of honor; his word was his bond. Once with him they had licked the Osages; now they would lick hard times.

Mary Rogers was born May 31, 1873. To keep from confusing her with her mother and grandmother she was called May. But life was hard in this rough, undeveloped country and, especially, it was hard on infants. How hard it was is indicated by the fact that Clem Rogers started a family graveyard on his farm. Two other children were born: Homer and Zoe. Both died in infancy and were buried in this family plot. Thus seven children had been born. The eighth and last (as he proved to be) was Will.

And now word might be set down as to the financial condition of the family. It was better than most; in fact, the family soon became the third most prosperous one in the community. Most of their neighbors were of Cherokee blood and were proud of it. The Cherokees were the aristocrats of Indians. They looked down on most of the other Indian tribes. There was even a paper, printed half in Cherokee and half in English — *The Cherokee Advocate* — and this was the first paper that young Will ever saw.

A good report on the family's finances is contained in the 1890 Census of Cooweescoowee District, of the Cherokee Nation. Will was ten years old then, but the report gives a glimpse of how a pioneer family lived. It reads:

Rogers, Clem V, Native Cherokee — 51 years — male — farmer

Rogers, May   "   "   15   "   F

*   *   *

Rogers, William P   "   "   10   "   M

*   *   *

All can read and write. 3 dwellings; 7 other structures; 3 farms; 300 acres enclosed; 300 acres under cultivation; improvements valued at $15,000; 3000 bushels of corn; 1000 bushels of wheat; 1000 bushels of oats; 200 bushels of apples; 5 mules; 36 goats; 50 domestic fowles; 5 plows; a machinery plow; wheat drill; 1 reaper and mower; 1 self-binder; 2 farm wagons; 1 hack; 1 piano; 1 clock.

It will be seen from this how prosperous the family was. The most important item is the value of the buildings. Another striking item is mention of the piano. It was the only one in Coowees-

coowee District. Will loved to try to play it. But he never quite
made it. His mother, however, could play and she could sing.
Will loved to stand beside her, as she played, and sing with her.
Neighbors liked to come in and he and his mother would put on
a little entertainment.

CHAPTER 2

Poor Willie Is Sent Off to School

THERE are not many authentic stories about Will's early childhood. The first that can be accepted has to do with his lateness in giving up the bottle. He was still pulling on it long after the age that most children have gone on to new adventures. But not our hero. He wanted his bottle and he said so at the top of his voice which, even then, was quite a considerable affair. The family, as has been indicated, lived near the Verdigris River. The river, on this occasion, was up. Sallie decided to row across to call on one of the neighbors. She loved her little brother and asked her mother if she could take him with her. To this the mother consented. To keep the boy quiet, as she was rowing across the river, Sallie gave him his beloved bottle. Peace, contentment and happiness came over him. The world was a great success and all that was in it. Suddenly the bottle slipped from his grasp and settled into the water. The boy was sitting in such a position that he could see it disappear; he blinked in astonishment, seemed to weigh the situation — that's what Sallie always said — and then gave up without a whimper. And never again after that did he have to hook on to his bottle.

The next story, chronologically, that can be accepted is told by Mrs. Andrew J. Lane, a friend of the doctor who helped bring Will into the world. One day she came to call. Will's mother was getting ready to bake bread and had a pan of yeast sitting on the floor letting it "rise." Will came along, saw the tempting mess, and put his foot into it. Mrs. Lane expected to see Will's mother spank him, or at least announce that the yeast would have to be thrown out and a new batch started. But not at all; instead Will's mother said, with a sense of humor, "Willie has a good idea. That'll make it sweeter. It'll be the best bread we ever had." And so, declared Mrs. Lane, it was.

Two who became important in Will's young life were a Negro couple, "Uncle Dan" and "Aunt Babe" Walker. They did not live on the Rogers ranch, but nearby. Dan worked for "Mr. Clem" and, when needed, "Aunt Babe" would come over and help Will's mother. This was typical of how the better-to-do Cherokees, after the war had done away with slavery, employed the Negroes. The two — employer and employee — seemed to have had each other's respect.

Since the Walker cabin was near, Will spent a great deal of time with Uncle Dan whom he found fascinating, especially since Uncle Dan could do wonderful and unexplainable things with a rope. Young Will would watch with concentrated attention, then try to do what Uncle Dan had done. But he failed. Uncle Dan, who was a kindly soul, began to show Will how to do some of the tricks. The boy was delighted. When his mother couldn't find him, she knew where to look: at Uncle Dan's and Aunt Babe's. Also they had good things to eat, and young Will liked to eat.

One day an exceedingly trying situation arose. A boil developed on Master Willie's head. His mother tried to get him to let her lance it, but he would have none of this. Uncle Dan came over, this day. His mother sent Will out of the room, then told Uncle Dan the unhappy situation. Uncle Dan didn't relish the idea, but if Mis' Mary want it done, then he do it. He showed the boy his knife, then coaxed him up to take a closer look at it. Willie got into his lap, eager to see the fascinating instrument. Suddenly Uncle Dan pinned the lad's arms to his side, the knife flashed, and the boil met its end. Young Will yelled till he could be heard to Four Mile Branch (as it's told by the old-timers) and for a moment, completely lost faith in the once-kindly Uncle Dan. But after a time the breach was healed and their world was again roses and sunshine.

A matter that helped Uncle Dan return to the boy's good grace was a pony that Uncle Dan had, certainly the most wonderful animal a boy ever climbed on top of. Willie would sit astride, Uncle Dan's hand hard by. Back and forth, up and down, the two would go, Willie in seventh heaven, Uncle Dan just around the corner. But this was not all. Uncle Dan began to show him how to catch things by throwing a rope. And then it was that Willie got a pony of his own.

Willie was certainly the happiest boy in the Indian Territory. A pony, a rope, and a wonderful friend to show him how to manage them. And Willie had plenty of friends to play with; in fact, Uncle Dan had twelve children. Will's playmates were white children, colored children, and Indians; the latter were mostly Cherokees. Will's family looked on themselves as white, but were also proud of their Indian blood.

Another reason that Willie liked to go to Uncle Dan's was that he had a boy of Willie's age named Mack. Willie would get down on his hands and knees and have a boy's saddle put on him. Mack would climb in and Master Willie would become a wild, bucking bronco, uttering fearful grunts, groans, and whinnies, until he pitched poor Mack off. As Willie grew older, Uncle Dan proceeded to teach Willie to rope calves. This was far more exciting than leaping around on the floor under a saddle.

When Will was four years old, a blow came to the family. Will's brother Robert Martin Rogers, was in Vinita, Indian Territory, living with his Aunt Margaret and attending the Worcester Academy. One evening he came home from school and said that he was not feeling well. A doctor was called; it developed the boy had typhoid fever. He died two days before his fifteenth birthday. Now there was only one son in the family; and Will became even more the center of attention.

A difficulty arose. Will's mother wanted him to be a preacher and often spoke of it. Will's father said little in opposition, but did remark that so far as he could see there wasn't much money in preaching. On top of this he did something that disturbed Will's mother: he worked on Sunday. Not only this but made Rabb and Huse, and Dan Walker work on Sunday. Will's mother wished he wouldn't do this, but it wasn't important enough to make an issue. Another matter was grace at meals. She expected Clem to ask the blessing and he did, but at breakneck speed. In just no time at all he would have his head in the plate, eating.

The food was what was called "substantial." "Con-hennie" was one dish; and there was canuchi soup, hickory nut hominy, "curd," and a great pitcher of blackstrap molasses. "Sofkey" and hickory-smoked ham and corn pone made without salt. The family did not think much of white bread; they called it "wasp's nest" and served it only when fancy company came. In addition there was the "white" food of beans, "cracklin's," and "chitlins."

It was at about this time that Will made his first recorded bright remark. He liked to spend all his time outdoors, either on his pony, or trying to rope. His mother kept urging him to study his books — something that seemed to go against the very grain of his soul.

One day his mother told him that he should be ashamed of himself because he didn't want to know how to read. Will thought it over; the appeal was a powerful one. But he conquered it. "I've got such a good pony," he said, "that I don't want to waste my time learnin' to read."

His mother was considered well educated for the time and place. She had gone for a while to an academy in Arkansas and, later, to the Cherokee Female Seminary at Tahlequah. The latter school was where the wealthier and more important Cherokee families sent their daughters.

The years went along for Will about as they did for any boy of his age on a ranch in this section. He played outdoors; most of his playmates were either colored or Indians. Then the Musgrove family moved in. Quite a help there, ten children, all white. If Will was brighter than any of the other boys in the neighborhood there is no record of it. But he was the biggest talker. He was the loudest and noisiest boy in any group. But also the best-liked. He liked everybody and everybody liked him. He was fun to be with. But he was a puzzle to his hard-driving father. The boy didn't like to work.

When he was eight years old exceedingly bad news was imparted to him. He would have to go to school. His mother had been trying to teach him, and sister Sallie had taken a whack at it. But so far he had completely escaped the deteriorating effects of education. But he didn't know the power of adults, for he was whisked off and sent to live at his sister Sallie's at Chelsea, which was about twenty miles away and where they had a damned ol' schoolhouse. It almost destroyed his sunny nature. But there was one good thing about it; he could ride his pony to school; the distance was three miles.

Then he could really live; and when he got home from school his father would not be there to make him help do the chores. After all, there was something to be said in favor of education. But not much. The name of the school was Drumgoole. The school was for Indian or part-Indian boys and girls, and was supported by taxes paid by the Cherokees. If a white child went he had to pay a dollar a month. The school had about twenty "scholars." Some of the boys and girls talked Cherokee among themselves. Will listened and picked up some of the language. The building itself was a one-room log affair. The seats were split-log benches which had been smoothed with an ax, and were wholly and completely without backs. The floor also was made of split logs, with splinters lying in wait for bare toes.

At the noon hour Will could escape the academic grind: the teacher allowed the boys to race their ponies, and this they did, with as much yelling as at Custer's Last Fight. No one could yell quite as loud as Willie. There was another scholastic matter that he shone at — passing the water bucket. The teacher allowed each boy to take turns going to the spring and dipping up a bucket of water; then the boy could pass it around to the suffering students. But ill luck was always with Will, and some way or other the water always got sloshed in the others' faces, or spilled on them, or down the girls' backs. Next time he would try to do better. He never quite succeeded.

A ray of sunshine came through the clouds. Sallie and her husband were the mainstays in the little country church. Sallie wanted an organ for the church and sent off to Kansas City and for forty dollars bought a secondhand organ. She kept it for some days in her house. A musical instrument was never safe around Will; he would try to play and sing. Finally Sallie got the thing to church and peace again settled over the little farmhouse.

The novelty of having an organ in church attracted the Indians. They came to church and liked to sing as Sallie played. The Indians sang by note and could, it is said, carry a four-part harmony. Will sang along with them. Old-timers still talk about it.

But Sallie and her husband liked to have Will around. He was "good company." The neighbors liked to drop in to hear "what the boy had to say." But he never worked. Sallie's husband had several cows which had to be milked; he tried to shame Willie into helping, but he never quite made it. One time the tortured boy gave as an excuse that he had a sore knee. His ingenuity at evading work was the talk of the neighborhood. He never quite let shame defeat him.

In the meantime, Will's mother was not strong; so a woman who lived in the neighborhood was engaged as hired girl. Her name was Mary Bibles. She ate with the family and was considered part of the family.

A picture of Will's early days was given me by Miss Gazelle Lane who was, when I talked to her, deputy county clerk in Claremore. She was Will's cousin, and grew up with him. He stayed at the Lane house at least once a week, she said; and he never came without bringing his lariat. One day he swung at a turkey, gave the rope a snap, and broke the turkey's neck. He was greatly disturbed and repentful, for he could not bear to see anything suffer. As the turkey stopped its flopping, Will said, "I'm sorry. I'll never do such a thing again." Then he brightened. "But I'll stay till we eat it up." And he did. Will was always willing to help in this way. "One of his deepest traits was kindness to animals; most boys in our section went rabbit hunting; when they caught a rabbit they would kill it with their clubs. Will would never do this.

"Although I was quite young, I still remember his mother. She had a buckboard and drove a white horse. She would take Will and the two of them would go visiting together. I have always thought this was where Will got his interest in going to see people. When anybody in our section saw a buckboard and white horse coming they knew they were in for a good time. Will's father wasn't that way at all. Sometimes he would be silent for a long period at a time. But he was just; when he said he would do a thing he would do it."

There was a barrier between Will and his father, a barrier that neither could quite breach. Will spent more and more time roping and in working out fancy loops and throws. If anyone could show him a rope trick that he didn't know, Will would hang around him like a honeybee around a sorghum pan. He still went to Uncle Dan's and Aunt Babe's. Sometimes he stayed overnight; then he and Mack would have a high old time.

Ill luck again knocked at his door. His father announced that Will would have to go to Tahlequah to attend the Cherokee Female Seminary — the very one his mother had attended. The words must have sounded like the clap of doom. It was bad enough to have to go to school, but to go to a girls' school was more than a person could stand. The reason was that his sisters — May and Maude — were attending the school, and Willie could go along with them. He would be the only boy in school. And so he was shipped off, no doubt kicking like a steer. Will didn't like the school and he didn't care who knew it. He yelled in the hallways, crept up on girls who were studying at night, and let off war whoops that would have thrilled Chief Claremore. He got into arguments with his teachers; he liked to argue and here was a golden opportunity. It worked. In two weeks he was back on the ranch, pale and shaken.

Now he could live. The outdoors, horses, cattle. But he counted his blessings too soon, for another disaster befell him. His father said he would have to go to school again. This time his father chose the Harrell Institute at Muskogee. It was a Methodist School inhabited mostly by girls. In fact, Will and the president's son were the only boys there. Will started in as before, teasing the girls and arguing with the teachers. It was not long before the president (the Reverend T. F. Brewer) wrote Clem Rogers: "I regret to inform you that your son is not doing well in school and would suggest you remove him." Will was removed and he rejoiced.

Soon after he was home he came down with the measles. Real tragedy entered the ranch house. His mother became gravely ill. The family doctor was out of the district, so Will's father sent a telegram to Dr. Oliver Bagby, at Vinita, to come in desperate haste. And this doctor did; he drove across the prairies by team and buggy the distance of thirty-six miles in four hours. But he was too late. Will's mother was dead of "flux."

Will himself was too ill to attend the funeral. He was ten years old and was disconsolate, for there had been a bond of love and understanding between them. The two were, in main, of the same nature and it was from his mother that he got his predominant traits.

For a time Will had a saddle under him but not for long. His father was still bent on education, and soon (September 5, 1892) the boy found himself at the Willie Halsell Institute, Vinita, Indian Territory, the youngest boy in school (he was not yet thirteen) and certainly the most discouraged. This institution of learning was called a college, which was kind of people. It had been founded by William Halsell, who had a daughter named after himself — Willie Halsell. She had died, and, in memory of her, he had given her name to the school.

Here's a stereoscope picture of what Vinita was like at this time:

"Vinita was sure one muddy town. Besides being flat, with little natural moisture drainage, there were no sewers, no curbs, no pavement. When it rained, the moisture stayed until it was dried by sun and wind. Meanwhile every passing vehicle churned the black, sticky mud deeper and deeper.

"One day, when the mud along Illinois Avenue had settled into chug-holes, the fire alarm sounded. The gallant fire laddies responded. Merton Raines was standing manfully on the back step of the fire wagon, holding tight with both hands. He was resplendent in his blue uniform, with great, shiny brass buttons.

"As the fire wagon dashed by, some of the girls from Willie Halsell called out, 'Hello, Merton!' Merton (the complete gentleman) let loose with one hand, gallantly to lift his hat to the young ladies. Just at this unhappy moment the fire wagon struck a chug-hole and Merton was flung far and wide into the boggy street, in front of the girls he was seeking to impress. Fortunately he himself was not hurt, but his uniform was never again quite the same."

Willie Halsell was a towering institution of four stories; the boys' dormitory was on the top floor, the girls' on the third. The first and second floors were given over to classrooms. The dormitories were not big enough to contain all the students, so those who were not contained took rooms outside. Will was placed in the boys' dormitory, where he had as roommates John McCracken, Charles McClellan, and Tom Lane. The older boys looked him over and nicknamed him "Rabbit" because of the size of his ears.

This was the most congenial school Will had got into (it was his fourth). It didn't look too bad. Knowing how dull the educational process was, he had brought along his lariat. Every free minute he was practicing; the other boys and girls liked to watch him and he liked to have them watch him. He loved to be out in front of a crowd.

He pursued two studies about as far removed from the needs of a ranch boy as anybody could think up: piano playing and oil painting. He struggled manfully against both of them. His piano teacher (Eugenia Thompson) held forth in her home, and there Will pecked away. The lessons were given of a morning before classes began at the school proper. Will was popular and the other students liked to walk to school with him. One morning two or three of them stopped in front of the house to see if Will had finished his thumping. He came from the torture chamber and said, "Don't wait for me. I forgot to practice yesterday and I gotta do it now before I go to school." Then he dragged himself back.

The other students started on, but before they got to the

school they heard a whistle and there, behind them, was Will jogging joyfully after them. "I'll tell you how it was," he said. "She kept pointin' her finger at the notes and sayin' over and over, 'What's this? What's this?' So I said, 'It looks like yore finger to me.' This made her mad and she handed me a good slap and told me to get out an' go to school. I'm goin' to use it every day."

The life of the students was regulated by a gong. A gong to get up by, a gong to march by, a gong to study by, a gong to send them to bed. Will didn't like this regimentation, but, on the other hand, the school wasn't bad. Especially when he could lasso the girls. When he caught a girl by the leg he said he was roping calves.

At eight in the evening the gong boomed — time to go to the study hall. Will went as if to the gallows. Sometimes he would study ten or fifteen minutes, but soon would be whispering and playing pranks. He had the ability to absorb information rapidly, and had a truly remarkable memory. Sometimes he used a short cut to knowledge. He would, when the study period was over, ask someone to tell him what had been in the book; and usually the person would do so, for everybody liked him, so genial, so full of fun was he. Another short cut he developed was to seize his textbook and study it as he walked from one classroom to another. But this was not the end of his scholastic attainments; when the teacher called on him to answer a question he didn't know, he would, in an adroit manner, manage to side-step it, or to involve the teacher in an argument. He was quick-witted and so mentally alert that he could down almost anybody in an argument. The other students liked to hear him argue; usually he made them laugh.

He had a trick of sitting at his desk, seemingly deep in his studies, but actually watching like a cougar. When a girl came along, he would whip his rope out from under his desk and throw it ahead of her so that she would step in the loop; then he would haul away. The trick was not popular with his teachers.

One time, at recess, he went too far and tripped one of the girls until she had a fall; her friends, provoked by this constant source of annoyance, rushed upon Will and began to pummel him and threaten him with all sorts of dire punishments.

"Aw shucks!" said Will. "You wouldn't hurt a Rabbit, would you?"

The girls laughed and soon the incident was forgotten.

He came under the influence of the school's elocution teacher. She discovered that he had the ability to stand up in front of people and talk, and she encouraged him in this. Once a week, at chapel, one of the students "spoke a piece." When she put Will on, he chose to deliver a burlesque sermon in the manner of a backwoods colored preacher, a kind of entertainment popular at the time. He stepped out in front and began as he had planned, "Breddern and Cistern." He spoke a few lines of the material he had elaborately committed to memory, then his mind fled. Suffering the tortures of the damned, he tried again; again he stuck. Finally he gulped and said, "Amen," and crept back to his seat. It was his first public appearance and it was a complete and dismal failure. He told his teacher that he would never try again. But, later in the term, he did try again; this time it was not a burlesque speech, but one he had made up himself called "The Terrors of Education." No doubt he put his heart into it. Anyway, he seems to have come off fairly successfully. That winter a school play was put on; he took part. There is no record to show how well he did, but it may be believed that he was fairly good.

At nine-thirty at night, lights were turned out; all talking in the dormitories was supposed to cease. But it never did with Will. He always had a few more things that it was necessary to say. Demerits were clapped on him, but he wasn't cured. The boys liked to hear him. Next day they would tell the boys who did not live at the dormitory what Willie had said.

Some of the half-Indian half-white boys were rugged characters; now and then there was a fight. But Will never got into one. He was not pugnacious; he bore no one ill will. He liked to have a good time and to make those around him have a good time.

One term, when he came back from school, he received a shock. He found that his father had married Mary Bibles. Will had not known anything about it in advance. His father was just twice as old as the bride.

Will had always given his address as the Rogers Ranch, Cooweescoowee District, but now a town had sprung up: Oologah.

Bicycles were coming into popularity in the Indian Territory. Will had one of the first; one reason was that his father was rich and he indulged his son. But he didn't understand the harumscarum child. The boy ought to work harder.

Will tried all kinds of fancy tricks on his bicycle. He even tried to rope calves on it; his success was not notable. His father watched all this with growing pessimism. Why did his only son have to be such an irresponsible turnip?

Will had a bit of financial luck in 1894, for that was the year the "Cherokee Payment" was made. This was the money that the United States Government paid the Cherokee for taking over "the Outlet," which was the land the Cherokees had been leasing to cattlemen. Will got $265.70 and so did all the other Rogers children. It paid to be on "the Rolls."

Will, who was becoming inured to the hardships of education, went back to Willie Halsell for the second year. The school plays were continued; more and more the "funny parts" were assigned to him.

He was becoming restless; by now he had gone to Willie Halsell four years; he told his father that he wanted to give up school and go to work. His father must have been pop-eyed. "Let me think it over," said the baffled man, fighting for time. In a few days he imparted devastating news to Willie — he would have to go to school again. Willie must have been profoundly depressed.

Scarritt Collegiate Institute (to give it its full name) was run by the Southern Methodist Church of Neosho, Missouri, which was about eighty miles from Will's home. In the fall of 1895 Will packed his lariat and dragged himself off to school. He lacked two months of being fifteen.

The name had originally been Neosho Collegiate Institute, but it had been having hard sledding. In desperation the board met, looked around, and approached Nathan Scarritt, who had made a fortune in Kansas City real estate. His heart had been touched and he had made them a handsome donation. The appreciative board promptly changed the name to Scarritt Collegiate Institute. The school remained about the same.

Will did not live in a dormitory, for there was dormitory space only for the girls; the boys lived in boardinghouses where they had their meals. Will was soon the cutup of the campus. Here, too, he was the only boy who realized that a lariat was a necessary part of education. Not far away from his boardinghouse was Clark's pasture (where the Neosho Pet Milk plant stands today) and where Will liked to rope calves. The boys and girls would gather to watch him. He liked to get his rope around a calf's neck and then maneuver the calf so that it would sweep into the girls and play havoc with their dignity. He especially liked to tease the girls; wherever he went girls' squeals could be heard, "Don't, Willie!" But in spite of this he was popular. He had more fun than any boy or girl in school and the boys and girls around him had fun. Now and then he studied a little.

A glimpse into the loves and sorrows of a young man of seventeen is given by Mrs. Garland Price, 416 Ripley Street, Neosho, Missouri, who was his girl friend when he was at Scarritt College. At that time she was known as "little Maggie" Nay. I did not get to interview her, but she gave me a glimpse by correspondence. The glimpse:

"My mother would not let me go with Will because he was considered 'wild.' It came about this way. A German family lived a few miles outside of Neosho. It was considered exceedingly wicked to go to their place because they made and sold wine, so wicked, in fact, that only boys went. They would buy a bottle of wine and pass it around among themselves. All of them together would probably not drink more than a bottle. But one day one of the boys drank enough to make him unsteady and he fell off his bicycle. Our conservative town was shocked. Just at this time, Will asked me to go to a party with him. I was eager to go, for he was lots of fun, but my mother would not let me go out with this wild Indian boy from the Territory who drank wine. It is hard to realize today how carefully mothers in those days guarded their daughters. I was tactless enough to write Will and tell him that I could not accept his invitation because he drank wine."

Will's response is written in lead pencil and here it is, just as he wrote it, punctuation, underlinings and all:

Neosho Mo
Nov 27 96

My Dearest Friend if you can not be my sweetheart. I received the note a little bit ago and was more than glad to hear from you but was sorry to hear my fate. I did not think of getting such a note but it is all right. Of course I am sorry as can be but then if your mother does not want you to go with me why it is all right. I would hate to do anything contrary to her will. I know I drink and am a wild and bad boy and all that but you know that Marvin is a model boy. he never did anything in his life, he is as good as an Angel. I am an outcast I suppose so. Of course I don't do anything that will get you with a *drunkard as I am.*

And as far as me not coming back after Xmas I will be here but then that is all right. I know how it is when you don't want to go with a boy. A girl has to make up a good excuse to tell him, so you see that is the case with you. You want to make things as smooth as possible, so that is all right, but I would rather you would have just told me that you did not dare quit Warren and go with me. I would not have got mad at you for it and that would have been all that there was to it.

I was a fool for trying to go with you any way. I might have known you would not have gone with me.

But then you said for me to write to you when I went home, but what do you ask that for you would be Marvins Sweetheart and he would not like for you to be writing me and going with him. And then you would not want to be writing to a *drunkard* like I am. I am to far below you to write to you and then you do not want my picture. You want the the one you are going with not I.

Well, I suppose you have heard enough of the *Drunkard* that they call Will Rogers, so I will close hoping you all a merry evening, as I expect I had better not go as your Mother might object to me. And as Jess says that no decent person would speak to me and I know all of you are decent but I am very sorry that I can not come.

But don't think that I am mad at you in the least and I like you more than I ever did before, for the truth never hurts me.

I will send this by Harry Basye, as he is going up.

I will close,

> From a drunkard who likes you but whom
> you never cared for.

Now please dont let any one see this Maggie and I will not let any one see your note.

> Your would like to be Sweetheart.

*   *   *

Mrs. Garland Price finishes with: "Soon after the incident mentioned, Will was called back home because his sister's husband was shot and killed, and Will did not return after Christmas. Instead, he went to Kemper. I never saw Will but twice afterward — once in the *Follies*, in New York. But I was too bashful or timid to go back stage to speak to him. Later he was in Joplin, Missouri, and I went up and spoke to him. He looked at me and said, 'Why, you ain't growed a bit.'"

On the campus was a drinking fountain to which tin cups were chained. (This was before people had learned how deadly germs are.) On top of the fountain was a figure of a Grecian goddess bearing a stone pitcher on her shoulder. It was too much for Will and too much for the goddess, too, for he roped and yanked off one of her arms. The school authorities didn't like this, but let the goddess do the best she could with one arm and a pitiful stub. Then one day Will went to the pasture and roped a colt. The colt bolted down the street as fast as its legs would take it. Will lost hold of the rope and the colt started across the campus. It so happened that President Woods was walking across it when he was startled to see a colt racing past him with a rope trailing behind. He made a snatch at the rope and managed to seize it. In a moment he was going across the campus faster than he ever had in his life. The colt turned aside and shot into the back yard of a house, the president still hanging on. A clothesline caught the president under the chin and sent him sprawling in a most undignified way. He picked himself up and asked who had started all this. Of course, there was but one answer. The president threatened to expel Will (Will probably hoped he would) but Will held on the rest of the term. But he was growing more and more restless; finally when school was over for the year, he went home and informed his father that he was not going back.

His father was disturbed; in fact, he was always disturbed

about Will. The boy wouldn't study, he wouldn't work; all he wanted to do was to swing a rope, ride horses, or go visiting. Anything to have a good time. So his father thought it over . . . what could he do with the boy? His solution floored poor Will.

CHAPTER 3

Will Goes to a Military School in Missouri

IT WAS NOTHING less than to send Will to a military school. Again the poor boy must have heard the clap of doom. It was the fashion, at this time in the Territory, to send hard-to-control boys to military schools with the hope that the stern discipline would make them toe the mark.

Will conceived the idea that if he was good during the summer, his father might relent and not send him off to more of this damnable schooling. An incident happened almost at once. He and a boy of his own age rode horseback into Oologah and while there Will thought he would show off by smoking a cigar, just then the supreme test of manhood. Will bought a product known as a Pittsburgh stogie. After he'd bought them, he was afraid somebody would see and tell his father, so Will kept them out of sight until he started home. He ripped a sulphur match on his boot sole, started a stogie going, and nonchalantly tossed the match over his shoulder, as he'd seen the men do on the store porch. The cigar was downright strong; but he wasn't going to let a cigar conquer him, so, when he finished this one, he set another going. It was strong, too.

It was not long until he discovered something was wrong with his stomach, also he began to experience trouble remaining in the saddle. Then he smelled something and looked back, and, great guns! the grass was on fire and the blaze was running before the wind. The boys raced their horses to Will's home, snatched gunny sacks, wet them, and raced back. Will's head and stomach were swirling, but he had to fight the prairie fire. Neighbors saw the smoke and soon there was a line of fire fighters. They wet their sacks in Four Mile Creek and fought as best they could. It was not until after dark that the fire was conquered. When it was over one of the men said, "What if we hadn't licked the fire, Willie? What would you be doing?"

"I'd be ridin'," said Will.

Will's father did not get home that night. But the next day he returned from one of his political trips and there, before him, were the blackened fields. Then he called for Will who, whatever his weaknesses, was not a liar. He told all. His father did not say much, but Will knew what he was thinking. Will was exactly right.

These days Will liked to ride in to Oologah (no cigar) and stand in front of the store and do tricks with his rope. As usual he liked to have people watch him and, as he twirled, he would exchange witticisms with them. Sometimes he commented on the trick.

His restless nature began to assert itself (and possibly it was because he liked to get away from his father's disapproval of his unconventional ways); anyway, he decided to see a little of the world and went by himself to Buffalo, New York. On May 21, 1896, a rather remarkable thing happened. He was walking down the street, looking for a barbershop where he could get his hair cut. He saw one in the corner of the Brown Building at Main and Seneca Streets and was about to cross the street to go into the barbershop, which was in the corner of the building, ground floor. Just then a street beggar solicited him and Will stopped to talk to him. Finally the man turned away and Will started to cross the street. The space under the building was being excavated; suddenly there was a frightful roar and the structure collapsed. There were nine barbers in the shop, a cashier, a boot-black and several patrons. Three of the barbers were killed and every patron was either hurt or killed. If the beggar had not stopped him, Will would have been in the barbershop. Will felt that this delay to talk to a beggar had saved his life.

The dreaded day of return to school drew nearer and nearer, and on fateful January 13, 1897, Will arrived at Boonville, Missouri, enrolled at the Kemper Military School. He was the most exuberantly dressed boy who ever came to that institution of learning. He had on a cowboy hat; at this time there was no such thing as a "ten-gallon" hat, but he had its brother. Encircling the crown of the hat was a horsehair cord that could have hung a horse thief. He had a flamboyant shirt, a vest that talked for itself, and high-heeled boots. No other boy arrived wearing boots, but that made no difference to this young scholar. And around his neck, protecting it from the elements, was a flaming red bandanna handkerchief. But most noticeable of all — most astonishing of all — was that his trunk was tied with a lariat. In those days, trunks were "roped" and Will had killed two birds with one stone. No other boy had ever come to Kemper with these educational aids.

He cared not at all for the glances shot at him. He spoke to everybody and it wasn't long till everybody was speaking to him. And soon they began to like him. How could anyone not like such an exuberant cowboy?

When the material was collected for his "autobiography," Will devoted three sentences to his career at Kemper. It is worth a great deal more than that, for the qualities that were to make him began to show themselves. There were, when he entered, seventy-two students, many of them from the Indian Territory, many part Indian. I was fortunate enough to meet his roommate — John H. Payne. He was, when I talked to him, assistant superintendent of Creekmore Park, Fort Smith, Arkansas. He lives at 1010 West Dodson Avenue, Fort Smith.

On the first day of drill, the commandant ordered the boys to hold their hands high above their heads, and bend until their fingers touched the ground. As young Payne was doing this, he moaned, "It hurts."

The boys took it up, after drill, and that's how he got the nickname of Hurt Payne.

"I had the pleasure of rooming with Will," said Hurt Payne, "— that is, if you could call it that. The reason he chose me as a roommate was that we had met each other at Webbers Falls in 1894 (I think it was). We had gone there with our fathers to get our Cherokee allotment money from the Government. We got the money and pushed it in our pockets. Did we feel rich? Did we feel important! We had a double bunk; that is, it was one section. One bed above the other. It was Will's favorite trick, when he saw me asleep in my upper bunk, to creep quietly up, seize the bunk, uptilt it and slide me to the floor. And there he would stand, laughing and 'hurrahing' me. I couldn't get too mad for he hadn't a mean bone in his body. His father was an important Cherokee politician in the northern part of the territory, and mine was one from the southern part; and we both had Indian blood, so all this made a common bond.

"Will was seventeen and entered what today would be equivalent to the sophmore class. He always pretended that him and education were strangers but that was just part of his waggery; as a matter of fact he was better educated than nine-tenths of the people of the Territory. I've looked it up to make sure of what I was sayin' and here are the subjects he studied: arithmetic, algebra, grammar, history, bookkeeping, letter writing, elocution, physical geography and Bible study. I remember elocution, letter writing and Bible study came only once a week. He was a dogie at arithmetic, algebra and bookkeeping, but when it came to a talking subject he led the herd. Nobody in class could talk as much as he could. And good, too — especially when he was dodging an answer to a question. Sometimes I had the feeling the teachers were giving him the rein so he could cavort around. He was good in history. But when he ever studied was a full-blown mystery; he was too active to tie down to a book. Sometimes, after the class bell had sounded, he would say, 'Hurt, what's the lesson about today? Tell me so I can see how well you know it.' Of course I knew he hadn't opened his book, but I liked to tell him, and so did the other boys. Bein' a natural-born talker like he was, he would make a wonderful showing in class — better'n the rest of us who had really laid our running-irons on the book.

"A trying occasion was elocution. We had to get up and recite such things as Patrick Henry's 'Give Me Liberty, or Give Me Death.' We'd do it seriously. But Will wouldn't. He'd torture his face till it looked like a wrinkled saddle blanket, make funny motions with his hands and roll his eyes and, some way or other, manage to make us laugh. I never saw him get up in front of a class without making them laugh before he sat down. That lassoo! He had it with him most of the time. The profs hated it like Adam hated snakes. He liked to take it out to the campus an' rope with it. But the officers would grab it and take it away from him. His greatest scholastic trouble was gettin' his rope past the guard officers. One time he wanted to take it out, and knowin' the guard officer was watchin', Will pulled up his shirt an' coiled it around his middle. When he passed the officer he saluted most correctly; the officer returned it — then stared at the malignant growth on Will's stummick. He called Will back — and that was rope's end. But it didn't discourage Will. He would practice with his rope, even if he knew an angry mob was goin' to seize it and hang him with it.

"I'd put this down as a notable thing about him: how much he could get out of nothin'. Our superintendent had a belligerent way, when he was goin' to reprimand a cadet, of roaring out his name with a 'Mister' attached to it. One day the superintendent bawled out, 'Stand up, Mister Rogers.'

"Will got up an inch at a time as if he couldn't understand why such an ignoble thing had been saddled on him, worked his eyebrows up and down, and said, 'Yes, sir' in such a manner that it made us roar with laughter. If one of us had got up and done exactly the same thing, it wouldn't have been funny, but it was when Will handled the situation. That's what I mean when I say he could get much out of practically nothing.

"I call to mind one night him and another cadet — it wasn't me — worked out a prank. There was a fire hose in the hall. I reckon it hadn't been used since the time of Geronimo. Well, Will and this cadet I speak of got an alarm clock, set it ringing and ran down the hall shouting 'Fire! Fire!' The boys leaped out of their bunks and into the hall in a little less than no time at all. And there was Will and his compatriot dousing them with the hose. They had never had such a good time in their lives. I'm now speakin' of Will and his confederate. Of course they had to pay for it — demerits. This didn't set too well with the teachers. Will was always hangin' on to his scholastic career with one hand.

"About the only enjoyment he got was to arrange for his beat to pass the kitchen. Then he would ask the cook if he wouldn't do something for the vanishing American. Another thing he didn't like was to clean his rifle. The commandant hardly ever gave the rifle his eye without finding it lacked its natural grace an' brilliance. Then onto the beat Will'd go.

"Now and then on Friday night we had a chance. The girls had to be rustled from the town supply. Will was smitten on a town girl named Mamie Johnson and asked her to go to a dance. She turned him down. He never said much about it, but he was hurt. When anything touched him deeply he did not talk about it. It was a way of his, a mixture of Indian in this, I guess.

"His jokes today seem simple, but they were hilarious to a set of lively young boys ready to haw-haw at anything that came along. One time, in physics, the teacher said, 'Where can a person go to get H_2O?'

" 'To the circus!' said Will.

" 'Why to the circus?'

" 'Because it has so much pink lemonade.'

"Well, that was funny to us. On the other hand he was so good-natured and had such a warm smile we were ready to laugh at almost anything.

"Will's father would send checks and Will'd go into the Commercial Bank in Boonville to get them cashed. Hangin' on the wall was an ornate chromo of 'Custer's Last Fight.' One day Will looked at it and said, 'That's the only picture I ever saw where the Indians got the best of it.'

"There was a chili parlor in the town. Will liked to slip away from the dormitory and go to the chili parlor. We'd all sit on round-topped stools and he'd talk and we'd laugh and have a good time. It was here that he developed his great attachment for chili."

At the end of the first term, Will returned to Oologah. He was proud that he had been "away" to military school; indeed he was the only one in his immediate section who had gone. One day, shortly after he got back, Dick Nicholson, a neighbor boy, came to visit him at the ranch and Will launched into his school adventures. Dick asked how they drilled. "I'll show you," said the obliging Will and, going in, got his father's rifle. Will shouldered it and began going through the manual of arms with a mighty display of military efficiency. But things did not go quite right; he struck the ground too hard and the gun went off with a roar. The startled Will almost leaped out of his clothes. It was really quite serious, for the bullet grazed his left temple; he carried the scar for the rest of his life. Will had never cared for guns and had never hunted with guns, as the other boys in the neighborhood had. And now he cared for them even less.

"The mischief Will was gettin' into mounted up," continued Hurt Payne. "Demerits kept pilin' up. He said, 'If I had to walk off all my demerits I would cover more territory than Daniel Boone!'

"Springtime was comin' on and he was growing more and more restless. He wanted to light a shuck for any ol' place just so it wasn't school. But getting his hands on the money — that was a considerable problem. He didn't write his father, because he knew his father wouldn't send it. So he dispatched letters to two of his sisters tellin' them he was in need of money, but not mentionin' what he was goin' to use it for. He didn't tell the sisters he was writing to both of them; he made each letter seem like the only one. The sisters each sent him ten dollars and he hopped a train for Texas. Sometimes that statement has been glossed over by sayin' he decided to try his hand at ranchin', but the facts are he just plain vamoosed. He departed the halls of learnin' toward the end of his junior year, which would be about parallel to now being a junior in high school. When he went, about half our fun went, too."

Roy D. Williams, now an ex-judge in Boonville, gave me this graphic picture of Will's schooldays:

"He used to say to the little boys, 'You be a calf an' I'll rope you around the left leg.' And he'd do it, too. The left, not the right. The middle-sized boys were the cows and as they ran away they had to *moo-oo-oo*. He would rope the cows around the right leg. The tall, rangy boys were the steers. He would rope them around the middle. To the short, stocky boys he would say, 'Now run like a bull after a heifer.' He always roped them. We got twenty-five cents an hour. We got lots of bruises and rope burns and sometimes we would, when jerked up, land on our heads. But also it was fun. We would have let him rope us for nothing. Sometimes, after a roping spree, he would take us out for a chili spree. He was the most popular boy in school. We even liked him when we had welts and bruises."

CHAPTER 4

Will Runs Away from School— Turns up in Higgins, Texas

As a result of all his mischief and demerits, Will had been threatened with expulsion. But he didn't know where to go. He did know he didn't want to go back and face his father who had pretty well made up his mind about his harum-scarum boy. One of the boys at Kemper had been Billy Johnston and he had told Will Rogers about a ranch near Higgins, Texas, run by W. P. Ewing. It is from his son Frank Ewing, who was about Will's age, that I get the true story of what happened when Will dusted out (at night) from Kemper. Frank Ewing lives on the old Ewing Ranch.

Will arrived at Higgins, in the spring of 1898, without knowing a soul. The post-office address was Higgins, Texas, but the ranch was on Littlerobe Creek, across the line in Ellis County, Oklahoma. The distance was eight miles. There was no mail; that is, the mail the family received was picked up at the post office when the family came to Higgins.

Will got a job driving a delivery wagon for a grocery store; the wagon was horse-drawn, and up and down the street went the young military man guiding the destiny of the ancient animal. Will discovered in his professional rounds that Frank Ewing had a sister living in the town. He hastened to see her; she said she would send word by one of the neighbors that Will was there; and so, while waiting, Will went to live at her house.

Frank Ewing tells the story: "We heard at our Littlerobe

Ranch that a young man in Higgins was trying to get out to our place. We had not inquired for a hand. . . . Who was this mysterious young man? Finally my father and I came to town in our horse-drawn buckboard. A young man darted out from what might be called a sidewalk and asked if this was Mr. Ewing? Will Rogers said that Billy Johnston had told him about our ranch and that he wanted to get a job on it. 'Exactly who are you?' asked my father. 'I'm Will Rogers, from Oologah, the Territory. I was in school but I decided to quit. I am a good worker.' A ranch always needs help and so my father told him he would take him out to the ranch. One thing I noticed about the stranger's grips was that he had a lariat lashed around them. It seemed a bit unusual equipment for an educational career, but we did not say anything about it. My father recognized that our puzzling caller was from a good family, and wrote to Will's father announcing that Will had arrived. Will's father was thoroughly miffed at Will's desertion of school and wrote back for him to keep him and that if he could get any work out of Will it would be better than he'd ever done. It didn't look very promising for our visitor, but he surprised us all by pitching in and working as hard as any hand on the place. He would sing 'coon' songs and he would say things that kept us constantly amused. He was the life of the bunkhouse. The other men would play cards and gamble, but Will wouldn't.

"We were putting on an extensive cattle drive — six hundred head — from our ranch to Medicine Lodge, Kansas, and Will went along, making a full hand. Flood waters came up and we had to camp for four days at the mouth of a creek. Taking care of cattle during rainy weather and especially when they're being driven is hard work, but Will never complained; in fact, he enjoyed it. His good nature made him a favorite.

"When the drive was over, my father offered him a check for thirty dollars, which, at that time, was top wages for a month's work, but Will refused it, said he'd had such a good time he wouldn't accept pay. And he didn't. He stayed with us four months — until he heard that there was to be a cattle drive from Amarillo, Texas, to the Mule Shoe Country of Kansas. He hustled to Amarillo, got the job, made the drive, and came back to us. I think he accepted pay for this one. Finally his hippity-hoppity nature made him move on. We all felt lonesome and wished our fun-maker and good fellow would come back."

Will was one of those boys who can't be induced to work at home, but who simply tears into it when they go visitin'.

Will finally headed home, his scholastic career at an end; six schools had done all they could. He beat his way on a freight. Almost the first thing he did was to repay his sisters; he had saved the money for this by riding the freights. And now he must face his father. His father had moved to town — that is, Claremore. Clem had become more and more interested in politics; his money was piling up. He owned the Rogers Ranch, he was vice-president of the bank, and he had a livery stable. It was usually considered beneath the dignity of a banker to traffic in anything so humble as a livery stable, but Uncle Clem trafficked wherever there was money, and everything he turned his hand to made money. And now happy-go-lucky Will was to come before him. There is no record of what his father said. It's probably just as well.

This is typical of the kind of humor Will enjoyed at this time. He owned two hounds; one he called "You Know," the other "Did He Bite You?" When a visitor arrived, Will would make it easy for the dogs to come up. Almost always the visitor would indicate one of them and say, "What's his name?"

Will would look at the visitor and solemnly say, "Did He Bite You?"

The person would disclaim this and say he merely wanted to

107766

know his name. Will would look reproving and say, "You Know." It was his favorite joke; he never seemed to tire of it.

July 4, 1899, Claremore put on what was known as a "roping contest" — later such affairs became rodeos. Will won first prize. He was the noisest contestant there, and the funniest. He had a good time and so did the people. (He didn't know it, of course, but this was his start in show business.)

And now began a strange experience. Will was restless; on top of this he did not like the family that was running the home ranch. He boarded with them, but as soon as a meal was over he darted away and kept out of sight as much as he could. He had a cousin named Spi M. Trent who lived at Fort Gibson. Occasionally the two were together; in fact, they had known each other all their lives. Spi, however, was four years younger. Will, in his sea of discontent, proposed to Spi that they build a log cabin and live in it. In this way, Will could get away from the hired family and its depressing influence.

Spi acceded and immediately the two started to build a log cabin on a hill about a mile from the ranch house. With his usual foresight Will got somebody else to do the hard work; this was the cutting and the dragging of the logs to the place where the cabin was to bloom. The unfortunate man on whom this job fell was colored. But Hayward did not complain. If Mr. Willie wanted it that settled it.

At last, after a great deal of activity, the cabin was built in 1899 and Will and Spi moved in, certainly as queer an event as had yet happened in Will's life. They bought furniture from the ranch house, procured a kitchen stove, and were ready to partake of the joys of a carefree life. Their troubles began almost immediately. Food. Eats. They hadn't given very intensive thought to this, so now they brought some cows from the ranch. But who was to milk? That was a knotty problem.

Will gave thought to the subject and developed the idea that Spi should milk since he (Will) was supplying everything. Then they would share the cooking and dishwashing. Will was never better than when working out such problems.

Spi agreed to this and they began their adventure in contentment.

At first it was wonderful. Get up any time they wished, no one to make them work, trips to Oologah. Of course there were the damned ol' cows. That annoying matter came up twice a day. Sometimes it almost seemed to hurt Will to sit around the house and let Spi milk. But, some way or other, he always overcame his pain.

Then together they would wash the dishes. This did not take long.

When it rained, their enthusiasm was considerably damped, but they managed to stick it out. Now and then they rode to Will's sister's, or to one of the neighbor's, and got a home-cooked meal. Will was never so friendly in his life; he loved everybody, especially if they set a good table. He especially liked Navy beans and he liked the chili which he had learned to eat at Kemper. In fact, he liked almost anything that a friendly neighbor would cook. As he and Spi ate, Will would talk about the fun they were having batching.

Neighbor boys came in and enjoyed this Boys' Heaven. They raced their ponies. Will took part in this. Sometimes they would ride as far away as Claremore; the other boys would get cigars, but Will wouldn't. The ones he had smoked the day of the prairie fire had made him sick; he wanted no more truck with tobacco. The other boys swore; they prided themselves on the frightful oaths they could turn loose. But Will did not swear. (Was it the influence his mother had had on him?)

One day Will found one of his steers dead; examination

showed it had been shot. In the ranch country this was a serious offense.

Will's suspicion fastened on a man who lived not far away. The man had a cornfield; around it he had put up a makeshift barbed-wire fence with only one wire clinging to wobbly posts. Will's steer had knocked over a post and gotten into the corn. Will was thoroughly and completely mad. The man had shot his steer without warning or justification. He should have come to Will and told him of the damages and Will would have paid him. Now Will would have the man arrested; the jury would take care of the steer-killer.

So Will and his cousin mounted their horses and started to the man's cabin. It began to rain and they became soaked and chilled. When they arrived in sight of the cabin, they were surprised to see what a miserable shanty it was. They knocked. A tired, over-worked woman came to the door and invited them in. Will and Spi took their horses to a pole stable and then went to the house, where they found five children living under the most depressing "poor white trash" conditions. The wife said, "Sit down. My man'll be along soon, I reckon."

Will and Spi sat down, taking in more and more of the starving conditions the family was living under. At last the man returned — a fierce-looking bearded specimen.

Now was the time to demand an accounting. Instead Will felt sorry for the man and his impoverished family.

The rain continued to fall mournfully on the poor cabin. They had a "sowbelly" supper. Then the man went to the door, looked out, and said, "'Tain't fitten weather to travel, so I'll invite you to bed down with us. We cain't offer you much, but such as it is you're welcome to it."

The next morning they had a pork-and-beans breakfast. When time came for Will and Spi to leave, the whole family lined up outside the door and waved good-by. Will's and Spi's visit had been a godsend in the way of news and talk to the wretched family.

"I was sure mad when I started on this trip," said Will as the two rode away, "but I'm not now. That poor man could kill two steers and I wouldn't care."

The strain of cooking and trying to get out of milking began to tell on Will. They went visiting oftener and oftener and brought back more and more pies and cakes. Finally Will proposed that they call it off. And this they did, each pretending it was against his earnest wishes. But the surprising thing is that the two stuck it out for eight months.

Will engaged in pranks which today seem crude, but at that time were accepted as a way of life. David W. Hazen tells this story in the *Portland Oregonian* for August 17, 1935. In substance it reads:

"I was a printer on the *Advance*, Chetopa, Kansas; the town was about two miles from the Kansas-Indian Territory line. Just inside the Indian Territory was a hamlet called Bluejacket; about the only good thing that could be said for it was that it had a dance hall. Once, when Will was visiting in Vinita, he brought some of his rough-and-ready friends to one of our dances. They had a good time and it was not all on the dance floor. I had hired a livery team in Chetopa, got my girl, and had driven to the dance party at Bluejacket. Will Rogers was there. Everybody knew him, for he was always the center of attention. He could think of more devilment in a minute than an ordinary person could in a month. The dance went along all right; knocking off time came and I escorted my girl out to my hired livery rig. Instantly, even in the dark, I knew something was wrong. In fact there was a quite considerable bit wrong. Will Rogers and his friends had taken the harness off my horse, put it on backward, and turned the horses around so that their heads faced the buggy. Not only this but they had changed wheels so that the big wheels were in front and the small wheels in the rear. I was mad and I was embarrassed in front of my girl. How to change the wheels by myself? I heard a snicker in the dark; the pranksters were enjoying my embarrassment. Then I heard a voice I knew was Will Rogers's. He was telling his lively friends they should come and help me. And this they did. If it had not been for Will Rogers they would have gone off and left me to manage the situation as best I could. After the change was made, I started with my girl on the return trip to Chetopa. It was like Will Rogers to engage in such a prank; also it was like him to help me when the fun was over."

In spite of his pranks he was, in many ways, more sober-minded than his lively friends, for he did not play cards, gamble, smoke, drink, or get into situations with girls. Sometimes, in a card game, his friends would bet their horses. This was considered hitting rock bottom. Will would not dream of betting his horse or his saddle.

Another characteristic was his kindness to animals. Especially horses. The Reverend A. G. McCown, 325 East Main Street, Edmond, Oklahoma, sent me this story:

When Mr. McCown was sixteen years old, he was living on his father's ranch in Lincoln County, Oklahoma. Some of their horses had strayed away and young Mr. McCown and two cowboys from the ranch mounted their horses and rode off to search for the missing animals. The horses they rode had their tails bobbed which, at this time, was the fashion in this section. At last they came in sight of some cowboys lounging in the shade of a tree, playing mumblety-peg. They would flip knives for points, and the loser would have to pull the peg out of the ground with his teeth, then he would spit out the dirt he had accumulated. One of the players was Will Rogers.

As young Mr. McCown and his friends rode up, Will Rogers called, "Are you lookin' for horse thieves?"

"Yes," they said.

"Well, you've come to the right place," said young Will. "Look at these fellers here with me, don't they all look like horse thieves?" Mr. McCown and his friends explained they were looking for their horses which had wandered away. When Will saw the bobbed tails of the horses, his manner changed. "Say, that's a shame," he said, pointing to the docked tails. "If you treated your other horses like you've done these, I don't blame them for runnin' away. Why do you want to cut off their tails? Don't you know it hurts them and does no one any good? If God hadn't wanted tails on horses, he would have borned them that way."

Here's an anecdote from Joe Galbreath, my favorite rancher and storyteller:

"Here's something you might like to put in the book you say you're writin' about Will. Has the advantage of never havin' been published before, least so far as I've ever seen. Begins in Territory days. Cattle was branded by their owners and turned out on the open range. Each spring and fall the owners would have a get-together, round up their cattle, and each owner'd 'cut out' his animals. They were nicknamed the 'Greasy Roll Outfits' from the fact that their bedrolls were usually of waterproof canvas, also from the fact that the rolls accumulated a greasy surface from rubbin' against the horses. They didn't have no Christmas Night perfume smell. They smelled like something under the porch.

"Well, in the fall of 1898, there was a roundup and both Will and Hamp Scudder were along. They were roundin' up in that part of the Dog Creek Hills which is northeast of Claremore and southwest of Foyil. Lots of Indians in these hills, mostly Cherokees, all had cattle. Will and Hamp bein' the youngest were delegated to 'hold' the cattle as the others brought them in; this was near a place known as Sageeyah Switch. On the day I'm leadin' up to there was quite a number of cattle and Hamp and Will was havin' their trouble keepin' 'em herded, cattle nature bein' what it is. Will was ridin' his black pony Nigger Baby. Will took advantage of every lull of activity to practice ropin'. He would run his horse and toss his rope at anything on the ground from a weed to a buckbush. His horse got heated. Finally come the time Will wanted to cool off, so he unloosened the saddle cinch and went and set down under a tree with Hamp for that purpose.

"Will said, 'You see that black steer? If he leaves the herd, you watch me catch him!'

"Sure enough the steer made a run, and so did Will, the latter toward his horse. Will forgot to tighten the saddle girth an' leaped on the horse and tore after that steer like a coyote after a jack rabbit. He threw a Johnny Blocker which landed on the steer as neat as a bride's veil. In just no time flat, things happened. Will's saddle was yanked half around and Will went sailin' through the air like a bullfrog into a pond. He got up, holding his left hand clamped over his right arm. His arm was broke.

"Hamp took him to the home of a family of full bloods named Tincup, borrowed their horse and buggy, and took Will to the doctor's in Chelsea and had the arm set. Will's oldest sister, Sallie McSpadden, wanted Will to stay with her in Chelsea until the arm knitted, but Will was too restless and said, 'Oh, it won't kill me. I'll get along all right.' And he did, but after that he always saw to it that his saddle girth was tight, a good idea for anybody to follow."

Will's restlessness continued. His energy seemed to grow rather than to wane. His interest in work remained about the same.

One day there came what seemed to be a wonderful chance to get away from home and have an immense amount of fun. This was to take part in a roundup at the mouth of Caney River, on Big Lake, and travel northward to the Kansas line. Most of the cattle were owned by his father. His father engaged a man known as "Uncle Blue," who was to be in charge. Will was to be his helper. But Will didn't know what a hard-driving man Uncle Blue Starr was; he got the hands up at four o'clock in the morning and kept them hopping until nine at night. Even with Will's tremendous energy, this was a pretty demanding program. Every morning Uncle Blue would have a hard time getting Will out of his blankets. Will always had wonderful excuses: he hadn't slept well, his back hurt him, could he lay a few minutes more?

Uncle Blue did some thinking on the subject. One morning he took a set of chain harness on his shoulders and went to the blankets where Will was peacefully slumbering. Suddenly Uncle Blue began to stomp the ground and yell at the top of his voice, "Whoa! Whoa! there, you damned mules," and at the same time to shake the harness.

Will thought the mules were running over him and jumped to his feet with a speed that made wide-awake men rub their eyes. The hint did help; after that Uncle Blue did not have to prod quite so vigorously.

Fun and excitement could not last forever. At last the roundup was over and Will went back — to the ranch and the same discontent.

But he was industrious at roping. He would go to anyone who could teach him. One was Jim Rider, another was Jim Hopkins, a tramp roper from Texas. Will would spend hours with them. In the meantime he was interested in girls. Kate Ellis was his favorite. Her father ran the little hotel in Oologah. But there were others; Belle Price, Mary Bullette. But Kate Ellis was *the* one. There was talk that the two were going to get married, but her father was opposed to it. Will was too wild, he said; even his own father couldn't control him. And then, to make matters worse, Will bought a rubber-tired buggy — the first in that section — and showed the girls better times than ever. He was so careful of it that, when he wasn't using it, he hoisted it by ropes and let it hang from the rafters to keep the tires from being flattened. In addition, he got a derby hat and the fanciest clothes that could be procured in Kansas City and became the flashiest dresser in the Cherokee Nation. Roping, girls, dances, parties, good times. That was his life. The cakewalk was all the go. At a "tacky party" in Oologah, Will won a prize for doing the cake-walk — a ginger cake. At these parties he sang "Coon, Coon, Coon," which was popular just then, and "I Ain't Got a Dollar I Can Call My Own." Most of the young people, when asked to perform, had to be coaxed as was the fashion of the day, but not Will. He would pop up like a jack-in-the-box and sing as long as anyone would listen.

Will's unceasing restlessness continued; he proposed to his father that instead of shipping their next load of cattle to Kansas City they send them to New York. His father didn't approve, but Will talked him into it, and so Will and Spi Trent's brother, Dick, started with the Rogers steers to New York. It was a long hard trip; the cattle had to be watered and fed. The two boys slept in the caboose in their work clothes. Now and then they would have to go back to see if any of the steers were "down." If a steer was knocked off its feet, the others might trample him to death. But the important thing was that the boys were going to New York. At last they arrived, sold the cattle, put on their "good" clothes they had brought in their valises, and started out to see the sights. They stayed four days — two green, country boys in a big city — and then started back. Will's father was eager to hear the news. What he heard was not very good. They had lost money. They would have done better to have sold the cattle in Kansas City.

Will grew more and more discontented; his father more and more concerned. When was the boy going to settle down? In May 1901, his father told Will he could go to Kansas City with a load of cattle and see how successfully he could market them. Will was eager to try, since it meant going somewhere. While in Kansas City, Will met a stock shipper who told him that Memphis, Tennessee, was going to hold a big Confederate Veterans' Reunion. Will saw vast possibilities. As soon as he'd sold his cattle he went straight to Memphis and met the officials. Yes, they were going to have a reunion. "How would you like me to put on a ridin' and ropin' contest?" asked Will.

They looked him up and down. He appeared a bit young. (He wasn't yet twenty-one.) But he was self-assured and finally they agreed he could bring a group of cowboys to the reunion.

Will rushed back home with the good news.

His father was thunderstruck. He had sent the boy to Kansas City to sell cattle and he had come back saying he was going to put on a show in Memphis.

Will threw himself into organizing the Oologah end, working day and night, which must have completely mystified his father. On May 25, Will Rogers and J. C. Law left with their riders for Memphis—forty in all. (Their horses and cattle had been sent in advance.)

This advertisement appeared in the *Memphis Commercial Appeal*, May 29, 1901:

Cowboys and Indians at Montgomery Park
Grand Roping Contests, Indian Parades and War Dances
Miss Lucille Mulhall, the Daring Broncho Rider
Will Appear Daily and Rope the Wildest Texas Steers
49 Indians and Cowboys
Contests Daily at 3 P.M.

This paper, two days later, described the event: "Charley McClellan, a quarter-blood Cherokee, and his seventeen-year-old brother, Steve, are among the most daring and skillful riders. But

Charley was badly hurt Wednesday by his horse falling on him. Charley is a typical-looking Indian, with long black hair, black eyes and high cheek bones."

Will Roger's name appears for the first time outside of the home papers, but briefly, for this is all that it says: "Messers. Sharpe, Franklin, Rogers and Hopkins entertained the crowd with fancy roping on horseback." Charley McClellan, his old roommate at Willie Halsell, had done much better.

The show lasted four days. Will and his cowboys put on exhibitions of roping and riding; they would come down the field at full speed, yelling at the top of their voices. The boys in gray must have thought they were back on Missionary Ridge.

At last it was over and Will and men returned to Oologah. The affair had been a tremendous success; the only fault anyone could possibly find was that Will came back broke. There is no record of what his father said.

His father told Will he could now run the home ranch, which must have been bad news for fun-loving Will. That meant everlasting work. But Will said he would. His father was living in Claremore with Will's stepmother, when Will started to manage the ranch. Almost the first rattle out of the box, he had a wooden platform made so there could be dances in the yard. This was a new idea in ranching; even the oldest cattlemen had never heard of it. But this was what the young ranch manager wanted: excitement, laughter, gaiety, flying heels, swishing skirts. And that is exactly what he had; he hired a band from Muskogee, and invited people from as far away as Kansas. The Rogers Ranch was the liveliest spot in the Indian Territory.

Miss Gazelle Lane told me how Will got up swimming parties; in fact, any kind of party suited Will. Swimming suits had not yet entered the mind of man. People put on their old clothes and hopped into the water; it was that simple. The boys would go behind one clump of bushes, the girls another. One day Will came charging toward the clump of bushes where the girls were, shouting at the top of his considerable voice, "You can look now, girls. I've got my hat on." The girls screamed and prayerfully closed their eyes. Of course, it was a joke, for he was dressed from head to toe. "He was always thinking up things like that," said Miss Lane. "He was the leader of our stomp dances. They were held outdoors Saturday nights on the little round knoll north of the Oowala Schoolhouse. Will always wanted us to dress up like Indians and mostly we would do that. He would dress up, too, and, now and then, would let off a war whoop that sounded like the battle of Claremore Mound. He wasn't the best dancer present, but he was the loudest; he brought more fun and good times to our stomp dances than did anybody else. What energy! He could dance all night, and when the dance was over, would be going as strong as when the dance had started."

And then something exciting happened. A new girl arrived in town — Betty Blake, from the Ozarks in Arkansas. She was a year younger than Will.

CHAPTER 5

Betty Blake Is Born in the Ozarks of Arkansas

BETTY BLAKE was quite a remarkable person in her own right. She was born in a log cabin in the Ozark Mountains of Arkansas. The cabin was blown down and destroyed in 1928. There are still faint outlines of where it stood. The collection of houses where she was born was called Silver Springs. But the name didn't last long; it was changed to Monte Ne, and this is what it is called today.

She was one of the many daughters of James Wyeth Blake. He ran a "grist mill"; this meant that he ground corn, wheat, and small grain. He was a poor man with a large family and had to keep his mill wheel turning. He was respected by everyone in the hills. The Blake family had come from eastern Tennessee after the Civil War. Young Jim married Amelia Crowder, whose family had come from Buncombe County, North Carolina.

Betty's father died when she was three years old and now the family had a problem, indeed. How was the widow to support all her children?

The name of the town where Betty was born is Monte Ne. (The latter part is pronounced Nay.) At one time, and in a curious way, the little town was famous; it was known from one end of the country to another, for here it was that the fabulous William Hope ("Coin") Harvey made his headquarters in his later years, and it was in this town that he stood on a platform in 1932 and nominated himself for President of the United States as a member of the Patriots of American Party. He was not elected.

But he did kick up an immense amount of excitement. His nickname came from his theory of silver coinage. I have had this theory explained to me a couple of times but have not yet quite grasped it. However, I do not mean to give up. He wrote a book on the subject — *Coin's Financial School,* and is credited with having made a half-million dollars from it. It makes my mouth water. He did other amazing things. He built a railroad from Lowell to Monte Ne, a distance of six miles. The first passenger was William Jennings Bryan. That afternoon he made a speech in which he said that he envisioned Monte Ne as becoming a great and powerful city. The town now is not quite as large as it was then.

When Coin Harvey arrived on the job, the town had another name. He thought up Monte Ne; he said it was Spanish for Mountains of Water. I asked a Spanish-speaking person or two what the words Monte Ne meant. They didn't know, so I told them in a way not to hurt their feelings.

The Reverend J. G. Bailey was not only a minister of the Gospel but also postmaster on the side. There was another Silver Springs in that section, so he wrote the post office department asking the name be changed to Vinola. But the letter was written in longhand and when the experts in Washington bent their talents to it, the name came out Vinda. And this, for a short time, was the town's name. Until Coin Harvey came along with his happy inspiration.

He did other remarkable things. (Somebody ought to write a book about him.) He saw a wonderful future as a summer resort for Mountains of Water and built a Roman amphitheater. Under the amphitheater was a natural spring which still spouts up volumes of water — a new idea, I believe, in amphitheater construction. Then he sent to Venice and got a pair of gondolas and put them on the lake. Evidently he expected Nature to take its course. But Nature did not and in all the Ozarks today there is not a single descendant of the original pair.

This is a brief picture of him by Erwin Funk, in the *Rogers (Arkansas) Daily News*, for July 1, 1950: "My first impressions were not very favorable. I found a slender, hawk-nosed man of medium height who stood and walked so straight that he gave the impression of being taller than he really was. His manner was curt and, while he was not discourteous, he was not interested in either speech-making or giving interviews. In other words, I got exactly nowhere."

Harvey ran a monthly magazine called *The Liberty Bell*, published in Monte Ne. For the April 1935 issue, he wrote an article entitled, "It Is Now or Never, If This Civilization Is to Be Saved." The methods he outlined have not been followed. It would seem to look pretty dark for civilization.

He planned an Egyptian pyramid to be built on the top of the highest mountain near Monte Ne. The pyramid was to be 32 feet square at the bottom and was to rise 130 feet and was to be of Portland cement: in this way it differed from the Egyptian. The earth would wash down, fill the valleys, and cover the pyramid. Then a new civilization would come along. He planned for that, for on the topmost point on the pyramid there was to be a brass plate which said:

> *When this can be read, go below*
> *and find the cause of the death of*
> *a former Civilization.*

Then he was going to put in the pyramid what civilization had died of. Inside, in printed form, was to be the history of the world since the dawn of civilization and the names and addresses of all who had contributed money to the building of the pyramid. The pyramid was to last as long as time itself. Alas, this did not quite work out, for it was never finished. The concrete work for the foundation support was put in, but that was as far as the work got. Seems too bad.

Coin Harvey had three children and this is why I am dealing with him at some length. One of them was Tom Harvey, and he is important to us because he was Betty Blake's first sweetheart. He used to court her by taking her on the railroad and on the gondolas. There really must have been something romantic about gliding along a lake in the Ozarks in a gondola. But it didn't get him anywhere. He used to say that his railroad was not as long as some railroads, but that it was just as wide. It is said that he used to write to other railroads and exchange passes with them.

After Mr. Blake died, Mrs. Blake moved the family to Rogers, a distance of about seven miles. The roads are bad today; they must have been heavy going then. Mrs. Blake had quite a houseful — six daughters and two sons — at 307 East Walnut Street.

I talked to Albert Graham who has lived in Monte Ne all his life and knew Mr. Blake. "Jim was a fine type of man, an asset to the community, respected by everybody. When 'Melie got to Rogers she was faced with the problem of supporting such a good-sized family, so she began to take in sewing and became the town dressmaker. It wasn't long before she married J. O. Boyd and there was a daughter. The marriage did not terminate well; he went to Texas, I believe, and she changed the name of the child to Blake. She growed up a Blake and became one of the Blake sisters, although she was only their half-sister. J. O. Boyd passed out of my ken and I don't know what happened to him. The family wasn't prone to speak of him.

"Her mother put Betty in the Rogers Academy. Her teacher was Professor J. W. Scroggs. It was run by the Congregational Church. She had to pay tuition; ran, as I recall it, about eighty dollars a year. But she never graduated. Her education was on the meager side. 'Twasn't as good as Will's, which comes in the nature of a surprise to most people, him belittlin' his like he always chose to do.

"The Blakes were a jolly living family. If you passed there on Sunday you'd hear laughter and see young people havin' a good time. Sometimes they'd overflow out into the yard, there was so many of them. Seven daughters, all seemed to get along well. The mother put the oldest ones to work; they had to help the young ones. It's really on the remarkable side how well they got along. 'Melie was a good manager."

I talked to Hugh Puckett who lives on a small farm just outside Rogers. "Yes, I knew Betty Blake well, for we clerked in the same store together off and on for several years — the H. L. Stroud Mercantile Company. Mr. Stroud passed away and today I'm to be one of his pallbearers. The store was always proud Betty worked there and used to advertise it, after Will got famous. Two of her sisters worked there, so, for a while, there were three Blake girls all working in the same store, something that's not too commonplace. She was always cheerful, customers liked her. She'd work awhile to get herself some clothes, then stop. She was always a tasty dresser. She took up railroad work. We always considered the Blakes a railroad family. She had two brothers — Sandy and John — and both engaged in railroad work. John was killed in an accident on the 'Frisco. Her sister married Will Marshall, who likewise was engaged in railroad work. Her sister Virginia married Bruce Quisenberry, who was in the drug business here, then moved to Joplin, Missouri, where he became engaged in the drug business and where he was deceased. He has a son, bearing the same name, in Washington where he is employed in the Pentagon Building. A publicity expert, I understand. Once served as Will's lecture manager.

"I'll relate an incident that comes to my mind. One time, after they were married, Will came here to our Victory Theater to raise money for flood sufferers in Arkansas. Of course the place was packed; you couldn't put another in with a shoehorn. He made a wonderful talk; then, as he was finishin', looked toward the wings and said, 'Bring Betty out.' When she came out he put his arm around her, looked down at the floor in that way of his, and said, 'I'm givin' this little talk free and in addition I've wrote a check for five hundred dollars for you folks here in this town. I owe you more than that for raisin' this girl for me.' Then he kissed her, something he didn't often do in public."

Erwin Funk, a well-known citizen of Rogers, Arkansas, said: "I was editor of the *Rogers Democrat* and Betty Blake worked for me, setting type. She was the first person in town to get a dollar a day for setting type. She did not work regularly, only when some crisis arose and she needed the money. We all liked her. She was sunny and cheerful."

Glimpses of Betty's life in Rogers: She was a high-spirited girl who was, as they said, in everything. One night the Board of Trade gave a banquet in the Harvey dining room. It was a most impressive occasion and everyone was self-conscious and eager to have the best of manners. Consommé was served in coffee cups. This was something new; the guests sat gazing at it stiffly, not knowing what to do with this odd-looking concoction that had been plunked down in front of them. Betty, however, was a girl of action; with the air of having handled this situation many times, she put cream and sugar in hers and stirred it politely. The others, who had been watching the young social leader, now put cream and sugar in theirs. Then all drank, pretending it was a rare and exquisite beverage. Just then the woman who had prepared the meal came in and proudly asked how they had enjoyed the soup? There was an agonized silence, then all burst into laughter. It was the first time that consommé had come to Rogers, Arkansas. It became the town joke; in fact, poems were written about it.

Shortly after this the Woman's Study Club presented *Mrs. Jarley's Wax Works* in the Miller Opera House (no town in those days was so small it didn't have an opera house) to raise money for the new city library which was soon to open. The players were wax figures who had come to life. Betty Blake and a married friend of hers, Mrs. C. D. Short, were two wax figures who came to life and sang a song entitled "Consommé with Sugar On the Side." It was the hit of the show.

All this shows how simple life in Rogers was; and how wholesome. And in addition it gives a glimpse of what a vivacious and attractive girl Betty Blake was.

Hugh Puckett continued: "Her brother Sandy — real name was Jim — got a job on the Iron Mountain Railroad at Jenny Lind, Arkansas, as depot agent. The town was named after the famous singer. Betty landed a job as his filing clerk. It was an up-and-goin' town then. There was a man workin' in Sandy's office named Guy O'Kelly, was a cripple an' handicapped in getting about. So Betty'd put on rubber boots and a slicker and go out in the darnedest weather you ever saw an' go up and down the yards, checking empties and cars filled with slag and slate. There was all kinds of rough characters in the yards, but she could take care of herself. It was remarkable how she handled that job and she should be given plenty of praise. She worked there, I understand, about a year."

In Jenny Lind, Betty boarded with the Mumey family. I talked to John Mumey whose aunt ran the boardinghouse where Betty stayed, but he was too young then to remember anything about her days in Jenny Lind. But I was able to get an authentic glimpse into her life there. It was from Mrs. P. N. Knotts, 605 East Fifteenth Street, Okmulgee, Oklahoma. Her letter:

"Yes, I knew Betty Blake well when she lived in Jenny Lind. She roomed across the street and took her meals uptown. Sometimes the people where she roomed went away for a week-end;

then Betty would come and stay with us, not as a boarder but as a guest, or visitor. We loved to have her come, for she was light-hearted and full of fun, loved pretty clothes and liked to eat better than anyone I ever knew. Sandy was transferred to Atkins, Arkansas; they didn't have a place there for Betty, so she went home. We all missed her."

A glimpse into life in America at that time was given me by Edward Tatum Wallace who, as I arrange these lines, is a feature writer for the *New York World-Telegram and Sun,* and author of the novel *The Moon Is Our Lantern.* His father courted Betty in a way that is curious reading today, but seems to have been accepted then as normal. His father was Arl B. Wallace, a brakeman on the St. Louis and Iron Mountain Railroad. Twice a day his train ran with loads of coal between Fort Smith and Jenny Lind. Each time it pulled into Jenny Lind, Arl would go around to call on Betty Blake. Once she asked him to bring her some shoes from a store in Fort Smith. She would try them on, she said, and send back the ones she did not want. And this Arl did, but it was so pleasant to talk to Betty that purposely for two days he hid the shoes he knew would fit her. But he lost out. Other men with direct methods of courtship took her away from him, and so it would seem always to be with people who try to win by subterfuge and evasion.

She seems to have had plenty of admirers; in fact, far more than a town that size would normally provide. This was brought out in a unique way. I talked to William P. Mahoney who "went" with Betty. He was, for many years, the electrician at the Ward Hotel, but is now retired and lives at 1103 North Forty-seventh Street, Fort Smith, Arkansas. I talked to him in his car parked beside his house. Later we drove to the market together.

"I went with her when she worked for Sandy Blake at Jenny Lind. Sandy didn't have good health and she went there to help take care of him. I was employed by the Fort Smith and Western Railroad and could get access to a gasoline-powered handcar an' I would hop it and in no time would cover the twelve miles to Jenny Lind. I would go to see her at her boardin' place. We had an opera house in Fort Smith where they put on traveling plays. I'd go down after Betty, fetch her to the show, then I'd take her back, and come home, all on my borrowed handcar. It was fun. Nobody thought of lookin' down on us; in fact, some of them were jealous.

"After a time she gave up her job at Jenny Lind, then I courted her in Rogers. That presented more of a problem. It was eighty miles there and there was no handcar. There was three of us, and all interested in the Blake girls — myself, Jim Hinton, who is now a big lawyer in Oklahoma City, and Tom Boles, who used to be head man in the Carlsbad Caverns, New Mexico. We'd leave on a Frisco train leavin' Fort Smith about midnight. We'd snooze as best we could on the train, or play seven up, arriving in the mornin'. We'd have breakfast wherever we could find it, then the three of us'd meander over to East Walnut Street. Mrs. Blake would have a good Sunday dinner. There was a late afternoon train returning to Fort Smith and we'd catch it, and after a time, would find ourselves home.

"One Sunday I was there payin' my respect to Betty when who should walk in but a fella I learned was Will Rogers, which was the first time I ever heard the name and if it'd been the last I wouldn't have shed any tears. He was plenty astonished an' he didn't look on me in any too wholesome a way. An' it was plain to be seen that Betty wished things were otherwise, but there they were and would have to be resolved. He was as bashful and shy and ill at ease as a new rooster, but he had come unannounced, so no blame could be saddled on Betty. He sure won out over me in a neat way! He eased the talk around to where he could suggest we go out in the yard, which we did, me unsuspectin'. He produced a rope and began ropin' everything in sight, includin' some of the boys. Betty had eyes only for him. I might as well have been in New Mexico as far as she was concerned. Finally I had to return to Fort Smith. Will stayed all night.

"After a time Betty pulled out of this section. Traveled around a good deal, used to send me a card now and then. I haven't got any of them, wish I had. It'd be interestin', in light of later events, to read 'em."

(Note: the story of how Will Rogers came to town to court Betty appears later.)

CHAPTER 6

Will Goes to South Africa and Becomes "The Cherokee Kid"

SOMETHING HAPPENED that at first did not appear important: Betty Blake, in Arkansas, decided to visit her sister in the Indian Territory. Her sister was married to Will Marshall who was the station agent in a little two-by-four town no one had ever heard of; even when you heard the name it was hard to remember it. And thus, in 1900, Miss Betty Blake — twenty years old — arrived in Oologah and moved into the depot with her sister and her sister's husband. It was the first time she had ever been so far from home — one hundred and thirty miles. In size she was larger than the average girl; she had brown eyes and hair that approached, but did not quite arrive at, blondness. She was counted good-looking.

There was a bay window in the depot where the telegraph agent sat so that he could look both up and down the track; at another window Betty would sit, surveying the town, an easy matter. It was a one-street town, with about three hundred inhabitants. Only in the very heart-center of the town was there a sidewalk, a wooden affair. Now and then a board would get loose; if you were walking with someone and if he stepped on the loose end, you would trip and sprawl all over Coowooscoowee.

She had not been there very long before she heard of Will Rogers, counted the wildest boy in the Valley of the Verdigris; and the wealthiest; and the best-liked; and (sometimes) the shyest. Will had gone to Kansas City and one morning got off the train at Oologah. He had bought a banjo in Kansas City and had asked for it to be sent in advance so that it would be there when he arrived; and so now, freshly off the train, he went to the office window to see if the banjo had come in. He came face to face with a disturbing element: a new girl in town. He was shy and fled without speaking.

He went to Oologah Hotel to call on Kate Ellis, his sweetheart — if a boy of twenty-one can be counted as having a real sweetheart. It was always awkward to call on her because of her parents' opposition. He was too wild for a girl to tie up with.

Finally he got the horse he had left at the livery stable and rode back to the ranch. The next day he returned, ready to face the terrors of the unknown: he went to the window and bravely asked for his banjo. Betty Blake and he exchanged a minimum of words, a matter Will could do to perfection when he felt shy. This incident has been romantically repeated a thousand times, but it was no more love at first sight than it was a green corn dance. He was shy with all new girls. He snatched his banjo and fled. Oddly enough it was Kate Ellis who brought them together. She gave a taffy pull, inviting the girl from Arkansas. One of the boys who was there was none other than young Colonel William Penn Adair Rogers.

Also it has been told a thousand times that Betty Blake so flustered Will that he dropped his taffy. I'm afraid the romanticists have touched this up. He did see her at the taffy pull, but there is no evidence that his taffy fell on the floor. It seems almost too bad. Betty could play the piano and Will could sing; at least, he could try. Betty and Will played together that night. Kate Ellis watched the proceedings.

Will wanted to make an impression on this new and captivating girl. And he did it in the only way he knew: he brought, a few days later, a horse from the ranch and rode it up and down in front of the depot to show the girl he was a master horseman. Not only this but he brought his bicycle and rode it up and down, too. The girl must have been bewitched by his talents. It is even on record that he tried to rope a calf from his bicycle. He must have been pretty far gone to attempt that. As he got better acquainted with her, he began taking her out in his rubber-tired buggy — the one he slung up at night by ropes. If that didn't win her, then nothing would!

However smitten he might be on Betty Blake, it did not keep his wanderlust from wanting to knock about. He had seen more of the world than the average Territory boy; he had been to Buffalo, to Memphis, to New York, and now he set his pegs on California. His father financed him, and Will left in the fall of 1900 for California with his only ambition to see the world, to go some place. The night he arrived in San Francisco he went to a cheap rooming house lighted by gas. Although he had seen quite a bit of the world, he was still thinking in terms of the coal-oil lamp. When he started sleepily to bed, he blew out the gas, lay down on the floor, and curled himself up in his blankets.

After a time the disturbed and suffering Will unconsciously rolled to a window which was partly open. Someone passed the door, smelled gas, and summoned help. Will was rushed to a hospital where he was kept for three days. A wire was sent to Clem Rogers and money was rushed to Will. He was put on the train and arrived back in Claremore.

John Smith told me the end. I talked to him in a saloon in Collinsville, Oklahoma. He said:

"I was working as a hired man on the Rogers Ranch when a telegram arrived asking us to meet a certain train. I was told to take the buggy and go to meet Will. He was so weak that I had to help him into it. He sat there, his eyes half-closed, hardly speaking all the way to the ranch. He told me he had blowed out the gas by mistake. His father came from Claremore, saw Will's condition, and sent him to Hot Springs, Arkansas, to rest and let the hot baths steam the gas out of him. Even when he came back home, he was still weak. This was one time when he didn't want to do any roping. We all realized that it had been a close call in that gas-filled room in San Francisco. A few more minutes in it and we would have lost Will."

(Note: this was the third time that Will had narrowly escaped death. First, from the gun, then the incident in Buffalo.)

His father was pressing Will more and more to "settle down." There was the ranch, his father said; Will could go into that and make a tremendous success. Not only the ranch but also there was the bank; he would take Will into the business and make a banker of him. This was the last straw.

The family pressure, however, was so great that, for a while, Will did operate the ranch. His father, still ensconced in Claremore, watched hopefully. What he saw was not very comforting. Will was still giving parties, still doing the cakewalk, still singing ragtime songs, still having a wonderful time, still the favorite of every crowd he was in.

One of his high-spirited friends was Dick Paris who was just as quick with a quip as Will was; indeed, some of the people said, quicker. When the two appeared on the streets of Oologah, people clustered around. Dick was working on the Rogers Ranch and was, like Will, part Cherokee.

Meantime, Will was taking in every roping and riding contest in striking distance. He roped and he rode. The latter meant that he "bulldogged" steers; and this, in turn, meant he would mount a horse and go racing down the field until the horse came abreast of the flying steer, then Will would catapult himself from the saddle onto the steer's neck, his own feet hitting the high places. Will would grab the steer's nose and twist his neck until the steer keeled over — all pleasant, outdoor work. Of course there was the dust; sometimes it would get in one's throat and make one cough.

Will was not as good at this as some of the other men; he was, however, as adept at trick roping as any of them. He was a roper rather than a rider.

There was a roping and riding contest at an Elks Carnival in Springfield, Missouri. Will was there; and so was Betty. She had gone back to Arkansas, but she managed to be at Springfield.

Teddy Roosevelt's Rough Riders were going to have a re-union in Oklahoma City, and Teddy was to be there. Off Will went in a lope. He roped and rode, but did not win any prize money. But that was all right. He was learning.

There was a roping and riding contest in San Antonio, Texas, and Will turned up. Charles H. Tompkins, one of the ropers, lives, as I write, in El Reno, Oklahoma. He told me in an interview:

"Us riders, for the most part, lived at the Southern Hotel. After hours, we'd sit out in front of the hotel, in chairs on the sidewalk, and lean back against the hotel and enjoy ourselves. This time there was a vacant chair in front of me an' a young fellow came along and sit down in the chair facing me, with his legs looping the chair and his chin on the back of the chair, comfortable like. He was on the smallish order and I knew at once he carried Indian blood. 'You sure made good time today on that steer,' he opened. 'You had a good horse. Is he yours?'

" 'No. He belongs to Scott Nance, of Kyle, Texas, and is a running-bred horse.'

"I ast him if he was goin' to rope tomorrow, thinkin' he was pretty light.

" 'I'm goin' to try,' he said. I ast him where he was from and he said Vinita, Indian Territory. Our conversation continued, during which I became interested in his flow of language. Finally he abruptly stopped talkin', looked at me and said, 'I see you're lookin' at my diamond stud pin.' I told him I hadn't noticed it specially, which seemed to put him down. He fingered it proudly and said, 'My father gave it to me to stay in school. But school was too much for me and I lit out.' He roped the next day but didn't get in on the money, bein' too light.

"The ropers were real cowboys right off the range; didn't go to a contest every week as the professionals do now. They had to load their roping horse in a freight car and ship him to where the contest was being held; they rode in the caboose to take care of him. There was a limit at the San Antonio Fair of sixty men, with prize money that began at one thousand dollars and tapered down to two hundred and fifty dollars — a lot of money to a cowboy making forty dollars a month, so they had to limit the number of entries. They drew numbers; the first thirty roped the first day, the second thirty the next day. The steers were big, powerful animals, weighing in the neighborhood of one thousand pounds. Many of them could outrun a horse for a hundred yards, and they had a fifty-foot start. When you caught one, you had to throw him high and handsome, or he would bounce up and run like a jack rabbit. When the cowboy started in pursuit, he could not have a rope already made, but had to make it as he went along. The steer's speed was accelerated by a flagman who had a five-gallon tin can filled with rocks. He would throw this at the steer, and the steer would start to travel. When the steer crossed the deadline, the rider could start, not before. He had to catch his thousand pounds of moving meat and tie him down so he would stay tied at least eight seconds. If he got even one foot loose you were disqualified. Another point worth putting in your book: you had to have a head catch, namely the rope had to go over the steer's head, either around his neck and horns, or around one horn and his neck, or he could have one front foot in the rope and the catch counted. But if the steer had just one front foot and one horn in the catch, that did not count and the steer was turned loose for some other rider to have a try at later.

"Now here's the way it's done today — sissy compared to the old ways we had to rope: the steer has a start of only twenty feet; the rider can have his loop made. After he catches and ties his steer all he has to do is to hold up his hands. The judge looks at the steer and if he is tied he says Okay, and orders the steer turned loose. Today's roping is parlor stuff to the way we used to have to go about it," said Charlie Tompkins firmly.

Meantime Will's father, in the bank at Claremore, was becoming more and more important in what was called "politics"; that is, in the Cherokee Nation. In size the Cherokee Nation was larger than Connecticut. It was to be divided into counties; so far it had been in "districts." It was, it will be remembered, in one of them that Clem Rogers had been born — Going Snake District.

To encourage Will, his father told him that he would give him the profits on the cattle, if Will would take care of them and market them. Will began to do this but not at the neglect of his good times. That would hardly do. Finally Will took the cattle to Kansas City and sold them with a profit of two thousand dollars, a handsome sum. The red soil of Oklahoma made his feet itch; he thought of Dick Paris. Will admired him immensely for his humor and quick take-up. And so he suggested to Dick that the two go to South America. Dick was wholeheartedly for the idea; the only catch was that he didn't have any money. By this time, Will was so eager to get away and to hear Dick's droll remarks that he told Dick he would finance the trip if Dick would go along. Dick was immediately interested. And so Will went to his father and told him that he and Dick were going to South America. Will's father was shocked; he had never been farther away from home than St. Louis, and now Will wanted to pack off to South America! What in the world was the matter with the boy?

Will began preparations for travel with as much enthusiasm as he had for parties and dances. One of his classmates at Willie Halsell had been Jim Rider. Jim had a fancy saddle that Will wanted more than anything in the world. The saddle was about the most impressive bit of leather in all the Indian Territory; it had been made in San Francisco by a saddler who knew all the tricks. Will was determined to have the saddle; Jim said he would not sell. So they got together. It all ended with Will giving Jim his own saddle, a saddle blanket, and fifty dollars in cash. And now the saddle was his. He would show the boys down in South America what a saddle was like.

In May 1902, Will and Dick Paris set out for South America. They reasoned logically that since South America was south, the way to get there was to go South. But logic has its flaws; in no time at all they found they were going in the wrong direction. Not a boat was sailing from New Orleans for South America; the way to get there was to go to England.

A strange change took place in the inimitable Dick Paris. As soon as he was out of the Territory and away from conditions and people he was familiar with, he was no longer humorous. In fact, he was downright gloomy. The good times that Will had looked forward to did not materialize at all. On top of this, Will promptly got seasick. Just why a stomach that could handle beans and chili con carne so effortlessly should quake at a body of water is not known. But quake it did; Will was as white as a buffalo skull.

They stayed in London eight days until a ship was ready to sail for South America — the *Danube*. They found that first-class passengers were supposed to "dress" for dinner, an idea that two Indian boys had never heard of before. They faced it with the courage of their race. They bought dinner jackets and went bravely aboard. Then the ship started for South America and Will was again promptly sick. Dick — reviving a little of his back-home spirit — boasted how fine he felt. He would go to the dining room in his dinner jacket, then come back and describe the wonderful meal he'd just polished off. Will would look at him weakly and wish to God he'd left him in the Indian Territory.

It took twenty-three days to Rio de Janeiro. Now and then Will's seasickness would seem to abate and he would put on his dinner jacket and go to the dining saloon and try to be a gentleman. It was hard, demanding work. He began to hate the sight of a dinner jacket and especially Dick's propensity for enjoying food.

Will kept his prize saddle in the cabin he and Dick occupied. He planned to have a wonderful time with it in South America. At last Will and Dick landed and started out to savvy the country. It proved to be quite a remarkable odyssey of five months. The two went here and there in the Argentine; sometimes they had a job; oftener they hadn't. When they did have one it was at the rate of seven dollars a month. Sometimes they slept out at night. This was adventuring and it was what Will liked. But Dick became gloomier and gloomier and more and more homesick, and finally said he wanted to go back to God's country (the Indian Territory). Will, always generous, told him he would give him the money. Will bought some souvenirs for the home folks and the two parted — Will to continue his adventuring, and Dick to go back to wonderful Oologah.

But there was a holdup. There were customs dues to pay in New York and Dick didn't have the money. So he wired Will's father. Dick got the money and finally arrived home. Mr. Rogers made up his mind about Will. Will had started out with two thousand dollars; evidently that was all gone. Soon Will would be wiring for money to get back. Maybe this time, when he got home, he would settle down.

Will's eyes were open to the difference in ranch methods between Oklahoma and the Argentine. The thing that appears to have astonished him most was the way the gauchos drove their cattle on a run. In Oklahoma, fat cattle were handled as carefully as jewels in a lady's watch.

Through an interpreter, Will asked about this.

"Oh," said the man, "we don't mind that. They soon fill up again."

It shook Will to the foundations.

After the first glamour had worn off, Will did not like the country. His letters home and his letters to the Claremore paper are filled with criticism. "This," he said, "is a fine country to stay away from. My parting words are for all you people to fight shy of this part of the globe." Sometimes his letters mentioned things at home dear to his heart. "Papa, don't let Comanche be touched till I get back. Take good care of my buggy."

Days and weeks passed; and then Will was offered a job on a cattle boat going to South Africa. This was it! More excitement. More travel. The only catch was that he would have to act as nursemaid to horses and cattle. It would be worth it, he reasoned; so he got his precious saddle and put himself on the boat, August 5. In no time at all he was sick. Little by little he recovered and went about making the horses and cattle comfortable.

It took thirty-one days to get across. By this time Will hated all the horses and cattle in the world. But he had to take care of them just the same.

The ship stopped at Cape Town and Will went to a vaudeville show. During the act Will heard the juggler speak and knew he was an American. When the show was over, Will went backstage. The man was W. C. Fields. The two were the same age. Fields was important enough to be on a juggling trip around the world. Will was picking up any old job he could.

Then back on the ship. As it was approaching Durban, in Natal, he was told that no one would be allowed to land who did not have an equivalent of five hundred dollars.

He went to the Englishman who owned most of the horses and cattle and told him his plight and offered to work for the man when the stock was landed. The man was looking for help, and he signed papers to give Will a job. And so Will was able to put a shaky foot on the soil of South Africa.

Will worked for the man until he had paid off his obligation, then started to Ladysmith, South Africa, eager to see the Boer War. It ended two days before he got there, and again there was the problem of a job. Finally he landed one breaking horses for the British Army.

Will went on a "mule drive." Anyone who thinks he can drive a mule is not in full possession of his mental faculties. There were seven hundred mules and they had to be driven two hundred miles. Finally, he got them to the Mooi River Station, an embittered and disillusioned man, and never again wanted anything to do with those unfortunate creatures.

He decided to return by train and took his saddle to the station and checked it. When he got to the Orange Free State, he went to claim his saddle, but it was gone. Transportation had been upset by the war and their system of caring for baggage was different from what he had known back home. The officials said they accepted no responsibility for the safety or delivery of baggage. It was a severe blow.

His wanderings thereafter are too long and too complicated to detail here, but they do give glimpses of this part-Indian boy so many miles from home. He wrote many letters home; his sisters suddenly found him very affectionate. Some of the letters were published in the *Claremore Progress* and can be read by any person who wants to go into detail. One glimpse is worth while: before he had left home, he had taken out life insurance, and now, as soon as he had saved the money, he went to the post office in Durban and sent his father one hundred and forty dollars to pay the insurance. It must have made the old gentleman blink.

In his wanderings he came to Johannesburg and there, as he was going down the street, he saw something exceedingly thrilling — a sign which said, TEXAS JACK'S WILD WEST SHOW. Was it possible that an American was over here and that he had a show? In no time at all Will was out at the show grounds to ask for Texas Jack. He was pointed out — a tall, picturesque-looking man in a picturesque hat and picturesque clothes. Will edged up.

"Are you Texas Jack?"

"I am," said the busy individual, then glanced at the young man asking the question. Why, that wasn't a British accent!

"I reckon I'm a neighbor of yourn," said Will. "I'm from the Indian Territory."

Texas Jack was pleasant and talked to Will nicely.

Finally Will came to the point: did Texas Jack have a job for him?

Texas Jack looked him over with even deeper interest. "Can you handle a rope?"

"I can, some."

"Come around before the show starts and show me what you can do."

Will was there when the time came, and taking hold of a rope, proceeded to do what, back home, was called the Crinoline. This consisted of starting with a small loop and gradually playing it out until it was large. Finally Will had used up the rope. Texas Jack stared, and when Will dropped the rope, said, "I guess you're good enough to join. I'll hire you." Sweet words.

What Will didn't know was that Texas Jack had a standing offer of fifty sovereigns to anyone who could do the Crinoline! Now that Will was a member of the show he couldn't collect.

Texas Jack gave the people their idea of what life was like in America, where the whites lived in hourly dread of the Indians who descended on them, from time to time, and bloodily scalped them. One of the scenes — "plays," Texas Jack called them — showed an emigrant family slowly lumbering across the plains in a covered wagon. Suddenly a band of bloodthirsty Indians bore down and cruelly murdered every one in the defenseless band. Will was given the job of being an Indian. To make the show more realistic, Will, dressed in feathers, was to come running down the aisle in the audience, screaming and flourishing his tomahawk. The catch was that he screamed so fiercely that he scared the cash customers and was demoted to cowboy.

Will practiced constantly with his rope and became so good that Texas Jack told him he would feature him and that Will was to select a name for himself. Will chose "the Cherokee Kid," and soon was one of the stars of the show. His riding and roping went so well that Texas Jack himself began to introduce him as the world's greatest roper and rider. This might have come in the nature of a surprise to Jim Hopkins, Jim Minnick, Black Chambers, Johnny Blocker, Jim O'Donnell, Clay McGonigle, Dal Walker, Chester Byers, Charlie Tompkins, and various and sundry back in Texas and Oklahoma. But Texas and Oklahoma were far away.

Will was so pleased with his rise in the world that he had a professional card printed:

The Cherokee Kid
Fancy Lasso Artist and Rough Rider
Texas Jack's Wild West Show
U S A

Texas Jack's show must have been worth going a long way to see. Here is an advertisement that appeared in the *Pretoria News*, July 20, 1903, and two or three times after that. It makes the show almost irresistible.

COMING

Texas Jack   Entire New company
                              including —
Clarence Welby Cook, in his famous Jockey Act
Miss Violet Welby Cook,
    queen of the wire
Miss Lyle Marr, equestrienne   Ajax, the flexible marvel
Mr. Constance, daring trapeze   Mr. Eric Ward, the dash-
                                        ing rough rider
The Cherokee Kid, lasso expert   Apollo, feats of strength
Tony and Alvarez, clowns   Miss Williams, and her
                                        trained pony
                  Splendid Mounted Cowboy Band
                  Scenes in Prairie Life

For a time an attraction billed as "Frank, the Human Crockodile" traveled with the show, but, for some reason or other, did not reach Pretoria. It seems almost too bad.

Texas Jack and his titillating company played in Pretoria from July 23 to August 8. Each day there was a write-up of the show, but the Cherokee Kid does not get a mention until July 25 when the paper says briefly: "The lassoing of the Cherokee Kid and his Bucking Broncho were especially good."

On July 27 the paper really spread itself:

"A matinee performance was given Saturday afternoon when there was a crowded audience of enthusiastic children and many grown-ups to witness the show, amongst whom were noticeable the daughters of the Lt. Governor. Wonderfully successful matinees attend Texas Jack always, owing no doubt to the fact that the performance presented falls nothing short of the evening's entertainment. The turns have already been noticed in these columns, but mention must again be made of Ajax whose marvellous contortions drew great applause. Texas Jack gave an exhibition of his skill as a marksman and the Cherokee Kid proved himself a champion with the lasso."

On Saturday the show is reviewed again. Will is again mentioned, but he does not do quite as well as Apollo:

"The introduction of monkeys riding on horses and the zebra caused much amusement, but the zebra was a little refractory and after the first jump refused to take the rail again. Apollo performed some wonderful feats of strength. He opened his performance by swinging a 56 pound weight with as much ease as a child would an India rubber ball. At 100 pound weight seemed almost as nothing in this strong man's hands. He then bent a solid pile of steel over his arm and he challenged any to do the same for 100 pounds. He also gave a further challenge of 20 pounds that no four men could straighten the same piece when bent, which he did with perfect ease. His next act was the breaking of a horseshoe. After these acts he tore in half a pack of playing cards and to further show his strength, he did a feat that only one other man in the world is credited to have done, namely the tearing of three whole packs of cards at the same time. (Sandow is the only other credited with this.) He then lifted a man of 11 stone and 6 pounds with one arm, after which he tackled and was successful in lifting to the full extent of his arm a weight of 200 pounds (one arm only).

Now comes Will:

"The Cherokee Kid performed some wonderful feats with his lasso. His double act of catching first the horse, then the man with the lasso, being very clever. The last performance was the enveloping of himself in a 'Crinoline,' letting the loop touch the ground and then bringing it back over the horse and himself, and allowing the loop to return to its former size."

Nor did he do quite as well as the talented Ajax:

"Ajax, the Flexible, is simply a marvel and his acts are quite beyond description. To see him once, you want to see him again. This man has a wonderful expansion of chest measurement, his normal size being 40 and he can expand to 46¾. His neck is also rather large, being 17½ and his weight 11 stone and 2 pounds. Do not miss him."

It would seem that Apollo, the strong man, and Ajax, the Flexible, were the stars of the show. Will, the monkeys, and the zebra seem merely to have added variety.

The show, after a time, returned to Durban; Will thought he would take advantage of this and go to the railroad station to ask if anything had been heard of his saddle. The clerk looked through some papers and said, "I find it was reported in. But there was no claimant, so it was raffled off."

"Raffled off?" repeated the aghast Will.

"That's what is always done to unclaimed property," blandly returned the clerk.

Will got the name and address of the man who had won it and hastened to see him. Yes, the man had it and when Will told him what had happened, the man gave it to him and Will departed with his precious saddle, his heart leaping high.

A year passed; he still yearned for home, but the fascination of the show business held him. He wrote to everybody back home and to the Claremore paper. But not often to Betty Blake, strange as this seems. Their alleged romance during these days has been burnished till it shines far more brightly than it did in cold truth.

He heard much discussion in the show as to whether or not a person could rope a zebra. Will thought a person could; with him to think was to act, so he hired a guide and went to a place where zebras were supposed to be found. There they were, just as Will had been told. Getting on his horse, he made a dash into the herd, swinging his lasso high and proud. But, alas, his horse stumbled and Will was thrown off; he landed on his head and was knocked unconscious. He was taken to the hospital where he had to remain several days. He was chagrined at his poor showing, and, to salve his pride, had a picture made of himself roping a zebra. But it was another zebra and at another time. This closed his zebra-roping career.

He wanted to see Australia, and after a time, bought a second-class ticket to Sydney. He went sight-seeing for several days, then the old yearning for the show business laid hold of him. Texas Jack had given him a letter to the Wirth Brothers Circus and soon the Cherokee Kid was in action again.

One of the feats he worked out for the delectation of the Australians was to pick up a handkerchief from the ground when the horse was going at full tilt. Will accomplished this by locking his feet around the horn of the saddle, holding on with one hand as best he could, then leaning back over the horse, and picking up the handkerchief with his free hand. The governor general of Australia saw the feat and sent an aide to ask Will to do it again.

Will said he would do it again for thirty pounds.

The emissary was shocked at the sum Will wanted and protested loudly.

"You go back," said Will, "and tell your boss that if he'll do it cheaper, I'll lend him my horse and handkerchief."

The aide went back but the governor general did not do the trick.

Will was much impressed by the skill of the natives — "wool-lies," he found they were called — with which they could throw a boomerang. He would try himself, but never could manage it

"Why," he said in great admiration, "they can knock your hat off going, and scalp you coming back!"

He was beginning to think more and more about home. This roaming was all right, but there was such a thing as home ties, old friends and family relatives. He sold his saddle, which was a severing of this part of his life and a turning of his back on the past, and prepared in earnest to start home.

An incident: planning to leave from Auckland, he got into the port by train. He dreaded the seasickness which he believed would be his. He had heard of a remedy and decided to try it: it was to go on board and be asleep when the boat started. This he tried, but when he heard the creakings of the ship he became seasick, just as he always had. Finally, to get his mind off his troubles, he dragged himself over to a sailor and asked how far, by now, the ship was at sea.

The sailor looked at him as if he thought Will was daft. "We haven't even left the dock," he said witheringly.

Will went up on deck, shuffled over to the side of the boat, and there it was, safe and steady. The boat had creaked, but the seasickness had all been in his mind. Later, he often checked up on himself to show the power of imagination and to help himself see things as they really were.

Of all the countries he had been in he liked New Zealand best. Later he wrote: "Say, that little New Zealand is just what I would call a regular country. The best government in the world, the greatest scenery and natural resources of the country are great."

At last he started home and arrived, third class, in San Francisco. This time, no gas. He had been gone almost three years. He was now twenty-three and was a widely traveled young man. The only catch was that he was also broke. He had no idea of becoming a professional showman. He thought of himself as a cowboy and ranchman. The next thing was to get back to

Oklahoma. He wasn't going to telegraph for money. He was determined on that. He started his world trip, traveling first class; he was back, traveling third. On the ship going from London to South America, he had worn a dinner jacket. Now he was snugly outfitted in overalls. But he wasn't too depressed. He would get along. He had confidence in himself. He would manage.

While he had been away, he had sent back four hundred and thirty dollars, a little more than a hundred dollars a year. The money had gone to pay his life insurance and to impress his father.

CHAPTER 7

Will Ropes at the St. Louis World's Fair

HE WAS IN AMERICA, but he wasn't in Oklahoma. He took care of this by going to the railroad yards and mounting a freight. At this time there were bitter battles between crews and unauthorized passengers; when a train crew found a man hiding, they marshaled their forces and threw him off, no matter how fast the train was going. It was hard on the man. When the train stopped, the crew would go up and down the train, looking under it, over it and in it. Will got on, anyway. He hid behind freight cars at the stations and in the switchyards, and then, just as the train was picking up speed, would make a dash and return to his travels. The trainmen discovered he was on and were determined to take care of him. The trail got hotter and hotter; the train crew was out to get Will, and Will was out to get home. In dodging here and there, Will met a nonpaying fellow passenger; they joined forces but even with two to watch and to help each other it was a precarious business.

Finally the two found a flatcar, covered with canvas, that was being used to haul chickens. But every available inch of space was occupied by coops; no place for passengers. Will and his new-found friend took care of this by stripping back the canvas and throwing a coop of chickens into the Colorado night, then creeping onto the space the chickens had once occupied. It was hard on the chickens, but it was heaven to Will. It was nice to have such comfortable quarters. But the train crew discovered the loss and then were more firmly than ever after Will and his friend. In fact, they were so hot on their trail that the two had to get off at Trinidad, Colorado, and stay until Will felt it was safe to resume his eastward travels.

At last bedraggled Will showed up at Claremore. His father was shocked. Here was his son who had started to South America with two thousand dollars in his pocket and now was back, broke, and with a slight chicken odor. "I hope you'll settle down now," he said grimly.

"I'm goin' to, Papa," Will promised earnestly.

In all the time he had been away, as we have observed, he had not written to Betty Blake, nor had she written to him. In fact, she did not even know where he was. The "affair" seemed over. He had liked many girls. She was just one of them.

He tried to settle down, but running a ranch was just plain hard work. Fun was still what he wanted more than anything else; fun and a good time; dances, parties, ropings, and "joshing" with the fellows on the corner. There is no reason to believe at this time that he looked on himself as a comedian, or humorist. He knew that he livened up a group when he came into it and that people around him were always laughing. But his ambition was in quite another field: he wanted to be the champion trick roper of the world. He never ceased to practice. Anyone who could show him a twist of the wrist he didn't know was a person he could admire wholeheartedly.

One of the persons he admired was "Black" Chambers who was an expert roper. Like himself, he was part Cherokee. His real name was Evans Chambers; he was called "Black" because of his swarthy complexion. Will would go to any roping or riding contest where Black Chambers might appear, just to study him.

Claude H. Wright, editor of the *Collinsville News*, Collinsville, Oklahoma:

"As a young man I belonged to the Collinsville band. There was to be a riding and roping contest — that's what we called 'em then — at Ochelata, and our band, full of vim and vigor, went along to add to the gaiety of the occasion. The roping ground was a flat open space at the edge of town, no building, no seats. The buggies and wagons were drawn up in a half-moon shape so as to make one side of the roping field. The cattle would be released from the chutes and the men, on their horses, would be after them. No calves; a cowhand would have been ashamed to rope a poor helpless calf at an exhibition.

"Well, the chute opened and out came a steer as big as a moose and after it came Will Rogers on his horse. Near us was a carriage filled with ladies; the lines were wrapped around the whipsocket, the ladies enjoying their outing. Just as Will's horse got up even with me, I gave my drum a hearty wallop. The team almost jumped out of their skin and started to run away, the carriage swaying from side to side and the ladies yellin' till you could hear them to Oowala. Instantly Will turned his horse and started for the carriage as fast as horseflesh could take him. The team had on blind bridles; riding up beside one of the horses, Will seized it by the bridle and began turning the terrified team in a half-circle. At last, by clever maneuvering, he brought the runaway horses to a standstill. Other mounted men were there, but Will was the one to grasp the situation and handle it. When this was over, Will rode back to the circle and another steer was let out. This time I didn't wallop."

Happy-go-lucky as he was, he also had plenty of courage. This was brought out by a story told me by John Smith, of Collinsville, Oklahoma, (who has already been mentioned):

"Clint Lipe was a neighbor a few years older than Will. I guess Will had known him all his life. Clint rode a horse that was not wholly trustworthy, but was a good piece of horseflesh. He had to be rode with a watchful bit. One frosty morning Clint was riding this animal when, all of a sudden, the horse plunged, threw Clint off and then rolled on top of him, crushing him.

"I ran to Clint and then called to Will, 'Clint is still breathing. We must get the doctor.'

" 'I'll go,' said Will.

"Most men won't get on a horse that has just thrown a man, but Will did. The horse was a killer, but Will wasn't afraid of him. Clint was dead before the doctor arrived. The saddle horn had gone through his chest."

As the summer passed, Will grew more and more hippity-hoppity. He had not looked on the ranch as home since his mother had died; and unconsciously he had always resented Mary Bibles and made no effort to be on friendly terms. And now, to get away from the ranch and his father, he rode to the Mulhall Ranch which was about thirty miles north of Guthrie. It was owned by Zacharias Mulhall who was always called "Colonel," but who was no more a colonel than you are. He was an up-and-coming man — really a power in the Territory — and had some up-and-coming people around him. And two charming daughters: Lucille and Mildred. In addition there was Mrs. Mulhall whom Will soon began to call "Auntie." And there was Tom Mix, a bartender Colonel Mulhall had brought up from Guthrie. He had been born in Pennsylvania, and had never been on a horse until he forked one at the Colonel's.

Mrs. Mulhall had a piano, something rare for this section. Will's mother had had one, but it had disappeared. Now Will pounced on this one. He loved to sit at it — when the other men were out building fence or putting up hay — and try to peck out tunes. At first, Mrs. Mulhall was patient, but the monotony of it, day after day, began to get her down. Will, little suspecting, plunked on.

The year was 1904 and St. Louis was preparing to celebrate the hundredth anniversary of the Louisiana Purchase. The "purchase" was in 1803, but St. Louis was slow and didn't get around to the matter until 1904.

In the meantime Colonel Zack had an opportunity to open a show, and this he did under the title of the "Cummins and Mulhall Wild West Show." He told Will he would take him along; Will was delighted and hurried home and got his riding and trick horse, Comanche. Soon Will was in St. Louis, at sixty dollars a month.

The show was not inside the grounds, but just outside on what was called "The Pike." Will was delighted; he was back in the saddle again; again the showman. Not as an Indian, but as a rider and trick roper. Not scaring the audience to death. The star of the show was Lucille Mulhall, who was becoming known as a "cowgirl"; indeed the word had to be invented for her.

Something happened that turned out to be important. Betty Blake came from Arkansas to visit her sister in St. Louis and to "take in" the Fair. As she was going through the Oklahoma State Building she heard someone mention the name Will Rogers. Instantly her ears were on the alert. The person said that he was "riding" on The Pike. This was the first word that Betty had had of him in three years. She would see what he was like. She wrote a note and sent it in care of the show. Back in no time came an answer. Would she come to the show the following afternoon and have dinner with him?

When he rode out she was shocked at the costume he was wearing. It was a red-velvet affair, with enough gold braid for a South American revolution. It was the suit that the Wirth Brothers Circus, in Australia, had made him wear when he had been appearing as "the Mexican Rope Artist." No Mexican had ever seen a suit like it. It was an Australian conception of what a Mexican rope flinger might wear. A real Mexican, proud of his country, would have called the police.

Will had put it on, instead of his cowboy costume, especially to impress Betty. It had, but in the wrong way. She chided him about it and he became self-conscious.

That evening, after dinner, Will took Betty on a tour of the midway. He bought tickets to the Irish Village and there, in this little touch of Ireland, they heard John McCormack sing. McCormack was, at that time, a great figure in the musical world and just to see and hear him was for Betty and Will an outstanding event.

Things did not go well at the Fair. Business was poor, and then, to make matters worse, Mulhall got into an altercation with one of his riders and shot him. The shooting on The Pike was front-page news in the *New York Times*, June 19, 1904, column 6:

"Col. Zack Mulhall, livestock agent of the St. Louis and San Francisco Railroad, and a friend of President Theodore Roosevelt, tonight shot three men. One of these, an innocent bystander named Ernest Morgan, was shot in the abdomen, and died. The other two men are Frank Reed, boss of the Wild West Show, and John Murray, one of the cowboys. They are being cared for at the Emergency Hospital on the Fair Grounds. Mulhall, Oklahoma, was named for the Colonel."

The same paper, three days later, page 5, column 4, carried the sequel: "As a result of a shooting affray in which three men were shot on 'The Pike' at the World's Fair grounds, Saturday night, 'Zack' Mulhall was today, by order of the World's Fair officials, excluded from further appearance in the show where the trouble took place."

There was a trial and Mulhall was sentenced to three years' imprisonment. Meantime, Will returned to Oklahoma. And now, after this brief touch of show life, he was again restless. Parties and fun weren't everything. One had a career to think of. The show business wasn't so bad.

Things became better for Mulhall. He appealed the case and the charges were dismissed. He was again a free man. And now he scurried around and opened a Wild West Show at Delmar

Gardens, in St. Louis. Back went Will and his faithful Comanche. One of Will's fellow entertainers was the Indian chief, Geronimo.

At last the summer was over; it had not been a good one, at least financially, and Will returned home no better off than when he had started it. But that was all right; he'd had a good time. The thing to do was to keep out of his father's sight, and this he did most of the time.

Then it was that Colonel Mulhall had a wonderful offer — at least it seemed wonderful; this was to take a band of cowboys to New York and put on an exhibition for the Horse Fair at Madison Square Garden. One of the cowboys he was going to take was Tom Mix, who, by this time, had learned to ride.

This was Will's third time in New York. Once he had come with a load of horses; the horses had been auctioned off in a stable where the Winter Garden later came to stand; and he had stopped here while waiting to get a boat to England.

The date: April 23, 1905.

The Horse Fair was to run from April 24 to April 29. Something happened.

CHAPTER 8

Will Ropes a Steer at Madison Square Garden — but Lets It Get Away

THE PROPOSED "cowboy act" was something new for Madison Square Garden. Each year there was the Annual Horseshow which was held in November; the other was called the Horse Fair and was in April. At the dignified Annual Horseshow there were no cowboys, no yipping, and positively no such thing as a girl in divided skirts mounting a horse and riding like mad around the arena. At the Horse Fair there was a little more latitude: cowboys could yip and girls could let out a few discreet lady-like squeals. (It will be understood that this was the "old" Madison Square Garden, which really was located off Madison Square, New York.)

There had been a Motor Boat and Sportsmen's Show which had lasted from March 2 to March 19. On March 21 Barnum & Bailey's Circus moved in and ran through April 19. Then Colonel Mulhall came and was to be there from April 24 to April 29. Things were really hopping.

Colonel Mulhall brought about thirty boys and girls to the Garden, and about forty horses. He was to be paid a thousand dollars a day. It wasn't all bankable money, for he had to take care of his expenses and pay his help. As a matter of fact he barely squeaked by. Early in the evening there was to be the horse fair: riding, jumping and equestrian acts. Then the Colonel was to come with his yipping cowboys. Among them was Will Rogers, and with him was his roping horse Comanche and also another horse, "Teddy," named for President Theodore Roosevelt. The act was to last an hour and ten minutes. Some of the older and more dignified members of the board thought this was plenty. But anyway Colonel Mulhall was engaged and arrived and all — so far — was well.

The star of the show, was Lucille Mulhall, who was heralded — and correctly — as the first "cowgirl" in the world. Will knew her well; he had lived for days on the Mulhall Ranch and he had roped with her at Memphis. And here they were together again. Lucille was to rope and ride; and when she rode it was not sidesaddle, something that must have profoundly shocked the ladies of the horsey set.

On April 25, 1905, the *New York Daily Tribune* mentioned Will Rogers — the first time his name ever appeared in a New York paper, and the second time in any paper except the faithful *Claremore Progress*, which would mention him at the drop of a lariat. The Memphis paper (as we've seen) dumped him in, with three others, under "Messers.," certainly no invasion of private rights. The Pretoria paper hadn't even used the name Rogers. He was merely "the Cherokee Kid" and that was all there was to it. The *Tribune* said: "Will Rogers, the fullblood Cherokee Indian, gave an exhibition of roping. It was announced that he is the only man in the world who can lasso both the rider and horse at the same time with two separate ropes." The next day the same paper said: "Rogers, the Cherokee Indian, repeated his performance of simultaneously roping a pony and its rider with two lassos." Each day the papers carried stories about the accidents, but otherwise the fullblood Cherokee Indian was not mentioned.

Then came April 27. (*Note*: I am going into this in some detail, for the reason that no episode in Will Rogers's life has been so often misrepresented as this one.) It was at the afternoon performance. Lucille Mulhall was roping to the soft music of the Seventh Regiment Band when suddenly the steer she was trying to snare made a run for it and leaped over the arena fence. He started plenty. The music was no longer soft. In fact, there was no music at all, for every man in the band ran like a jack rabbit. Every paper in New York mentioned the incident, but only one mentioned Will Rogers. That paper was the *New York Herald*, April 28, 1905, page 6, and this is what it said:

"Panic prevailed at the afternoon performance of the Horse Fair at Madison Square Garden, yesterday, when a wild, long-horned Texas steer leaped out of the arena, climbed two flights of stairs and ran three-quarters of the way around the Garden, back of the boxes, pursued by cowboys with ropes and leaving hysterical women and excited men in its wake.

"Many occupants of the boxes sprang into the arena and men, women and children tumbled over one another in their mad rush to get out of the way. There were five thousand persons in the garden at the time.

"It was during the act in which Miss Lucille Mulhall, daughter of Colonel Zack Mulhall, rides into the arena on a pony and ropes a wild steer. The particular red steer, which she was to rope and which made all the disturbance, is said to be, by all odds, the worst behaved animal on the American continent, and yesterday was one of its bad days.

"The moment he entered the arena, he began to paw the dirt and then made a bee-line for the aisle that leads up to the boxes near the front of the Twenty-sixth Street side. With the agility of a cat he leaped over the bars and ran clattering to the second tier boxes. There he turned to the right and made a wild dash to the spot where the Seventh Regiment Band was playing.

"When the steer approached the band, the music stopped abruptly, and the players started on the run, yelling like mad, with the steer in hot pursuit. Tom Mixico, a celebrated rope-thrower, ran up the Twenty-seventh Street side and tried to head off the steer; he missed with his lasso but caught an usher by the leg, bringing him down with a thump.

"Will Rogers, a Cherokee Indian, and three other cowboys had joined in the chase, and Rogers got a rope over the steer's horns as it turned to run down into the arena. Rogers clung to the rope, but was dragged over seats and down the stairs.

"Freed from his would-be captors the steer, trailing the rope, again sprang into the arena where half a dozen cowboys on their ponies managed to lasso him just as he turned for another race through the crowd.

"When the steer had again been turned loose, Miss Mulhall went on with her act and roped him with apparent ease.

"Scrub women were at work in the Fourth Avenue end of the Garden and in their mad scramble to get out of danger, one of them rolled down a flight of stairs and was badly injured."

The whole affair was a bit less glamorous for Will than it has always been said. He got the rope over the steer's horns but was unable to hold him, and the steer dashed away. "Tom Mixico" was Tom Mix who was registered under that name. Although he was a "celebrated rope-thrower" he completely missed the steer but, by a bit of luck, succeeded in catching an usher by the leg. The whole thing ended by Lucille Mulhall roping the steer and going on with her act.

Credulous writers have said that Will Rogers's name was on the front page of every newspaper in New York, and that this roping was the turning point in his career. A little research shows this hardly to be true; no reporters crowded around him; he was only one of half a dozen who went after the steer. He was, how-ever, the first who succeeded in getting a rope over the animal, short and useless as this incident proved to be — and the roping did not affect his career in any way.

But Will did get a quip out of the incident. When the steer went up the stairway, a policeman, a billy in his hand, charged toward the steer. "When you catch him, what are you goin' to do with him?" called Will.

It will be noted that the writer in the newspaper who said that the steer was by all odds "the worst behaved animal on the American continent" was taking in quite a bit of territory.

I talked to one person who saw the whole event: Mrs. Mildred M. Acton, who lives just south of Guthrie, Oklahoma. She was Lucille Mulhall's sister. She said: "We didn't think anything about the roping until we saw it played up in the papers; it was just an ordinary event. Will never pretended that he did anything unusual."

This story has been told and retold till the facts have been washed out of it, and the incident was used in a motion picture of Will's life, released in 1952. The script-writers must have enjoyed themselves, for they created it chiefly out of their imagination.

CHAPTER 9

Will Talks for the First Time.
He Fails in Business

THERE is this description of Will at this time from Tom Mix:
"We lived in the same room at the Putnam Hotel. Every time I
came in I stumbled over his ropes on the floor. Sometimes, when
I got up at night, I would step on one and think I'd landed on a
snake."

Will, now twenty-six years old, had no idea of ever becoming
a comedian. His ambition still was to be the champion trick roper
of the world. He wrote his father in all seriousness: "If I can become a good trick-roper I won't ever have to do manual work."
It must have made his father smile. And it must have made Jim
Rider, Dick Paris, Dal Walker, and all his old cronies smile. No
one in the Indian Territory had ever been so earnestly opposed
to work as Will. His father, who had done the extremely hard
work of "freighting," tried to defend him. "He'll settle down
some day," he said, making out that the matter didn't bother him
in the least.

The other men who had roped at the Garden went home; Will
sent Comanche back but kept Teddy, his trick horse. Will
wanted to get into vaudeville, but how? He had never been on
the stage in his life (except at school).

He hoped that the mention of his name in the paper after the
Garden episode would help him, but it did not. The fact that he
had been one of the cowboys who had tossed a rope at a wild
steer didn't cut too much sawdust. And now he was living in
New York, boarding a pony, and was without work. He had

been getting seventy-five dollars a week from Mulhall, but he had only worked ten days and some of that money had been none too easy to extract from the flamboyant Colonel.

In St. Louis, at the World's Fair, he had seen a man ride a horse on the stage, doing fancy acrobatics as the horse sped around and around. The idea had come to Will that he could put a horse on the stage, get a rider, and rope both horse and rider.

Will found there were such things as booking agencies, and plodded from one to another trying to interest them in his idea. They looked at him pityingly. The chilling thought must have come to him that he might have to return to the ranch and go to work.

But he kept plugging away. He bought some felt and had carpet slippers made for Teddy, took Jim Minnick (who hadn't gone back with the others), and with him went to New Jersey, where they staked out a plot of ground the size of a stage and began to practice riding and roping. And this, too, added to the expense. Would he have to wire his father?

One day, by chance, he heard one of the booking agents telephone Keith's Union Square Theater, Union Square, New York, to say, "I've got a man here who's making life miserable for me." There was a silence, then he went on, "He wants to rope a running horse on the stage. Put him on the supper show; in that way we won't have to pay him and I can get rid of him."

Will knew that the "supper show" was the low of the day and that actors dreaded it as they would the bubonic plague. In fact, no important "act" would go on the supper show; only the small fish swam then. This was the time when they tried out new acts. Will knew all this, but also he knew that Keith's was an important vaudeville house; if he could make good there, then he might be able to go "on the stage" and not have to ride in Wild West shows. That would really be getting up in the world.

Sunday, June 11, 1905, a few people were drowsing in the audience when a cowboy shuffled out on the stage, saying not a word at all; coils of rope dangled from his hand. He tossed the rope here and there and hopped through a loop or two, as silent as a giraffe. Then suddenly from the wings a horse darted out, a rider on his back. The cowboy threw his rope and caught the horse — the first time a running horse was ever roped on the stage in the history of the world. The people in the audience must have blinked; well, that was interestin'. What wouldn't they think of next?

The manager of the theater was impressed; usually a manager would not be impressed by a collision of the moon and Mars but this one was. He said, "Well, it wasn't so bad; some of the people appeared to like it. I'll put you on all day tomorrow."

Will's heart fluttered like a daffodil.

He was on the stage.

At least for a while.

He was kept for the rest of the week. The horse didn't break loose or slide into the orchestra pit. Teddy buzzed around and around, Will flung his rope, and all was well. Then came exceedingly good news. He was to have a chance to play at Hammerstein's Victoria Theater, in the part called "Paradise Roof." That was like a Christmas Santa Claus ringing a bell on the street suddenly getting an invitation to play Santa Claus at the White House.

Jim Minnick had to go back to his ranch in Texas. Buck McKee, an Oklahoma cowboy, had roped for Colonel Mulhall at Madison Square Garden, and so Will got Buck to take Jim's place. (Buck was a family name, not a nickname.) They practiced and then came the great, the wonderful, the thrilling opening night at the most important vaudeville theater in America. This would be the night that Teddy would slide into the orchestra pit and knock the bottom out of the bass drum and Will's career. But he didn't. His felt overshoes carried him through and all was moonlight and roses.

Will was now an actor. Or really the horse was and Will was his support. Everybody watched the horse. Would he fall? Would he dodge the rope? The novelty of having a running horse on the stage was exciting. Now and then someone asked who was the boy throwing the rope?

The climax came when Will gave the end of the rope to an usher who backed down the aisle with it so that everybody could see how long the rope was — ninety feet. Will would hold up his end of the rope and get on Teddy. Then Will would start a loop, gradually making it larger and larger. As it grew he would back Teddy upstage until the rope was swishing above the heads of the audience. Finally he would have it all in the air at once — the Crinoline, with which he had captured Texas Jack's attention — and then, at the right moment, he would let it go on the floor with a plop.

He was getting one hundred and twenty-five dollars a week. His agent had to get a whack out of this, and Will had to pay Buck McKee, and Teddy was quietly eating his head off. Not much left for the cookie jar.

During the act Will didn't utter a peep. He had worked out an additional fillip: this was to throw two ropes at once and catch both horse and rider, as difficult a trick as you can scare up. And he did add it, but the audience didn't pay much attention to it. It was just a fellow throwing two ropes instead of one.

Will was put down, but didn't know what to do about the lack of appreciation. Then one of the actors said that he should tell the audience what he was going to do so they would watch with added interest. The next time on he stopped the act, stepped forward, and spoke to the audience directly, "Folks, I'm goin' to call your attention to something in this act worth lookin' at, and

that's to ketch both horse and rider at one an' the same time . . .
if I'm lucky an' I'm not sure I'm goin' to be."

He meant it as a straight announcement and never dreamed
there was an element of humor in it. But with his personality
added, it made the audience laugh. Will was flabbergasted. They
were not taking him seriously; they didn't appreciate the trick.
He went through the roping depressed. Next time he wouldn't
say a word. If they had sense enough to see it was a difficult
rope trick, then well and good; if they didn't, they could just
sit on their hands.

One of the actors, in the wings, said when Will came off,
"That was fine."

"What was fine about it?" asked Will moodily.

"Making them laugh."

"There wasn't anything to laugh at. They laughed at me instead of appreciatin' what I was tryin' to do."

"You get every laugh you can," said the old and experienced
actor.

Will, thinking of the difficult rope trick, said, "I'm not goin'
to say another word. They can miss the point of the trick, if they
want to; I don't care."

But other actors counseled him. Get in and get the laughs. And
so he tried it again; and again the audience laughed. Will was
puzzled; if that simple thing made them laugh, and the old boys
said to do it, why, he would keep it in.

Will was an astute showman. If laughs were what they
wanted, he'd give 'em plenty; he went to Fred Tejan, who was
a big hearty fellow with a ringing laugh, and engaged him to sit
out in front and laugh at everything that he said. And so every
time Will came on there was big, booming Fred Tejan, who
simply roared at Will's alleged witticisms. Instead of being in the
position of not wanting the audience to laugh, Will was now
working hard for laughs.

And, a bit to his astonishment, Will found that he was a comedian; it was exhilarating. He had always liked to have fun when he was in a crowd and to make people laugh; and here he was merely standing in front of the crowd and having fun. And getting paid for it. Not bad.

He was nervous before going on. He told this to one of the actors, who advised him to chew gum just before he went on. This Will started to do; one day, by chance, he came out on the stage with the gum hard at work. The audience was amused. Sometimes he missed his rope trick and began to plan what he should do when this happened. He worked out an idea. One day, when he missed a couple of times, he stopped, walked over to the sign that had his name, took out his gum, and spread it over the "W" in WILL. The audience laughed. Then he went back and this time performed the trick successfully. Thus he learned the value of his gum, and he kept that part in. Almost unconsciously, little by little, he was building up his act.

He began to use the little things that happened in the acts ahead of his. In one a Swiss did a "William Tell" by shooting an apple off a boy's head with a crossbow. Each time, before he shot, he said in a thick German-Swiss accent, "I neffer make meestake, onderstan'?"

Will captured this. Following the Swiss act, Will said in an imitation, "I now make der rope yump. I neffer make meestake, onderstan'?" Purposely he missed the trick. The audience laughed. Will appeared to be embarrassed, brushed his hand across his mouth, and said, "Except dis time, onderstan'?" It wasn't brilliant, but it was going in the right direction.

The effect of what he said was heightened by the fact that he didn't look at his audience, but kept his eyes on his rope and seemed to make the remarks to himself.

He began to comment on his act in a casual manner as if the idea had just suddenly come to him. When he failed and the rope flopped on the floor, he would look at it in pretended embarrassment, smile, and say, "Well, I got all my feet through but one." When the rope business went all right, he would say, "Well, that worked out fine — my trick and my joke came out even." He had a variant: "I've got jokes for only one miss. It looks like I've either got to practice up and be a better roper, or learn more jokes."

His jokes were not such casual, offhand remarks as his audience may have liked to believe. Here are some of them. They are written in ink in his own handwriting on two pieces of wrinkled paper; evidently he had carried them in his pocket in order to refer to them from time to time. There is no date. They are on stationery from the Saratoga Hotel, 155 Dearborn Street, Chicago, and labeled "Gags For Missing the Horses Nose":

1. I think I will turn him around and see if I cant throw one on his tail.

2. If I dont get one on pretty soon, I will have to give out rain checks.

3. Hi you, Jasper. I think I will see if I cant get just one on your nose, if it dont make any difference to you out there.

4. If I have a whole bunch of good luck, I will get this on about the 13th throw, if this salary wing dont give out on me.

5. I should of sprinkled a little musilage on his nose, this thing might then hang on.

6. There is hope. Well, we are all check full of hope. If there was a little better roping and less hoping, we would get out of here earlier tonight.

7. This is easier to do on a blind horse, they dont see the rope coming.

He learned tricks of showmanship not confined to the stage. He had a saddle blanket made for Teddy and the name WILL ROGERS embroidered on it in gold letters. Teddy had been trained to follow Buck McKee; just before time to go on, Buck would take Teddy out of the boarding stable, and then Buck would start down the street, without touching the bridle, and Teddy would follow. People stopped to watch and some would pace along the sidewalk to see where the horse and man were going. Then Buck would lead Teddy into the theater. Not bad.

The inevitable happened. It was told in an interview by Buck McKee: "One time our act followed a comic-barber routine during which lather had been thrown all over the stage. It was our first day on the bill and I didn't know about the lather, as I had been offstage holding Teddy. When the manager gave the signal, I leaped on Teddy and dashed onto the stage. Immediately things began to happen. Teddy's feet went out from under him and he fell and slid toward the orchestra pit. He knocked out half a dozen of the trough lights with a terrible crash. My leg was pinned under him; my head and his head were both hanging over the edge of the orchestra pit. You never saw an orchestra pit cleared of musicians so quickly in all your life. Not only the musicians but the front-row customers got out in no time flat. And such shouts and screams!

"Will could think and act with lightning rapidity and that's what he did now. He sprang out of the wings and roped Teddy's head and pulled him up tight with one hand; with his other hand he seized me and dragged me from under the terrified animal. As soon as I was on my feet, the two of us seized Teddy, and by pulling and hauling, got him back from the orchestra pit and, finally, onto his feet. The horse stood there, shaking and trembling — and me, I was doing quite a bit of it myself!

"Will went into action. Stepping forward he drawled, 'No cause for alarm, folks. This is just a little something extry we put in today to see how you'd like it!' He said it so calmly and with so much humor that the musicians came back — a bit hesitatingly it's true — and so did the front-row customers. A stagehand mopped up the lather and Teddy and I started around again. Thank goodness! Nothing happened. If Will hadn't done some quick thinking we might have had a situation on our hands."

He was now an actor. Not only this but a comedian — still a little to his surprise. Why! he and Dick Paris had talked this sort of stuff endless times. His salary went up to one hundred and fifty dollars a week. A little now for the jar. He engaged an agent, Mort Shea, who began to book him into the leading vaudeville theaters. He even played for a while with Buffalo Bill. The important thing was that he was learning show business; especially he was learning what he could do and what he couldn't do. Since the audience wanted comedy he would give it to them in hunks, and he began to tell jokes he had heard. They fell with sickening thuds. He saw that the comments he made up himself and which sprang from his inner being went best, so he gave up the artificial jokes and was just himself. Sometimes, even then, the talk didn't go. When this happened he gave them more rope. When the audience laughed at his jokes, he shortened the rope.

One day a dog strolled out on the stage and looked around in a bewildered way. Will threw, and, by a bit of luck, caught the dog. The audience laughed. Will saw possibilities. People liked to see things roped on the stage.

Eleven months after he played the "supper show" he felt confident enough to take a whack at Europe. Mort Shea booked him in the Winter Palace, in Berlin — quite a hop from Rabb's Creek. In a short time, Will, Buck and Teddy were on their way. He was now twenty-seven years old. Since his chance meeting with Betty Blake at the St. Louis World's Fair he had been corresponding with her; and once, when there was a gap between vaudeville engagements, he had gone to Arkansas to see her. In the meantime, Kate Ellis had got married. And so it was.

Something happened in Berlin that is worth setting down. He couldn't talk, but that was all right; lots of rope. The act went well. Roping a running horse on the stage was something new; and Will looked picturesque. Will's attention was caught by an impressively uniformed fireman who stood solemnly a few feet off the stage and out of sight of the audience, with no more expression on his face than a totem pole. Suddenly Will's rope went wreathing out and landed around that august individual. Will hauled him out, expecting the audience to laugh at his upset dignity; instead the audience sent up a clamor of protest. Will had imposed on an official. So great was the disturbance that the manager hurriedly beckoned Will offstage, then rushed out and said that he was extremely sorry for what had happened, but that the American's rope had slipped and that the American was humbly apologetic for the unintentional insult. Meantime, the American was standing offstage, gaping. After things quieted down, Will came out on the stage, trying to look crestfallen.

His rope never slipped again during all the time he was in Germany.

His act went so well that he was booked in London, and there the three headed: Will, Buck and Teddy. And now, five years after he and Dick Paris had arrived in London, Will was back, this time at the Palace Theater. Not bad, either.

He was not content to let things go as they were; he wanted to work out rope tricks. He was not going to use them in his act, but he was more interested in roping than in anything else and would go to the theater in the morning and practice with his rope for hours at a time.

He played three weeks at the Palace, then went on a tour of Scotland. He was beginning to think of home. He made a decision: he would go back, so onto the next boat went the invincible three. In New York he put Teddy in a boarding stable; Buck returned to Oklahoma and so did Will. He went to see his father, who was still puzzled by his ever-wandering son. It wasn't much of an honor to have a son who had to make a living roping a running horse on the stage, especially when there was a ranch which needed a good manager. Why couldn't the boy stay at home?

In a few days, Will headed for Arkansas. He had been corresponding with Betty and was becoming more and more interested in her. It was an exciting event when he arrived at the dressmaker's home with the yard full of girls. They all seemed to have liked him; at least, the neighborhood children did, for he brought his ropes (he never went anywhere without them) and roped the gatepost in front of Amelia Blake's house.

Will returned to the ranch, and there was a round of parties for him. Will's sister Maude gave one at her home in Chelsea. Half a dozen young people were invited for what now would be called a week-end party. Mary Gulager told me about it. Betty Blake came all the way from Arkansas, a distance of a hundred and thirty miles. But she couldn't come direct; had to change and zigzag.

The train pulled into Vinita (where Will had once gone to school) and, lo and behold! Will himself got on the train. But it wasn't really so remarkable, after all, for he had come by an early-morning train to Vinita to meet and escort her to Chelsea, a distance of about twenty miles. In spite of this preparation he came bashfully to greet her. But a calamity occurred. A man slid into the seat ahead of Will and sat down beside Betty. Will reached across the stranger and shook hands, exchanged a few words, then went bashfully to a seat in another part of the car and sat there until the train finally achieved Chelsea. But at the week-end party they became better acquainted.

Mary Gulager told me about another party. She was Will's favorite cousin and now lives on Route 1, Tahlequah, Oklahoma. At this party Will was already there and Betty and Mary were to arrive by carriage. "I know how we can make an impression on the boys," said Betty. "We'll each carry a white parasol and get out of the carriage very daintily and march up to the house with our white parasols over us." It was a fine idea, but there were no white parasols in the town, and the two had to plump up to the house devoid of their glamorous canopies.

Joe Chambers (quoted elsewhere) told me a story which shows how Will, on his travels, had thought of his relatives. Once when Will was in Rome he had bought a present for his cousin Mary Gulager — a pair of pajamas — which he called "Roman fireworks." Will's sister (Mrs. Sallie Rogers McSpadden) had a house party at her home in Chelsea and invited Mary Gulager. Of course, Mary wore her pajamas, which must have created more excitement than the burning of Rome. Anyway, Mary Gulager's pajamas disappeared.

A few days after the party, Mary Gulager came to Joe Chambers's office in Claremore and said she wanted to have some fun with Betty Blake. She said she thought that Betty had purloined them and, for the fun of it, wanted to pretend she was going to sue her. So Joe Chambers wrote Betty that he had been employed to file suit against her over the theft of a certain pair of pajamas, and that he must proceed with the action unless the pajamas were returned promptly. He received an immediate answer. Betty Blake said that her lawyer was out of town, but that as soon as he returned she would communicate. There was no letter from a lawyer, but Joe Chambers and Betty continued to correspond in a friendly way. Finally Betty Blake returned the pajamas to Mary Gulager, and the prank was over.

His taste of success in Germany and England made Will want to go back and, this time, do it in the big American way; he hired two other riders and got two other horses and left for England to show 'em riding that was riding. It was a good idea. The only catch was that it didn't work. He could get hardly any more money than for the single act, and in just a little less than no time he was broke. He sent the two men and their horses back home as fast as they could go and then he, Buck and Teddy patiently started out again.

As soon as Will could get enough money together, the three of them came home. He was discouraged; even worse, he was without funds.

CHAPTER 10

Will Is Married. Meets Fred Stone

HE PLUGGED along with his running horse act; he told the audience what to look for; he commented on the acts ahead of him; he chomped away at his gum. But he was an actor; he was on the stage. On top of this he was a comedian. This latter must have taken a little getting used to.

Will had quite a bit of spare time. He spent it practicing — always practicing — and going to ball games. He liked the players and liked to have them come to see his act. Then he would call them by name, point them out in the theater, and make some comment about them. He wrote to Betty and he kept in touch with his father, and so things drifted along; he was just another vaudeville player. And his act was limited. No one could get very far with a horse, a rope, and a wad of gum.

A year went by.

Then suddenly he came to Arkansas. Betty hadn't known he was coming, but there he was and he had something on his mind. He was now twenty-nine and she was twenty-eight. It had been eight years since the banjo. His courtship had been far from ardent; in fact, each time he met her he was shy. But he liked her.

Betty had to do some thinking. Her family was poor; her mother was still taking in dressmaking, and one of Betty's sisters was still working in the Stroud store and so, from time to time, was Betty. Another sister (Theda) was teaching school. The family was respected. Amelia Blake had done exceedingly well with the six daughters and two sons left on her hands.

Betty liked Will, but her family did not consider him any great catch. He was just a vaudeville player who roped a running horse on the stage. No future to that. Actors weren't considered very "much"; here was one who wasn't a "regular" actor. Just a rope thrower. It presented problems.

But Will meant business.

He went back to Oklahoma and told his father and sisters the good news. His father was pleased. It was time Willie was settling down. Would he run the ranch now?

The two were married the day before Thanksgiving, 1908, in Betty's mother's home. The home paper didn't spread itself; it took care of the matter in four paragraphs:

"Miss Betty Blake and Will Rogers of Claremore, Okla., were married Wednesday afternoon at one o'clock by the Rev. J. G. Bailey, at the home of the bride's mother, Mrs. A. J. Blake, on East Walnut Street.

"Only the immediate family of the young couple were present. Those from out of town were the groom's father, C. V. Rogers of Claremore, and two sisters, Mrs. C. L. Lane and Mrs. Stine of Chelsea, Okla.

"Mr. Rogers and bride left on the northbound evening train for New York City, where the groom is a prominent figure in vaudeville. We understand they plan a trip to Europe before they go to Oklahoma next spring, where Mr. Rogers has a large farm and where they will make their future home.

"The bride was born in Rogers and has grown to womanhood here. She has always taken a prominent part in the social life of the city and is one of the best-known young ladies of Northwest Arkansas. Her attractive personal qualities have made her a general favorite, and she will be missed by an unusually large circle of friends."

The last seven words in the third paragraph are especially worth noting.

The minister who married them was Betty's old preacher-post-master from Monte Ne.

Then the two drove down the muddy, deep-rutted street to the depot, got on the wheezy, cindery train, and started life together.

The day after the wedding, Man-of-the-world Will took the Girl of the Ozarks to the Planters Hotel in St. Louis and ordered their Thanksgiving dinner — not down in the dining room where the common people ate but in their own private room. Then he added his own idea of elegance — champagne. Thoughtful readers will know that champagne is not ordinarily served as part of a Thanksgiving dinner, but Will decided it would be a touch of elegance that his bride deserved. So he told 'em to send up plenty. Never before had Betty come face to face with champagne; it tasted like cider from the choice orchards of the Ozarks, so she helped herself liberally. It was nice cider. Will had bought tickets for Maude Adams in *What Every Woman Knows*, and when the champagne-turkey dinner was over the happy couple started for the theater. The only thing wrong that Betty noticed was that it all seemed uphill. The curtain went up. Soon she found that Maude Adams was not enunciating clearly and that the theater needed to have the windows opened. Suddenly the stage tilted; she was alarmed through and through. Seizing Will's arm she said, "Please take me out." He took her out, stopped at a coffee place, and finally got his bride home. And thus, the day after their wedding, Betty Blake Rogers learned that champagne is champagne, and cider is cider. It was her first champagne and her first stage play. The play was not as good as *Mrs. Jarley's Wax Works*.

There began a new and adventurous life for the bride. She knew nothing about show business. The people backstage . . . what strange creatures they were! How different from the reserved citizens of Benton County, Arkansas. And what free and easy ways. The first time she saw Will on the stage was at Proctor's Theater, in Newark, New Jersey. He had gotten her a seat down in front; and there she saw him rope Teddy, do a few tricks, and make some remarks just as he would talk offstage. It did not seem very thrilling; and when it was over, he looked at her eagerly to see how she had liked it. She tried to show enthusiasm, but he sensed what was in her mind and was disappointed.

They meant so much to each other they stayed together and saw hardly anyone else. He would go to the theater just in time to buckle on his chaps, put on his cowboy shirt, and tie his bandanna. As soon as his part was over, he would leave and go home to Betty. The two would go sight-seeing together. He showed her New York almost street by street. This part she liked — the sight-seeing, the interesting restaurants, their hours together.

Two friends from home came to see Betty: Mrs. Coin Harvey and her daughter Annette, who was Betty's age. And now Betty must have thought of her first sweetheart — Tom Harvey. Well, he was still in Monte Ne. But that was the way of life. One never knew. Tom Harvey was rated as the son of a millionaire. At least an off-and-on millionaire. Mostly off. But Will, the Indian cowboy, was wonderful. Of course, he was in an odd business.

Buck and Teddy were made ready, and Will and Betty started "on the road" for the Orpheum Circuit. It was a new life to her, but it was not long until she liked it. Will's restless, never-ceasing, amazing energy did get her down. He could never sit still, was always on the go. At night, when the show was over, they would have sandwiches in their room at the hotel, or would go to a restaurant where Will could get his beloved chili. This strange passion had grown until he was now a lost soul. Betty liked to rest of a morning, but Will was hopping early and would have all kinds of ideas as to places they ought to see and things they should do. She would say she wanted to rest; he couldn't understand this. Why, they hadn't done anything the day before! "Let's go sight-seeing this morning and get back early, then we'll have more time to do things this afternoon," he would say with logic that was hard to combat.

He was not known as a comedian and didn't think of himself as one; his comments were merely to make the "act" better. And the people he met backstage didn't think of him as a comedian. A comedian was a funny fellow who dressed up in tramp clothes, or one who blacked his face and talked in a killing way.

Up and down the land Will and Betty journeyed, from coast to coast. A week in this town, then hop to the next. Sometimes it was only one day in a town, then hop. Betty, in her book, tells this story: their expenses were heavy, with both Buck and Teddy nibbling at the pay envelope, so Will and Betty hit on a way to save. They bought a metal box with a slit in the top. Every day they would push a dollar through the slot; in the East it was paper, in the West it was silver. The box grew fat and rattled like a chicken car. One afternoon in Butte, Montana, they came home and when they opened the door they saw that their things were strewn about in disorder. And there, on the floor, was their strongbox — the lid pried open and the money no more. Betty was brokenhearted; their nest egg was gone. Will was cast down for a few minutes, then said, "It's all over, Betty, and there's nothing we can do about it except report it to the office downstairs. And since we can't do anything about it, let's not worry about it. Let's go out and have a good lunch."

But all the time Will and Betty looked on this vaudeville business as only temporary. They'd go back to Oklahoma and get into ranching. The Rogers Ranch still pined for a good manager. But, in the background of Will's mind, was that stern master: *work*. He had perfected himself in roping so he could escape it, but now, through his father's urging, he was about to embrace it. Will's father was getting old, so he said; sometimes he had dizzy spells. Will was the only son. He ought to take over the ranch.

Then Will got a vaudeville offer from the Percy Williams chain of theaters, the best offer he had ever had. Well, he would take this plush offer and when it was over he would go back to Oklahoma.

Will and his horse galloped along neatly; Will couldn't get along without him. To make additional money, the agent also booked Will and his act outside of vaudeville; he arranged for Will to appear before the Mercantile Club in Philadelphia. When Will got to Philadelphia, consternation came and perched on his shoulder like a raven. Teddy hadn't arrived. Will had never given a performance without faithful Teddy loping rhythmically around, and with Buck McKee manfully taking the ropes he hurled at him. What should he do? Well, he had his lariat and his gun, so, with his heart in his chaps, he walked on. He was nervous; after all, a horse was a mighty competent understudy. He cracked a few jokes; the audience laughed, then, gaining confidence, he really gave it to them. The show was a success. Will opened his eyes. Well!

He no longer had to worry about poking a dollar every day through a slot. His was still an animal act but it had comedy, an article rare in animal acts. His name began to appear in reviews of the vaudeville shows; now and then a reporter dropped backstage to report something the droll cowboy said.

Will began putting money in his father's bank. The old gentleman's eyes popped. Mebbe the boy could make a go of this theater ropin'. Now and then somebody from back home saw Will on the stage and told Clement Vann Rogers about it. He would listen with rapt interest. Finally he went to Washington, D. C., where Will was playing, and, with his own eyes, saw Will amble out on the stage and pretty soon get the people laughing. "Why, he ain't actin'; he's just bein' himself. He was always

cuttin' up and carryin' on — and now he's gettin' paid for it."
He was completely mystified. He stayed a week, visiting with
Will, and going to every performance. The astute banker began
to estimate the number of people in the theater and how much
the tickets had been sold for. It seemed to him — now wholly
and completely pro-Will — that the people were coming principally to see Will. One day he said, "Willie, I've been doin' a
little figgerin'. The people are spending a lot of money to come
to see you. The managers are not payin' you enough. You get
after them and stand up to 'em — you're worth it an' you can get
it." After a performance he would wait in the lobby, and, if he
heard anyone mention the Oklahoma cowboy, he would say,
"You might be interested to know that's my son. I'll introduce
you to him, if you want me to." Then he would lead the person
to the stage door, trying to appear modest, and, when Will came
out, introduce the sight-seer.

At home he loved to have people come to the bank; then he
would make it easy for them to ask about Will. He would
elaborately pretend he was in doubt. He would say, "Have you
heard anything? I just don't know whether he's makin' a go of
it, or not." Then, as the person praised Will, he would beam. But
he wouldn't openly give in. "I don't know, myself. We'll just
wait an' see." He carried crumpled newspaper clippings in his
pockets and would haul them out and read the flattering notices.
"Of course, you can't always believe what you see in the newspapers," he would say and shake his head doubtfully.

The passing of the years was having an effect on him not always to be found in people growing older. Instead of growing
bitter, he was becoming mellow. His early gruff, harsh ways
were passing. It was hard to believe that here was the man who
had once forcibly taken a store away from the Osages who
rightfully owned it. His advent in politics had made him more
agreeable. He found how important human relations and human

understandings were. He became a sort of father-adviser to the young people in Claremore. They all called him "Uncle Clem," and when they saw him, went squealing toward him. He now had a pair of fast-stepping driving horses and a swagger rubber-tired buggy, and he liked to pick up the young people and take them on a breathless swing down the streets of Claremore. When Will came home to see him, he took him to his rooms above the bank and there the two would sit and "visit." When Will would have to return to his work, the old gentleman would complain about being lonesome and would pack off and go to see his daughters and sons-in-law. There was one thing he did not change his attitude toward, and that was them damned autty-mobiles. He would not have one and would not get into one if he could possibly avoid doing so.

He complained about "not feeling as well as he should." Wasn't as young as he used to be, he said. He talked more and more of "old days." He told about the time he had helped drive cattle to St. Louis and how this was so far away it had taken him nine days to ride back. He spoke of how he "had freighted to St. Joe," and how he had opened a trading post at Oologah. But he kept away from mentioning how he had taken it over. He spoke of the "Constitutional Convention" and how he had been a member; and he talked with pride of how he had helped nab all the available land to make Rogers a big county.

A sulphurous, ill-smelling water had been discovered in George Easton's cow pasture; some imaginative person gave it the name of "radium water" — although there was no more radium in it than in a haystack — because it was a good tie-up with radium which was sweeping the country. Energetic citizens began to sell the water and advertise that bathing in it would cure anything that ailed you. One day, as he was walking down the street, "Uncle Clem" complained about not feeling well. He sat down on one of the Claremore's benches and said, "Bring me some radium water." A runner was dispatched, the water arrived, Mr. Rogers drank it, sat a few minutes, and said, "I feel all right now." Then he continued on down the street as if nothing had happened.

Meantime something was happening that, at first, did not seem related to Will Rogers. Fred Stone, the athletic comedian of the day, arrived in Louisville, Kentucky, to do his act. There was a play in town called *The Cowboy and the Lady*, and since the two matinees did not come on the same day, Fred went to see the show. Out stepped a tall, thin, dark-complexioned young man with the blackest eyes ever seen in a human head, and began to twirl a rope. Fred was delighted. Never had he seen a rope do so completely what its master wished. He looked again at the program. Who was this Black Chambers?

The reason Fred was so intrigued was that he was planning an act for a new show he was to appear in, *The Old Town* by George Ade. Fred sent word to the roper to come to the hotel to see him. But Black Chambers had never heard of Fred Stone. Fred sent a more urgent word for the young roper to come to see him; at last the tall, silent, black-haired, part-Cherokee roper showed up and waited silently.

"Do you think you could teach me to rope?"

"I don't know," said the visitor.

"I can do other things," said Fred modestly.

The visitor said nothing at length.

Then Fred, beginning to grow uneasy, explained that he was an eccentric dancer and could do athletic feats, and that he wanted to put a roping scene in his new play and that he would like to have Black Chambers teach him. Black Chambers said he would have to continue with his show until it closed; and this he did, a matter of five weeks, then joined Fred in Indianapolis and traveled with him. Every morning the two went to the theater and practiced. Finally Fred's show closed and Fred took

Black Chambers to his home in Freeport, Long Island, and there the lessons continued. But things did not go well with Black Chambers. He could do the paramount trick of turning a flip-flop through a loop. One day in doing this extremely difficult trick, he burst a blood vessel in his throat and had to go back to Oklahoma. There he died April 7, 1911. And now Fred was without a teacher.

Will Rogers, the perfectionist, was not making as rapid progress as he wished. He learned that Black Chambers had been engaged by Fred Stone. Will thought he could "borrow" Black Chambers, and went to the New Amsterdam Theater where Fred Stone was rehearsing for his new play. The diplomatic thing would be to ask Fred if he would mind if he, too, employed the talents of Black Chambers. Fred was worlds above Will, for Will was doing a "horse act" in vaudeville, and Fred Stone was the star of a musical show.

Fred happened to be sitting in the alley, just outside the stage door, when Will came up; he was wearing a blue serge, yellow shoes, a straw hat, had no vest and was carrying a folded newspaper. "Is Fred Stone in?" he asked the doorman.

The crafty doorman had dealt with pests before. "I don't think so. Who wants to see him?"

"Tell him it's Will Rogers, from Oklahoma."

Fred Stone sprang to his feet. "I'm Fred Stone," he said.

The two talked some, then Will told him what he wanted. "He broke a blood vessel and had to go back to Oklahoma," said Fred. "It's hard on me, because I was just getting started in this roping business."

"Maybe I can help you a bit," said Will. "I've been at it quite a while."

Without more ado the two went inside, took Fred's ropes, and began flinging them about.

Hardly realizing what he was doing, Will had been adding

more and more talk to his act. The players backstage and his friends who had seen the show from the front, said they liked his talk better than they did his roping. He was surprised, for, in Oklahoma, skill in roping counted for more than gab, but he was an astute showman. If they wanted talk he'd give it to them. And then came the big day: he sent Buck and Teddy back to Oklahoma, and now he was really on his own.

Something else happened. Will and Betty had been married three years and now a son was born. He was named for Will himself and Will's father. He was William Vann Rogers, and he was born at West 113 Street, New York. The exact date was October 20, 1911. The name of Will Rogers was becoming more and more important, and so the boy soon became Will Rogers, Junior.

CHAPTER II

Will Fails in Business Again

WITH NO FUTURE (seemingly) for himself in vaudeville, Will decided to become a producer, and looked around for an opening. (Did his mind go back to ill-starred Memphis?) A big "Western act." That was it! He would improve on that by having a Girl Show. That was what they wanted. He would give it to 'em. So he engaged the best and most famous riding girls to be had. (The country, by this time, was peppered with girl riding acts; no show or fair was free of them.) He engaged the most famous of all, Mabel Hackney, with her dancing horse Vardius; Goldie St. Clair, Flores LaDue, Hazel Moran, Tillie Baldwin and Arlene Palmer, a girl Cossack rider who had been in Buffalo Bill's Wild West Show. Most of the horses and some of the riders were secured through Charles H. Tompkins, whose present address has been given. He told me:

"Will and Petty came to New Hope, Pennsylvania, to see my riding stock. They left without Will sayin' anything specific, but I knowed he was impressed. He telephoned me in a few days to bring some of my stock to Bayonne, New Jersey, where he was goin' to put on the biggest Western act ever seen on an indoor stage. When I got there I was astonished to see the girls keep pilin' in. I said to Will, 'There's not enough big stages in the vaude circuit to handle this act.' He said, 'A good act always makes money.' The girls were most of the show; after the main part, the men were to ride bucking horses on the stage. This had never been done, and, when I examined the stage, I had a good deal of fear and trepidation; so I told Will we had better put up a wire fence in case one of the horses decided to graze in the orchestra pit. So we got some Pittsburgh wire, bored holes in each side of the stage and pulled the wire tight with block and tackle. Well, the girls came out, all mounted, in a pretty scene called 'Gathering the Garlands.' The girls circled around Mabel Hackney on her horse in the center of the stage. The act was good, but too long. After the girls were off, there came the climax of the show: the riding and bucking horses. The stage had been covered with matting so the horses wouldn't slide. No one in the group had ever ridden a bucking horse on the stage, so it fell to me to mount one of the horses. And this I did, with some confidence, also a bit of trepidation, for you never know what a horse is going to get into his head. Well, my horse did his stuff fine. Then he made a dash to go over the footlights and into the green pastures of the aisles. He hit the fence head-on. This threw him back to the middle of the stage. The audience was delighted, but me and the horse wasn't. That was givin' 'em too much for their money. At the end of the act, on the stage, I took the saddle off. The horse kicked at it, which made the audience laugh.

"The show failed and strapped Will financially. But he took it well. He was never down long. I took Mabel Hackney and Tillie Baldwin and put them in a show called 'Mabel Hackney and Her Bucking and Dancing Horses,' and went out on the road. It was a small show, and prospered."

After the interview he wrote me: "Oh, yes! be sure to tell about Vardius. He was a beautiful sorrel running horse from the stables of the Empress of Austria, price $750. He didn't like show business and developed the unpleasant trait of suddenly raring up and falling back on the rider. The rider had to scoot, or sqush. I had to re-train him which I finally accomplished. In 1912 a party in North Carolina offered Mabel $3500 for Vardius, which she didn't accept. I tell you this to indicate the kind of horses that Will had in his girl show. Will did not intend to give up his own act; he just wanted to augment his income, him havin' a wife and a family comin' on. We hated to see him lose out. Everybody liked him. He was the biggest hearted person I ever had the pleasure to know. If you can, I wish you would put in your book that Mabel Hackney was my wife.

"Where you say these were the first buckers ever used on the stage may bring in some hot letters. We had buckers with The Round-Up company several years before Will's act was staged. Will's horses were shod with rubber shoes to keep them from slipping on the coconut mats. I made the mats myself for the horses to travel on. Everything else in the chapter seems to square up."

The glamorous girls were no better than Buck alone. It must have been a big day for Buck. Will was back where he had started. And now, in his career, he had failed three times: he had come back from South Africa so broke that he had to ride in a chicken car; he had failed in London with his "big" show; and now in America, with his glamour girls, he had failed again.

Meantime, back in Oklahoma, Will's father more and more had become a politician. He was living alone over his bank; and now as he sought to win people to his way of thinking, he became less gruff. Many people had hated him bitterly and some of the stories they told about him were not pleasant. But that was all over now.

The Indian and Oklahoma Territories were going through birth pangs; they'd be a state, bye and bye. The districts were to be turned into counties; the Cherokee Nation was to be part of this new state. The Constitutional Convention met in 1906 and lasted for two months. The delegates from Oklahoma and from the Indian Territories met at Guthrie to draft a constitution. Mr. Rogers was chosen as delegate from Cooweescoowee District.

Most of the delegates had been chosen because they were good public speakers. Mr. Rogers wasn't a good public speaker, but no one could sit in a back room and manipulate things as skillfully as he could. He and C. N. Haskell really ran the convention, Haskell out in front, Rogers behind the scenes. The powerful William H. Murray ("Alfalfa Bill") was President of the Constitutional Convention.

Finally time came to name the county in the section in which Clem Rogers had been living. He had been anxious for it to be the biggest and best county in the newborn state; when the county was being laid out he fought to make it larger and larger. He would point to a creek, or a knob of land and say, "It's only fair to add that," and, to keep peace in the committee, the part would be included. One of the delegates scornfully called this new county "Little Texas"; there was a bit of truth in the idea. The members had become accustomed to the impossible name of Cooweescoowee, but now, in committee, it was pointed out that the name would defeat strangers. A debate resulted; the delegates shouted at each other and, at this kind of game, Clem Rogers was not a man to be taken casually. Finally someone suggested the county be named in honor of Clem Rogers. Mr. Rogers had secretly been hoping this would come about; and now it had actually happened and Cooweescoowee District was Rogers County. It was enough to make any man happy.

The Indian Territory became a state November 17, 1907. They celebrate it today as Statehood Day. The section of the Indian Territory where Will Rogers had been born was now Rogers County, Oklahoma. The county seat was Claremore, named after Chief Claremore. Will used the name Claremore as that of his birthplace and his home town. But, as a matter of fact, he had not yet stayed overnight in Claremore in his life. It was a name easy to be remembered. Will was too much a showman not to know the value of this.

In 1915 Will went to Atlantic City to fill a vaudeville engagement, and there saw something new and different — a "flying boat." It floated bravely on the water near the Boardwalk. The boat had been made by Glenn Curtiss, and had been purchased by an ambitious young man who was taking up passengers for five dollars a trip. There was a rather unusual way of getting aboard the flying boat. A man, broad of back and strong of shoulder, picked up the soon-to-be passenger and waded out to the boat, the prospective passenger clinging to the strong man and hoping for the best. Every day Will would come to the Boardwalk and watch the hardy passengers going aboard; he pined to go himself, but was afraid. Finally on the last day of his engagement, he walked up and laid down his money, as if afraid he might change his mind. In a few minutes he was being transported to the little boat, which must have looked about as big as a rabbit trap. The boat started up and, as it rose, he waved to Betty. . . . At last the boat came back and clunked down on the water with a hearty splash. Will was transported back by the sturdy ocean-going carrier. He was still nervous, but also vastly pleased. It had been an exhilarating experience.

Here is as odd a story as you would want. It appears in the *New York Times*, May 6, 1919, page 6. There was a "scourge" of deer on Shelter Island; the deer were eating the sturdy farmers' cauliflower and lettuce. Fifty game wardens and about the same number of volunteers (the latter mostly on the way) arrived to deal with the alarming situation. A great barricade was set up into which the deer were to be driven and captured. Unfortunately the deer broke through and loped off through the bayberry briars and the cattails in the swamps. The brave men came determinedly after them. One of the deer dashed through the yelling lines and made for the sea. Will Rogers had come out to see the mighty hunt. A powerboat — the *Muriel* — was sent after the floundering animal. Will stood up in the powerboat and directed its course. When he came close enough, he threw his lariat, snared the animal, and made it swim alongside the powerboat till it got to shore. During the exciting event, a Pathe newsreel man arrived with his camera and snapped Will landing the deer. Although the picture was only a flash, it marked Will's first appearance on the movie screen. The deer was crated and shipped back to the Adirondacks (its original home), along with its brothers and sisters, and the cauliflower and lettuce on Shelter Island were safe again.

CHAPTER 12

Will Joins the Ziegfeld Follies

FOR YEARS Will had been developing from the serious rope thrower into the humorous talker. To his delight he had found that he could entertain an audience without a rope, but usually he was afraid to risk it. So each time, out came the rope. And he had changed his ideas of giving up the stage and going back to Claremore to live. He'd do that in his old age; he'd buy a plot of land, build a ranch house and there pass his remaining days. It is an anomaly he had never spent a night in his life in Claremore, and never stayed with his father in the upstairs rooms over the bank; he always shindied out to the ranch.

In the meantime his father had been growing more and more proud of his once wayward son; oftener and oftener he maneuvered the conversation around to him; oftener and oftener his clippings came out of his pocket.

One of his other chief pleasures was to visit with his daughters. It was too far to drive his runabout to Chelsea to see Maude, so he would take the train, stay over the week end, then get back to his rooms over the bank. During the last part of October 1911, he went to Chelsea to visit Maude. He was always an early riser, but on Sunday morning he seemed to be sleeping late. Maude was quiet so as not to disturb him. Finally when he did not come down, she went to his room and knocked on the door. He had died in his sleep.

One of his last acts had been to mail a pair of tiny beaded moccasins to his grandchild, baby Will. Young Will was nine days old when his grandfather died.

Will was greatly upset by the news, and left immediately for Oklahoma. The thing that touched him was that he and his father were beginning to understand each other and to be closer than they had ever been before.

He came back to New York and his two-a-day. He had gone about as far as he could in vaudeville. He consulted with Fred Stone. The thing to do, Fred said, was to get into a musical show. Easy to say. Took scratching to do.

He kept his eye out for a musical show. At last he heard that George M. Cohan was going to put on one called *Broadway and Buttermilk*. Will hurried around, but Cohan said he wasn't good enough. The buttermilk, however, soon soured; the show lasted only six weeks.

Will continued to swing his lariat, chew his gum, and comment on what had happened in the act ahead of him; then out of a clear sky came a chance to go into a show, *The Wall Street Girl*. Blanche Ring was vastly popular from having put over "In the Good Old Summertime," "In the Shade of the Old Apple Tree," "Yip-I-Addy," "Rings on My Fingers and Bells on My Toes," and lesser songs. She was to be the star. Will had rings on his fingers and all kinds of bells on his toes.

The big, the wonderful opening night came April 14, 1912. Will and Betty were having to sail close to the wind, and they went to the opening in the subway. When the time came, Will went out, whacked away at his gum, and told a few jokes. He sensed something was wrong. People were getting up and leaving the theater.

Someone came backstage with the incredible news that the steamship *Titanic* had struck an iceberg and had sunk — the most dreadful catastrophe that had ever happened to a passenger ship; down with the ship had gone 1517 people, fifty-three of them children.

Will was called on to go out and tell the audience what had

happened. The show continued, but without spirit. When the curtain came down the theater was half empty. The play ran briefly. Soon Will was back in vaudeville with rope and gum.

He was discouraged. He was once again a small act in vaudeville. W. C. Fields was going gaily ahead and so were other entertainers he had seen, or knew personally.

Betty went to her mother's home and there, in the room adjoining the parlor where she had been married, a girl was born May 18, 1913, and was named Mary Amelia, after Will's mother and Betty's mother. Betty and the child continued to live there while Will tried to get ahead in New York. Will Junior was being taken care of by Betty's sister Theda.

Maybe he could do better in England, he thought; so in 1914 Betty left the baby with her mother, and went hopping to London with Will. Success smiled, and in no time at all he was in a musical show entitled *The Merry-Go-Round*. The only trouble was that it didn't go round. Also something was happening that alarmed Will. War clouds. And so the two came back to America, where Betty went to Arkansas and Will went looking for work. He was a "regular" actor now, with all the grim problems of getting work.

Musical comedy! He must get a part in one. But no musical comedy pined for his presence. Then suddenly one did want him. Good news. It was to be produced by the Shuberts; its title was *Hands Up*, but it turned out to be thumbs down; it soon closed its eyes and drifted off into a peaceful slumber. By now he had worked in three musical shows; all had closed as soon as they conveniently could. But he still believed in them. Certainly his chances would be better than in vaudeville, where he could swing a rope till he wore it out and not get anywhere.

A chance came to go into a spectacular review — *Town Topics* — to be produced by Ned Wayburn; it was to play at the huge Century Theater, on Central Park West. Will was

elated. He polished up his gum and his jokes and strolled out on
the stage with his ropes. He didn't have to lay in a new supply
of gum, for the show opened and closed like a lid on a box.
Back to vaudeville.

Will and Fred Stone had become even closer friends. Will
followed Fred to Amityville, Long Island, New York, where
Fred had a place for the summer. Will and Betty rented a house
across the road from Fred's and all was well. And there the
third child was born and was named for Betty's father — James
Blake Rogers. The date, July 25, 1915.

Fred had a boat on a channel of the tide water that came in
from Great South Bay. The water was deep when the tide was
in, shallow when it was out. Fred was a fish and tried to teach
Will to swim. All that Will knew about swimming was what he
had learned flopping around in the Verdigris River; he now
managed to kick up a great deal of water and to emit no end of
grunting and sputtering.

One day he ran on ahead of the others, dashed down the
wharf, and dived. But the tide was out; he struck on his right
shoulder and came out pretty well shaken.

Fred Stone said, "Didn't you know the tide was out?"

"We don't have tides in Oklahoma. We have swimmin' holes
which don't try to kill you."

The result was serious, for his right arm became paralyzed.
He had to continue in vaudeville, so he laboriously started to
learn to rope with his left hand. This was finally accomplished
and he became a left-handed roper.

When fall came Fred had to go on the road, and told Will that
he could move into his house on Olive Place, Forest Hills, Long
Island, which was about twenty minutes from the city. Will
liked Forest Hills, so when Fred came back Will moved into
Dr. Thompson T. Sweeney's house at 5 Russell Place. At the
time I was living in a potato throw, at 10 Standish Road — "The

Little House With the Big Mortgage." That's what I called it and, alas, I called it all too true.

Will kept his horses in Mae Wirth's stables on the Cord Meyer side, but exercised them on the lot where Public School 101 now stands. This was exactly and squarely in front of my mortgage. Nearly every day I saw him; sometimes we looked at each other and grunted. He was a vaudeville player. That was all I knew. He must have looked at me, at home during business hours, and wondered how I made a living. Well, I did, too.

One peculiar repercussion came from his roping. The children in the neighborhood were fascinated, and Will began to teach them. Almost every day, there they would be roping, or trying. The clothesline loss was appalling.

I never dreamed that my seemingly prosperous neighbor was having his difficulties, too. I looked on anyone who could afford to keep horses as a minor Morgan. But, as a matter of fact, Will was hearing scratching at his door. Some of the time he had no booking at all. Meantime his family wanted to eat; and so did his horses. So hard-pressed was he that he took jobs in vaudeville under other names. Sometimes he would be at a theater only one day; then hop. I was getting my mail at the post office, had a box. I would come out of the house and there would be my prosperous neighbor exercising his horses. We would grunt and I would go on down to the post office, open the box, and get my manuscript. Things grew progressively worse for me. It wasn't long before the grocer was carrying me. Now and then I sold something; many hands reached out for it.

And now came a turning point. Bad luck had followed Will like a farmer's dog, then suddenly it became his friend. His right arm returned to usefulness and once again he could rope with it. But this was not the important matter. One night Gene Buck went to the Forty-fourth Street Theater and there, on the stage, saw Will Rogers. At this time comedians were divided roughly into two classes — the "Dutch" comedian and the blackface comedian. Buck thought he saw in Will an opportunity for a comedian who represented the West and the great outdoors — a cowboy comedian, something unknown in America, later a scourge.

At this time, Florenz Ziegfeld, Jr., was the producer of two shows in the same theater — the New Amsterdam; one upstairs, one down. The one downstairs was the *Follies;* the one on the roof was the *Midnight Frolic*. The *Follies* was over at eleven-fifteen, and at the stroke of midnight the *Frolic* would open. Sometimes people who had seen the *Follies* would go up to the roof and Ziegfeld would nab them the second time. The *Midnight Frolic* was a glorified night club. There were tables at which drinks were served, there was food for the people to peck at, and there was a dance floor for them to bump around on. Entertainers were supposed to amuse the crowd. Mostly the entertainers were beautiful girls; no one in the world was so good at judging girl-appeal as Ziegfeld. Nature had given him this truly remarkable judgment, but it had taken away his sense of humor. He had none at all. He never laughed at a comedian. He sat as silent and as expressionless as a croquet ball, and when the comedian finished, Ziegfeld slipped silently and gloomily away, leaving behind him an aura of sadness and sorrow. No one ever knew what he thought; no one ever knew what he was going to do. Girls, not gags. That was the land where he was king.

Gene Buck was Ziegfeld's writer and had been largely responsible for Ziegfeld's success. Buck told Ziegfeld that he ought to hire the cowboy appearing at the Forty-fourth Street Theater and put him in the *Midnight Frolic*. Ziegfeld looked at Buck as a Boy Scout would at poison ivy. What! An uncouth cowboy before the richest and most sophisticated audience in New York! Surely Buck must be having fun with him. But Buck wasn't. He persisted and, in time, Will Rogers ambled out on the stage of the *Midnight Frolic,* with rope and gum.

The audience was startled. A cowboy in this garden of girls. But after the first shock, the audience liked him. Ziegfeld was there to see Gene Buck's find, and sat there with the sorrow of the ages on his face. "I don't like him," he announced.

"But the audience does," said Buck.

Ziegfeld came back again, and again gazed sadly and despondently. "I want you to let him go. He doesn't fit in."

"He hasn't hit it yet," said Buck, "but he will."

Three weeks went by. From time to time, Ziegfeld dropped in and shook his head. "I want you to discharge him."

Buck put it off as long as he could, then went to Will with the depressing news. But before he could tell Will why he was there, Will asked for a raise in salary. Buck blinked.

"I want fifty dollars a week more," announced Will.

Buck reminded Will that when he was playing in vaudeville he was doing three shows a day and paying his own traveling expenses. On the "roof" he had to do only six shows a week.

"I've got to have the money," said the obdurate Will, who did not know that the sword of Damocles was trembling over his head.

Gene Buck did not have the heart to tell him the bad news.

Finally, as they talked, Will said, "My wife says I ought to talk about what I read in the papers. She says I'm always readin' the papers, so why not pass along what I read?"

"You might get us sued."

"I think I could keep away from that. I'd keep it principally to public figures."

"Try it out," said Gene Buck and went away, leaving the sword dangling.

That very night Will began to talk about what he had seen in the papers. The audience liked it and so did the people backstage. Will made a tremendous discovery: that a joke does not have to be uproarious if it is timely.

Ziegfeld was away from New York for almost a week. When he returned he said to Gene Buck, "How did your cowboy friend take it when you let him go?"

"I haven't let him go."

Ziegfeld looked at him meaningfully. "It's my show, isn't it?"

"Why don't you come tonight and watch him?" asked Gene Buck.

Ziegfeld did, but there was no more smile on his face than on a flying saucer.

"You see," jubilated Gene, "the audience likes him. He gets the biggest laughs in the show."

Ziegfeld studied the puzzling situation. "We'll keep him another week."

He kept him another week, and another. Finally Gene Buck came to Will and said, "I've talked to Mr. Ziegfeld and he says you can have that raise."

Will was delighted. This put him up to $225. He hadn't known he was about to be thrown into the calflot. (Later he found out, but by this time he was safe in the saddle.)

And now, in Forest Hills, I was surprised to discover that my horse-loving neighbor had a car. (I was still going down to the post office and getting them back.)

It was at about this time that Will perpetrated his first big successful joke at the expense of a public figure. The war was decimating Europe, but the United States had not entered. December 4, 1915, Henry Ford originated the incredible idea of the Peace Ship, which was going to take care of the matter of Peace. An assorted group of pilgrims was assembled and left for Europe to "get the boys out of the trenches by Christmas." Just how this was to be done was a detail that had not been worked out. Anyway, the earnest peace advocates got together just before the ship sailed, and sent a cablegram to the Pope in Rome asking for his blessing and support. It was addressed to "His Holiness Pope Pius VII." This turned out to be useless, for Pope Pius VII had been dead one hundred and thirty-three years.

That evening Will shuffled out on the stage, his rope and gum going. Giving a brush of his hand at the lock of unruly hair on his forehead, he drawled, "There seems to be a good deal of talk about gettin' the boys out of the trenches by Christmas. Well, if Henry Ford will take this bunch of girls we've got here tonight, let 'em wear the same clothes as they do here, and march them down between the two lines of trenches, the boys will be out of the trenches before Christmas."

It was the biggest laugh he had ever had and was his start as an important humorist commenting on public affairs.

Most comedians used the same material for months — sometimes for years. But many of the people in the audience were "repeaters." Will knew they would not laugh at a joke the second time, so each night he had to incorporate new jokes. He studied the newspaper assiduously. Betty began to complain of being a "paper widow." He was up early of a morning — this driving, energetic, always-on-the-go man — and promptly seized a paper and buried himself in it, like a child in the sand on a beach. And there Betty would sit, trying to keep conversation alive. She never quite succeeded. But she understood and forgave. He was never so serious as when stalking a joke.

His audience in the *Midnight Frolic* began to mount. Since it was the one big, luxurious night club-theater in New York, people came back and brought their friends (or out-of-town customers), so Will's popularity continued to grow.

What was funny and what wasn't? What did audiences laugh at? What rolled across them leaving no more impression than a ball on the floor? Will began to see that it was truth that appealed to them — salted with exaggeration. So he tried to arrive at the basic truth in a situation, then exaggerate it until the audience laughed. He liked the people in the audience to nod approval, or to nudge their friends and say, "He's right." It was humor of truth. Most of the comedians told allegedly funny stories. Will didn't. His nose was poked in the papers, trying to analyze the events of the day.

Preparations began for the *Follies* of 1946. Gene Buck suggested that Will be put into the show, but Ziegfeld said he would be poison ivy in his Garden of Girls. Buck persisted until finally Ziegfeld made a half-hearted offer. Will discussed it with Betty and she said No. Betty and Will went opening night. She records in her book that they paid twelve dollars each for the tickets, and with them as guests they had Mr. and Mrs. Thomas W. Harvey, of Huntington, West Virginia — yes, her first sweetheart. Will watched the progress of the show with increasing discomfort; the show was too long, too dull, and too humorless. After all, one couldn't respond all evening to cloying sweetness and an artificial flower adjusted exactly right at a girl's beltline. He kept whispering to Betty, "I wish I could take a whack at it." But it was too late. She felt remiss that she had counseled against it. And now, as the show dragged on, he began to get peevish and ill-tempered. Tom Harvey must have thought she had married an odd lot.

The next day Will was still cast down. He had missed his big opportunity. One musical show after another had crumpled under him; now he had lost his chance to get in the biggest of all.

Again Gene Buck suggested that Ziegfeld put Will into the *Follies*. Ziegfeld still hesitated, master showman that he was. Will would cheapen his garden. But, finally, hesitant Ziegfeld telephoned Will he wanted to see him. Will loped in.

He was an instant success. He was playing in both the *Midnight Frolic* and *Follies*. This meant two matinees and two evening performances. It was eleven years since he had found that he was a comedian. He wouldn't ever have to go back to dreaded manual work.

Will's approach to a salary increase was his own. He was getting $350 a week but dreamed of $400. Going to Ziegfeld he said, "Mr. Ziegfield, I got somethin' I want to speak to you about." He stood there shyly. "I promised my wife and children that some day I would make $400 a week. They believed me. I just don't want them to lose faith in me. It's awful bad when your family loses faith in you." And that's how he got his raise.

One day the manager of the Gridiron Club in Washington, D. C., called up and said they wanted Will to speak at their annual dinner. Gene Buck took the word to Ziegfeld, who said that Will couldn't be let out of the show for the two days it would take. Buck insisted, and Ziegfeld hesitatingly agreed. Then Will was approached. Again he was all humility and self-distrust. Speak in Washington before the very people he had been flaying! They would eat him alive.

Buck urged him, telling him how extremely important this was, and that he would go with him and be his guide and comforter. The two got on the train and the big night arrived. Will was more nervous than he had ever been before in his life. Across from him was President Coolidge's cool and appraising eye. Nearby was General Billy Mitchell, head of the air force.

Will fumbled for some moments, feeling his way; finally there was a laugh and he began to have confidence. Once or twice he paused, not quite knowing what to say; then Gene Buck whispered to him to use one of his *Follies* jokes and this Will did. This happened two or three times; then Will began to go great guns. It turned out to be the best-received speech ever delivered (up to that time) at the annual dinner.

General Mitchell said to Buck, "I'd like to take him up in my plane tomorrow. Can you arrange it?"

Will hesitated; didn't like plane travel, he said; it was awfully far from where you was to where you might be. But Buck urged him and the next day General Mitchell called for Will at the New Willard Hotel and himself drove Will to Bolling Field. The time, curiously enough, was almost exactly ten years after Will's pickaback flight at Atlantic City.

General Mitchell gave him a wad of cotton. Will looked at it and said, "I only use cotton in my ears when I go to the Senate Gallery."

General Mitchell piloted him, himself. They flew over the George Washington Monument and over Washington's home at Mount Vernon. When Will got out he was still nervous, but also he was exhilarated, just as he had been the first time. As the two stood beside the plane, General Mitchell said, "You have been with me on the last flight I will ever make as a brigadier general. Tonight, at twelve o'clock, I am to be demoted to colonel and sent to a post far away where, instead of having the entire air force at my command, I will have seven planes." (Readers will remember that General Billy Mitchell was demoted because he had advocated that the United States should stand first in the air.) The date of this flight was May 9, 1925. It was this flight that made Will an air enthusiast.

CHAPTER 13

The Follies Become a National Institution. And So Does Will

WHEN WILL and Ziegfeld agreed on $400 a week, Ziegfeld said, "I'll have a contract drawn up."

"We don't need a contract," said Will. "We understand each other and that's what a contract is supposed to show. We'll shake hands and that'll be our signature." Ziegfeld, not knowing Will very well, was a little astonished at this offhand way of handling business matters, but finally agreed. However, he took the precaution to call in Charles Dillingham, who was in the office, and have him hear the oral agreement and witness the handshake.

The reason Will was such a success in the *Ziegfeld Follies* seems to have been due to three things: the first was the startling contrast between rough-and-ready Will and the cloying sweetness of the garden of girls; sometimes there was so much of the latter that it just about turned a person against gardens. Also Will was commenting on national and international subjects instead of the preceding act, or on the people in the show. And he was becoming more and more adept in "putting over" his material; he was beginning to learn to hesitate and seem to be at a loss what to say, then to arrive at the point with smashing suddenness.

My neighbor was becoming exceedingly prosperous. His name was in the papers and people talked about him.

September twelfth and fourteenth we had a Country Fair for the Red Cross. Will contributed the riding feats. (I'm ashamed to say I didn't go; I just monkeyed around at something else.) There was a big open tent on the land. Will brought his saddle there to leave it overnight. Someone had a different idea; the next morning it was gone, stolen. But he was not angry, as you would expect a person to be; all he said was, "I guess we have some thieves around here." Instead of refusing to go on with the show, he got another saddle and finished his part.

Forest Hills was known as the tennis center; the big matches were played there. One day someone asked him if he didn't want to go to the tennis courts and see Helen Wills play. He shook his head. "I'd rather go to the stables and see my horses."

Little by little Will was learning the art of showmanship, for his skill did not come at one full sweep. There was a convention of governors and Henry J. Allen, who was the governor of Kansas, came backstage to see Will. An idea came to Will. He asked Governor Allen to stand in the wings until the proper time; when this arrived Will said, "I've got a man here, Governor Allen of Kansas an' a mighty good governor, too." (Will always put in a pat somewhere along the line.) "Want to see him?" He roped him and led him out. "Y'know, he was supposed to be standin' out there watchin' me. But he wasn't. He was standin' there watchin' what you might call the backbone of the show."

The idea of seeing the governor of a state with a rope around him delighted the audience. Governor Allen made a nice speech, and the whole affair went off well. This gave Will an idea: the audience liked to see notables on the stage, instead of merely standing up in the audience and bowing, so why not bring 'em up? (But, as he continued with the idea, he brought some up; some he didn't.)

Chauncey Depew was the Grand Old Man of New York, a position comparable, later, to that held by Bernard M. Baruch, except that Depew was a famous after-dinner speaker. This was the age of after-dinner speakers. They roamed Broadway every night; no one could go out without having to hear one.

On Chauncey Depew's ninetieth birthday his family gave him a theater party. Word was brought back to Will that Chauncey Depew was in the audience, and so he prepared himself. When the time came, he called on the elder statesman to stand up and rattled some shots against his armor. Depew waited patiently. When Will finished, Depew said that he had been making speeches in and around New York for seventy years — and had never had to use a rope. Then he sat down. Will was taken so completely by surprise that he had no return and had to repeat what a fine gentleman Chauncey Depew was and how glad he was to have him in the audience. The laugh was on Will. But he didn't care. The audience liked it and that was what counted. Will saw that audiences wanted to feel they were rubbing elbows with notables.

Having discovered this, Will began to comb the audience. He had the box-office men and the ticket taker posted and had the ushers on the alert. In addition, he would peep through the curtain and inspect the audience. He did not catch a big fish every night, but often enough to make it worth while.

People from home began making themselves heard in the audience. He welcomed them, high or low. Sometimes, however, they proved a bit of a problem. A cowboy named Jim Tally had once worked on the Rogers Ranch. He had been taught by Cherokee Bill, Oklahoma's most famous outlaw, to gobble like a wild turkey. Cherokee Bill was part Indian; the Indians used this strange, weird cry as a danger warning. Once heard, it is never forgotten. On this particular night, as Will paused in his monologue, the cry rang through the theater. Will was startled; certainly this was the first time it had ever been heard on Broadway. He stopped and looked out across the audience (he always kept the house lights on when he talked) and at last located its source. Will called him up on the stage, then realized that he couldn't trust Jim to make a speech, as he had been doing with the notables, so he asked him to give the wild-turkey gobble. And this Jim did, with a force and vigor that would have startled any wild turkey that had ever roamed the Indian Territory. "Out in Oklahoma where I come from, that's our native language," said Will. "Our papooses learn it before they do Daddy." He got Jim back to his seat and all was well. But during a performance, Will never knew what was going to happen — nor did the audience.

These personal mentions were succeeding nicely. The audience liked them, Will liked them, and the notables beamed all over the place. One night Will found that Diamond Jim Brady was in the theater. "Guess who's sittin' right out there with you," he said when the time came. "Diamond Jim Brady! When I'm not workin' and haven't got a job, he takes me to a first night with him. Y'know, he always has a seat on the front row. Well, I stand at the back of the theater and if anybody steals one of his diamonds an' starts to run, I rope him."

His confidence grew. He had found something that was definitely good showmanship. So successful was it that people began sending him word (very discreetly, of course) that they were in the audience; sometimes a friend of the person brought back the exciting news. Will was a little cautious here. He preferred to find his own targets. His greatest — his biggest — his most outstanding triumph was when the *Follies* played in Baltimore and President Woodrow Wilson came from Washington to see the show — the first time in theatrical history that a President had gone away from Washington to see a comedy. Did he dare joke the President of the United States? This was vastly different from tossing a few quips at a private citizen. Will knew that everybody in the theater would be watching the President, and that if he disapproved of what Will said they would, too, and frowns would be his mantle.

He talked about current matters for a few minutes. The people watched the President to see if he approved. Then Will moved on to the Administration and discharged a couple of fire arrows. The President still beamed. And then — no doubt holding his breath — Will spoke directly of President Wilson, using his name, and sent a joke wreathing toward him. President Wilson laughed aloud and so, in a moment, did the audience.

What kind of joke did he use? This is an example. The war with Germany was on, although the Allies were not in it. Said Will, his rope and gum going: "I see by the papers that them German submarines cain't operate in the warm Gulf Stream. If we can only heat the ocean, then we've got 'em licked." The audience laughed, then he added seemingly casually, "Of course, that's only a rough idea. I ain't got the thing worked out yet." This was a rewarding laugh. Also it was a lesson: there should be a joke; and the audience should laugh. Then there should be another joke, advancing the idea a little further — "topping the gag" it was called.

When Will went off, his act finished, he had had the biggest and most successful night he had ever had in the theater.

This gave him new confidence; if he could joke the President of the United States, then he could go after anyone he chose.

He was learning the skills of his trade. One was that when an audience is not interested in the subject, drop it and take up something else. Usually he started his rope going. After a few whirls he would attack another subject. If this went well, he would continue until he had used up his material. He had mastered his most valuable secret: that a joke did not have to be too good if it was up-to-date. Sometimes ideas came to him on the stage; often these were the best of all. He never put on two performances that were alike. When he stepped out in front of an audience, he didn't know exactly what he was going to say. He would add or drop according to the way an audience responded. No other performer in vaudeville, or in musical comedy, was doing this. Their material did not vary an eyeflick from night to night.

His star was rising, and now reporters were coming around. This was a new problem for him. How should he handle them? Most comedians, important enough to be interviewed, told the reporters funny stories. But Will could not tell, and had no interest in, the so-called "funny" story. So he talked about himself and his experiences. There was glamour in the facts: he had come from Oklahoma and was part Indian, and had been a Gaucho in South America, and had been a roper in an American Wild West show in South Africa. He made good copy by just talking about himself.

The days were sweet. It was nice to be a rising young comedian.

In the meantime he was still deeply devoted to the old Rogers Ranch and he got back to see it as often as he possibly could. He stayed, on these occasions, at the ranch itself, or at a friend's house. The following story, illustrating one of his trips back, was given to me by Bill Hoge, of Skiatook, Oklahoma, who knew Will for many years and who has collected much W. R. lore:

"In 1919 Will had a man with a big family running the ranch for him. Now and then Will would come back to see how things were getting along. He sensed that Austin Hart — that was his name — was in a bad way financially and wanted to help him. Also he knew that Austin Hart was proud. The man had an old bronc mare, and a colt was born. The mare died. The man's children took the colt in hand and raised it on a bottle. It was a scrubby, undersized range colt. But the children thought it was wonderful and taught it some simple tricks, such as lying down, bowing, pawing, shaking its head, things of that caliber. Will saw his chance and asked Austin to see the pony perform. Of course Will knew everything in the book about horses, but pretended to be greatly impressed by the rare intelligence of the animal. He said he'd like to buy it.

" 'Why, Mr. Rogers, it's just a little pestle-tailed bronc pony the children play with an' I wouldn't want to see them lose it.'

"Will walked around pretending to be weighing the pony's wonderful possibilities. 'I'll tell you what I'll do, Aus, I'll give you five hundred dollars for that animal.'

"Aus was embarrassed and said, 'I couldn't let it go, Mr. Rogers. It's just like a member of the family. The children are all over it.'

"Will walked around again, pretending to be studying the hunk of wolf bait. 'You would confer a mighty nice favor on me, Aus, if you'd let me have that animal.'

" 'Well, I can't hold out on you, Mr. Rogers. I'll surrender the animal.'

"A day or two later, when Will was ready to leave, he saw them crating the jug-headed pony. 'Listen, Aus, I've got to leave the pony here for the time bein'. You go right ahead with the training, for that's a rare animal. I'll send for it just as soon as I get things whipped into shape.'

"The pony stayed there with the children and finally died of old age. Of course Aus figgered it out later, but it made him one of Will's greatest boosters."

Back in New York, requests to speak came in. Will wasn't an after-dinner speaker, but the requests were insistent, so he thought he would try. The first speech or two went all right. In no time people were offering him money to speak at banquets. He had discovered a trunk in the attic with gold in it!

One night he was able to attend a dinner at the Astor before his turn came at the *Follies*. The toastmaster was Will Hays who, later, became the mogul of the movies, and was, just then, a potent figure on Broadway. As a toastmaster he was on the flowery side, and as he introduced Will, rose to oratorical heights. As he finished the eulogy, Hays pointed to Will, who was sitting there with his tousled hair, trying to appear modest, and said, "There he is — the cowboy who has roped Broadway and who has something under his ten-gallon hat besides hair."

Irvin S. Cobb was on his feet as quick as a chipmunk. "Ladies and gentlemen," said Cobb, "I agree with every word that our toastmaster has just said, and I want to add that it's about time somebody said a good word for dandruff!"

Will never rehearsed with the *Follies*. The other members of the cast rehearsed until exhausted. The girls came on, dark-eyed from fatigue, dressed far from glamorously in odds and ends they had the appearance of having snatched up as they raced from their dressing rooms. Will sat in the empty house, watching; or sometimes he read a paper. When his time came he would amble out on the stage with his rope and would talk about the members of the cast and the things that had happened that day during rehearsals — but not a peep as to what he was going to say opening night. He wanted this to be fresh. His rehearsals always gave a lift to the cast and they all waited eagerly. He never disappointed them.

Fortunately this worked out all right. Ziegfeld rehearsed the others until they were as limp as dandelions, but he let Will have his way. If Ziegfeld had tried to tell Will Rogers what was funny and what wasn't . . . what would have happened? It saddens one to think of it.

At about this time my prosperous neighbor gathered up his children, his car and his horses and moved to Amityville, Long Island, and rented Fred Stone's house. I had never been on any of the committees that had worked with Will, or had any contact with him when he spoke on the Fourth of July, in Station Square. I had merely gazed at him when he had trained his horses in front of my house and had, from time to time, mumbled a few words to him, and that was all. I supposed he had gone out of my life.

CHAPTER 14

Will Meets the Great Comedians
of the Day

WILL AND ZIEGFELD did not care for each other; no two men could have been farther apart. Will was all friendliness and fun. Ziegfeld was no more responsive than a loose piano wire. But they respected each other; and they could work together to advantage.

Will was not getting as much as he thought he deserved, but made no protest. He waited patiently until Ziegfeld was ready to take the show on the road with the "original New York cast." It could have played in New York through the year, but by this time the *Follies* was an American institution; and Ziegfeld took pride in having it of national importance. It was Will's week. The upshot of it was that Ziegfeld agreed to pay Will $600 a week. A fortune. No danger now Will would ever have to go back to the ranch to do dreaded "manual work."

Will traveled in a strange manner. He took two horses with him and a man to look after them, Charlie Aldridge. It was Aldridge's duty, when the show got to a new city, to find a place for the horses — one was Dopey who had been trained in front of my house — and to have them ready every morning for Will to ride. And this Will would do while the rest of the cast slumbered. His amazing energy became more and more apparent. Six hours a night. But no head ever went to sleep quicker when it hit the pillow than his. And in the morning, when he awoke, he got up. No snoozing. Up and at something.

It seems strange, as one reconstructs Will's life, how few are the illuminating stories about him that come out of his days in the *Follies*. This is doubly strange when one remembers that the *Follies* had the greatest comedians in the world; one would think there would be endless stories. But this is hardly true. The authentic stories are few and far between. Yet the *Follies* housed such comedians as W. C. Fields, Eddie Cantor, Frank Tinney, Walter Catlett, Andrew Tombes, Bert Williams, Fanny Brice, Ina Claire.

Will took pride in being on the bill with W. C. Fields — the very W. C. Fields he had seen in Cape Town, South Africa, in 1902. Will was not a comedian then; in fact he had never dreamed of being one. But now he was a comedian and on the same bill with the greatest. It was nice.

Fields was an entirely different kind of person. He had a streak of meanness that is almost unbelievable; not only this but he was jealous, and hardly knew the meaning of friendship. Will, of course, was just the opposite. Everybody was his friend; and he was everybody's friend. (Later there will be a story illustrating the differences between the two men.)

In 1917 W. C. Fields bought a Cadillac. He wanted to show it off, and invited Will and Chic Sale to take a run out to Long Island to a friend's house. The three had attended a Lambs Gambol where drinks had been sloshing around all evening. Neither Will nor Chic drank, but Fields took care of that. The drinks hadn't sloshed in vain.

Chic Sale had just bought a pair of high-button, white-topped shoes, which must have had elements of comedy in themselves.

Fields took his place at the wheel. In no time they were on Long Island. "Now I'll show you what it'll do," said Fields, and proceeded to show them. Will and Chic were nervous, but Fields wasn't.

Also he showed them something he hadn't planned on and that was how the car could leave the road. The three were tossed around like dice in a leather bottle. They crawled out. Will was suffering and was taken to a hospital. Fields and Chic waited in the reception room to see what the result would be, Fields hardly mentioned what had happened to Will, but kept looking at Chic's soiled shoes.

"That's a shame," he said, "and it's all my fault. When we get back to New York I'll have them fixed up for you as good as new."

After a time, Will limped out. His ankle was so badly sprained that for several days he could not do any jumping tricks with his rope. But Fields hardly mentioned it, or paid any attention to it.

Eddie Cantor, who seems to have been more of a prankster than Fields, did get a joke on Will. It was during the summer of 1918 when the German "Big Bertha" was shelling Paris eighty miles away — a startling situation, indeed. Eddie Cantor said, "Will, I've thought of a gag you can use, and, if you can, it's yours. Tell 'em that no matter what the Germans invent, we can always go 'em one better. Tell 'em you have inside information that we have just invented a long-range gun that will shoot from Staten Island to Berlin and if it doesn't kill a man it will take him prisoner."

Will liked the idea.

Then Cantor went to Fields and told him the same story and cautioned him not to speak of it to anyone.

Cantor knew that Fields would go on first and that Will would be in the dressing room. Fields told the story, which brought a good laugh.

Will came on and told the same story, not knowing of course, that the audience had just heard it.

When the act was over, Cantor said, "How did the story go, Will?"

"It was a failure. I never had a gag fall so flat," said Will gloomily.

A bit later one of the actors told Will what had happened. Will was mad and sulked the rest of the evening and would not speak to Cantor. The next day, however, he was over it, for one of Will's outstanding traits was that he forgave easily and did not cherish a grudge.

Will used to tell Fields and Cantor about his old roping days; a name that kept coming up was that of Clay McGonigle, whom Will admired intensely for his skill with a rope. Fields and Cantor conspired. One evening, when Will arrived at his dressing room there was a note waiting for him, allegedly from Clay McGonigle, saying that he would be in the audience. Will bustled in to tell the two the good news. Anyone from home was a draft of wine to him.

When he went on, he kept peering out over the audience and walking from one side of the stage to another. Finally he said, "I've got an old cowpoke friend here who can write his name with a rope. I want him to stand up so you can see the best of 'em all." No one stood up and he had to pass over the situation as best he could.

When the show was over, Will hurried to the lobby and waited for his friend to come out, looking anxiously from one person to another. After the last person had left the theater, Will returned disappointedly to his dressing room.

Then one of the actors told Will the truth. Will was hurt and, for a time, was mad. But he soon forgave the pranksters.

At about this time Ziegfeld's daughter, Patricia, had a long illness. Will asked about her almost every day, for she was not only his employer's child but also his own children's playmate. One day, when he was talking to the Prince of Wales, an idea came to him — he would buy a polo pony for Patricia. The two — Will and the Prince — went off by themselves and stood under a tree and argued back and forth over the price like a couple of horse traders. Finally Will agreed to pay $2100.

Patricia was getting better, and to cheer her up, Will had the pony delivered at her house. She was delighted, and the family gathered around to see her pleasure. Someone in the group remarked that it would be nice for Patricia to have a pony that had belonged to the Prince of Wales. "That's right," agreed Will, "but it's goin' to be hard on the pony. Why! He'll think he's slumming."

His daily life at the *Follies* was simple. He was pleasant to the show girls, but made no advances. A few people came backstage to see him, but not many. His dressing room at the ancient New Amsterdam had Pilgrim simplicity. It had been years since the theater was new, but it carried the word in its name and, for that matter, still carries it as I write. Will's dressing room was on the third floor and was more of a cell than a star's abode. There was no rug; there was one dusty window that looked out on a forlorn alley. On the wall was a row of hooks, with a curtain that could be pulled over them; with a little imagination one could think of this as a clothes closet. There was a kind of make-up table; a mirror above it was flanked on each side by a row of electric lights such as could be found in any dressing room. There were two or three rickety-looking upright chairs, and that was all. The place looked like one of the better cells at Sing Sing.

Mrs. Rogers came in one day (she did not often go behind the scenes) and found Will lying on a blanket on the floor, resting, with an overcoat over him. Her heart was touched and, without saying anything to him about it, she waited until she knew he would be out of the room; then, with the help of a friend, decorated the place from top to bottom. She placed attractive curtains across the alley-gazing window; cheerful curtains were arranged over the hooks where he hung his clothes; new chairs stood proudly erect; but the most magnificent change of all was the resplendent new couch.

She went with Will the next day, after the job had been completed, so she could enjoy his surprise. Well, he was surprised all right, but also he was mad and said he didn't like anything about the new room. He said that he had always had the old kind of room, that it had brought him luck and that he didn't like this sissified thing. He was so disagreeable about it that she rushed out, found the ancient chairs and returned them to their trembling legs and stripped the jolly curtains from the alley window. He himself sent the couch to the basement where the musicians had a lounge room. Now, with the room restored, for the most part, to its original decrepitude, he settled down to enjoy it.

As the gravity of the war increased, he joked more and more about it. But always the roots of his jokes were planted in the subsoil of reality. His followers grew rapidly. Fifteen hundred people a day heard him, and they quoted him to others. But oddly enough the papers did not take him up. His fame grew chiefly by word of mouth.

He was too old to enter the war, and tried to make up for it by appearing at benefits and at money-raising meetings. Not only this but he began contributing out of his own pocket.

Here are some of his quips, typical of the period. Naturally they are out-of-date, but at that time their appeal was tremendous, for Will had the ability to put into a few words what the average man was thinking:

"I see the South American countries are comin' into the war. Let 'em come in. This is no private war. Since we give 'em the loan, they tell me Venezuela wants to cancel three revolutions to get in."

"Y'know, Germany cain't understand how we can get our men over there and get 'em trained so quick. They don't know that in our trainin' manual there's nothing about retreatin'. When you only have to teach an army to go one way, you can do it in half the time."

"One thing we got to be thankful for, our Soldiers can win

wars faster than our Diplomats can talk us into them."

"I thought the Armistice terms read like a Second Mortgage, but the peace terms read like a Foreclosure."

"Well, we finally handed Germany the Peace terms, eighty thousand words in length. It took that many to tell them what we thought of 'em."

His quips were being quoted so much that he collected some and added to them, and got out a book entitled, *Rogerisms — The Cowboy Philosopher on The Peace Conference*. The following year he got out *Rogerisms — The Cowboy Philosopher on Prohibition*. It will be noted that the name Will Rogers was not important enough to use in the title. The books had a mild success.

Something worth noting happened Sunday night, December 17, 1922, at the Thirty-ninth Street Theater, New York. Will was engaged to speak at a rally of the Molly Pitcher Club, which was a woman's "wet" organization affiliated with the New York Division Against the Prohibition Amendment. During the speech he said, "Here's what I want for my epitaph: 'Here lies Will Rogers who worked forty years in the *Follies* and when he died he had the same wife he had when he started.'" This was his first epitaph.

At about this time something new came into Will's life. On Fred Stone's place at Amityville was a polo field left by a previous tenant. Both Will and Fred had roping ponies and so the two decided to take a whack at something that was, just then, popular in America — polo. Neither knew any more about it than they did about smoke signals, but that was all right; they could learn. This they did, charily at first, boldly as they advanced. But there were many falls. Will came up with a quip: "The people who watch us play on Sunday afternoon know how to tell us apart. If a rider falls and lands on his feet, that's Fred. If he lands on his head, that's me. We're both equally safe."

After the first taste, the old roping and riding ponies wouldn't do; they had to have "regular" polo ponies. In this matter there was a present in Will's Christmas stocking: Jim Minnick, who had been the first to ride a horse on the stage for Will, had gone into the polo pony business. Will joked him about this. He said that Jim Minnick bought old buggy horses in Texas, brought them to New Jersey, curried them, and sold them to the unsuspecting. This, of course, was not true. But it was Will's approach to things.

Will and Fred bought some of Jim Minnick's ponies, and now the two were polo players. The two organized rival teams, brought in their polo-playing friends, and had high old times, sometimes on horseback, sometimes tumbled on the velvety grass which grows in such profusion on Long Island.

Will's life had gone through many changes. The first important one was when he had joined Texas Jack in South Africa. The next when he had talked on the stage for the first time. The third when he had joined the *Follies*. And now there was to be a new one.

Will Tries His Hand at Silent Pictures

HOLLYWOOD WAS BUBBLING. Show people were disappearing into its lemon groves and coming back with fabulous tales and impressive bank accounts. Men who had never been on a horse were now riding like Comanches. Tom Mix, his barkeeping days far behind him, was an inspiration to thousands of eager-eyed youths. His fame far exceeded Will's. Only a few cities knew Will; Tom was known from one end of the country to the other.

Samuel Goldwyn decided that the basic trouble with the movies was poor stories. So he organized a producing unit called Eminent Authors, Inc., and took eight Eminent Authors to Hollywood to give the movies better stories. The stories promptly got worse. The eight Eminent Authors wrangled among themselves, each one foolishly believing his own story was best; in no time Samuel Goldwyn was fighting for his bank account. The head of Eminent Authors was Rex Beach whose heart was in Alaska, but who had a substantial bank account in Los Angeles. He had sold Goldwyn one of his books, *Laughing Bill Hyde,* and Goldwyn was preparing to film it. But no lead player had been selected. It happened that Mrs. Rex Beach was visiting at Fred Stone's (the two wives were sisters) at Amityville, Long Island, and, at this critical moment, became possessed of an idea. Getting into her car she drove to the Rogers house and suggested to Will that he play the part of Laughing Bill. Her husband, she said, had great influence with Goldwyn and could bring this about. Will was pleased but fearful. He had to have the inspiration of an audience. On top of this he was not an actor, that is, in the professional sense of the word. And, too, he was tied down by his job.

Goldwyn, at Rex Beach's suggestion, came to see Will. He said the thing could be taken care of in the Fort Lee, New Jersey studios. The *Follies* did not play in the summertime and so, rather hesitatingly, Will entered this new medium.

One day Will sat down at a soda fountain to have a soft drink. As he was sitting there, a little colored boy came along and mounted the stool next to Will. Suddenly Will remembered something he wanted to do, gulped down his drink, and hurriedly left. The little colored boy looked hurt, then said to the attendant behind the counter, "I know why he left. He didn't want to eat by me."

Later the attendant told Will. Will, as we have seen, had grown up with Negroes and had great liking and respect for them. The last thing in the world he would do would be to affront a colored person.

The next day he kept a watch-out for the colored boy, and when he found him, said, "Say, boy, are you busy? Come on, let's take on a dish of ice cream."

And the two did, side by side.

The picture was made and released. No one was trampled trying to get in. However, Goldwyn was sufficiently encouraged to make another. But, he said, Will would have to move to Hollywood.

Did he dare? He had an assured place in New York in the *Follies*. What if he did not prosper in pictures? But Goldwyn offered him more than Ziegfeld could afford to pay. After talking with Betty, he decided to pull stakes.

Will was bubbling, too. On his way he stopped in Kansas City to make a paid personal appearance at the opening of a new motion-picture theater.

Two years before, when he was in the *Follies*, he had met the theater critic for the *Kansas City Star*, E. B. Garnett. Will, with his remarkable memory for names of people who could serve him, called up Garnett and invited him to go to the personal appearance. After this was over, the inevitable happened: straight to a chili parlor on Wyandotte Street, north of Twelfth, for, by now, Will was an addict to the deceptive influence of chili con carne. (Not only chili but also onion sandwiches; he loved them both; the combination was ideal, he always affirmed.) They climbed on stools — that's the way chili should be eaten, he also affirmed — and began to talk. Shortly a crowd gathered — something Will liked as a bear does honey. It was three o'clock in the morning when the two walked to Will's hotel. On the way, Garnett suggested that Will write down such things as he had been saying in the talk, and that he would print them in the *Kansas City Star*.

Will was struck by modesty. "Shucks, I couldn't do that! The only papers I ever wrote for were in Oklahoma and they had to run what I sent, or my father would take out his livery-stable ad."

Garnett, with the instinct of a Sunday editor, persisted. Will, it developed, had a portable typewriter. Finally Will said a bit shyly, "I might try. If you don't like it, you can tear it up. That would show you was a smart editor."

Several days passed. Garnett thought it was one of these early-morning promises. But then a letter, mailed in Hollywood, arrived; it was typewritten on both sides of the paper, with the spelling a bit haphazard, and signed in lead pencil. It was published in the Sunday edition of the *Kansas City Star*, June 15, 1919 — the first time Will ever wrote for a paper outside of his home town.

(It should be explained that Henry J. Allen, then Governor of Kansas, had just returned from Europe — a year after the end of the war — and had criticized Newton D. Baker, Secretary of

War, concerning the handling of the 35th Division in the Battle of the Argonne.)

ON BOARD CALIFORNIA LIMITED TRYING
TO GET OUT OF KANSAS

You asked me to drop you a few lines on my way West to Los Angeles where I hear the call of ART to act a fool for the Bucking pictures. I think they want to use me as the horrible example in some picture. However, you can never tell what a movie fan will fall for. We are making good time across Kansas. If it was not for having to stop to unload express packages for the bootleggers we could make it all in one hop. I have discovered a way to tell a bootlegger from the average hanger on around a railroad depot, the bootlegger is the sober guy. As I read the news today I see where Sectry Baker replies to Gov. Allen of Kansas. His reply was just as clear as the income tax blanks. Baker says he is willing to have an investigation but that Gov. Allen cant expect his investigation to take preference over all the others ahead of it. If Mr. Baker stays in to see all these investigations through he will hold office as long as Uncle Jojo Cannon. In the words of the Movie Director the Gov. has called for a retake. The Gov. claims when the 35th Division went into action, the artillery that should have backed them up claimed exemption. He claims they had plenty of airplanes there but they all belonged to the Germans. He says the only barrage our Doughboys had was laid down by the Krupps. While the boys were fighting, the officers in the rear were debating "Resolved that West Point turns out better Shimmie dancers than Plattsburgh." The Gov. says the whole thing was a frame up. It was a Prairie Division and they made them fight in a Forest. He says they made a mistake by removing the National Guard Officers as the men were used to them. That speaks pretty well for them as most officers are hard to get used to. Gov. says he will see this thing through if he has to be elected Gov. of Kansas again to do it. I claim that if you are going to investigate the 35th not being properly supported in the Argonne, then you should go further and investigate why the Democrats were not properly supported in November.

WILL ROGERS

P.S. Wallace Read is on this train, still got on his dress suit.

I feel more encouraged in my new endeavor, as the Porter just told me this was the same train Mary Pickford went out on her first trip. In fact everybody on this train is going to Cal. to go into the movies. Its the movie Special. The porters will tell you they are not black — they are only made up for a part. There is a Carona Typewriter in every berth writing Scenarios.

Will found a place on Van Ness Avenue, and wrote Betty to come out.

They were happy there, but suddenly tragedy appeared at the door. Their youngest child had been named for Fred Stone and was, at this time, eighteen months old. Diphtheria developed, and "Freddie" — as he was called — died at the house on Van Ness Avenue.

The shadow of the tragedy lay over the house; they would move. More than that, they would buy and they would settle in California. Film work was not nearly so strenuous as the stage. So Will bought the first house they had ever owned; ten years of hard work had produced a home. It was in Beverly Hills, near the Beverly Hills Hotel. The place was exactly what they wanted: commodious, plenty of play space for the children.

Goldwyn had hit on a short story by Ben Ames Williams, which had appeared in the *Saturday Evening Post,* entitled "Jubilo." It dealt with a happy-go-lucky tramp who got into all sorts of trouble, but also got triumphantly out. The eight Eminent Authors were put to work on it; in no time the story was all but wrecked. Finally the company went on location to shoot the film; the thing became so involved that no one knew what the story was about. The happy-go-lucky tramp was now getting into business and a successful career seemed unavoidable.

Will was troubled by the turn things had taken, so he suggested to the director, Clarence Badger, they throw out the high-priced authors and shoot it, scene by scene, just as the story had appeared in magazine form. The idea was revolutionary; many of the old heads said it couldn't be done. But the director sent to the library, borrowed a copy, had the story typed, and shot the scenes in exactly the order they appeared in the magazine. Immediately the story opened its eyes and began to breathe again.

Then came the cutting, during which the happy-go-lucky tramp survived incredible hardships. The picture was finished. Then Goldwyn took a hand; the title would have to be changed. He thought of *A Poor but Honest Tramp*. He may have had help in this, for poor titles are not arrived at haphazardly.

Will was upset. The story had a song running through it called "In the Land of Jubilo," which tied it together as neatly as a piggin-string around a calf's legs. So he sent Goldwyn this telegram:

Hollywood, California
October 17, 1919

Samuel Goldwyn,
469 Fifth Avenue,
New York.

I thought I was supposed to be a comedian, but when you suggest changing the title of *Jubilo*, you are funnier than I ever was. I don't see how Lorimer of the *Post* ever let it be published under that title. I suppose if you had produced *The Miracle Man* you would have called it *A Queer Old Guy*.

WILL ROGERS

Even a movie producer's deep and unswerving passion to change a picture's title can be beaten down, so Goldwyn let it stand. It shook Hollywood to the foundation.

The picture was successful, but not outstandingly so.

Will made an astonishingly large number of two-reel pictures — twelve, to be exact, in two years, all directed by Clarence Badger. The titles appear in the back under Sources.

One of the pictures was *Doubling for Romeo*. It had a good comedy idea. Will was a bashful cowboy deeply in love (of course) with a beautiful girl. But he couldn't impress her because he couldn't make love as they did in the movies. He is told that Shakespeare knew all about love-making, so the cowboy gets a copy of *Romeo and Juliet* and starts to read it. As he is reading he falls asleep and dreams he is in Hollywood playing the part of Romeo. He does some love-making that causes the girl's eyes to pop. Alas! Will wakes up and finds it is all a dream. But it ends all right; he gets the girl and that's what pictures are for.

Fatty Arbuckle was a comedy star of the day; this was when Hollywood believed that a comedian had to be fat to be funny. *One Glorious Day* was bought for him, but he got into a little mix-up in San Francisco and the picture industry threw him into San Francisco Bay. Will was engaged to do the picture. There was a girl in it — Lila Lee. He wins her, too, but the audience was left breathlessly in doubt until the last reel. The picture was fair; that's the kindest thing that can be said about it.

Another was *Cupid, the Cowpuncher*, adapted from Eleanor Gates's story *Alec Lloyd, Cowpuncher*. In this, Will is a cowboy who is so earnestly trying to marry off his cowpuncher friends that they call him Cupid. Finally the bug bites Cupid himself and he has a terrible time of it; but finally wins the girl — to the surprise and delight of the audience. In all these stories he played romantic parts.

James Cruze, who made the immortal *The Covered Wagon*, was Will's director in a picture in which the action called for Will to smoke a cigar. A nice tempting morsel was brought, but he refused to smoke it; he said it would make him sick. Nor did he smoke it, so vividly in his mind was the time he had smoked a Pittsburgh stogie and set the prairie on fire.

Things were not going smoothly; his pictures were not too good. Goldwyn refused to renew his agreement and Will was out of a job. Will thought — as have other actors — he would make his own pictures and get all the gravy; so he became his own writer, producer and director. He wrote a form-fitting story — *The Roping Fool*. He used a white lariat and made some of the scenes in slow motion. Soon he found he would have to rope more money; this was harder than the elusive zebra. He put a mortgage on his newly purchased house, borrowed on his life insurance, and even cashed his children's Liberty Bonds. But still more money was needed; a hundred greedy hands were reaching out for it. He had to go to the Bank of America and put up his film as security.

Under these discouraging conditions he made two additional pictures: *Fruits of Faith* and *One Day in 365*. They were all second rate. He was desperate. California — which had looked so sunny when he had first arrived — was now drenched with the cold rain of gloom.

He had made money in New York. He would return and make it again.

But when he got back, the *Follies* had run its season and was about to close. There would be no opening until fall. What could he do best? Speak in public. Entertain. He'd made a success of many an after-dinner affair. He would take up humorous speaking in a serious way.

He had spoken many times at the Lambs and at the Friars; a few engagements came in from people who had heard him, but he needed to make money faster than that, and in bigger quantities.

So he got an agent who booked him from one end of New York to the other. The variety of organizations he spoke before is surprising. One night he would speak to the Automobile Manufacturers' Association; in a night or two before the real estate dealers. And so on and on.

As he went he was perfecting himself in the art of the after-dinner speaker, one of the useless arts. But he was mastering it. When he had first begun, he had opened with the usual slow-paced introduction; he would address the chairman, mention the honored guests, and work his way on down to the humble diners. Then he would tell how delighted he was to be there, although generally he was a truthful man. He changed all this into an attention-arrester which seemed to carry an insult. When he spoke before the dignified American Bankers' Association he began, "Loan Sharks and Interest Hounds, I understand you have ten thousand here; with what you have in the various Federal prisons that must bring your membership up to around thirty thousand." (Of course, later, he told them what fine gentlemen they were.) To the New York City Advertising Club: "I am glad to be here tonight to address the Mother Lodge of Liars."

He worked hard, making two and sometimes three after-dinner speeches in a week. His digestion began to show the effect of thin consommé, broiled chicken, and head of lettuce with Russian dressing. However, he was not quite defeated, for he learned to protect himself. Before the so-called banquet, he would go to a chili parlor on Broadway, at Forty-seventh Street, and fill up on good, wholesome chili. Then he would go confidently to the banquet room. When the food was brought on he would toy with it. This simple solution pulled him through; his health returned to normal.

He was able to take care of his more demanding creditors. Every creditor would be paid. Meantime, Hollywood was booming. Tom Mix was busy killing stagecoach robbers, cattle thieves and low-down skunks. It was bitter to Will to think that his old roommate was doing better than he himself was. But he was not jealous; this was no part of Will's make-up. No one was more generous to his family and friends, or more helpful to other actors. He liked to show actors, who were not quite as expert as he was, how to get certain results.

His traits were becoming more marked, more personal. He never tried to tell a "funny" story. He recounted incidents that had happened to him, especially incidents that had happened on his world tour, but he never told any of those simply killing ones about Pat and Mike. That kind of humor was completely and wholly foreign to him. His sprang out of truth and had something to do with the subject under discussion; it was a crystallization of the truth of the situation.

He was being called on more and more often to appear at benefits. It is truly astonishing how generous he was with his time; also how extremely liberal he was in giving to "causes." He formed an attachment for the Red Cross and the Salvation Army. If they needed him to raise money, he would come on the run with his rope.

Out of the clear sky in 1923 came a Hollywood call. Hal E. Roach had done well in the movies, starting his career on an inheritance of $3000; now he was willing to risk Will in a series of two-reel comedies. His most famous and most successful was *Two Wagons, Both Covered*, directed by Rob Wagner. It was a take-off on *The Covered Wagon*, which was still rumbling across the screens.

While Will was working with Roach an incident happened that shows legend is not always to be accepted. One folk story was that Will never got mad and that he liked everybody. This is not quite true. He was asked, at this time, to appear before the wounded veterans at Arrowhead Springs, California. He would have to drive from Culver City, where the Hal Roach Studio was located, to Arrowhead Springs, about ninety miles. At first, he didn't think he could get there in time, but he had promised the men he would come, and to him a promise was sacred. He started out alone and at a pretty nimble pace.

All went well till he hit Azusa, California. A motorcycle officer who had been hidden out of sight, popped out, pulled up beside him, and told Will that he was going at forty miles an hour through a twenty-five-mile zone. Will did not protest it, but explained that he was on his way to fill an engagement at a veterans' camp.

"Can't help it," said the officer. "I've seen your face on the screen, but in this town one man is just as good as another. I'm taking you before the judge."

And in a few minutes he was before the judge. The judge asked him if it was true that he was speeding through a restricted zone. Will had to admit it was true. Then gave the reason. But the judge waved it aside. "I'm here to carry out the law and the law says you have to be fined. I'm fining you one hundred dollars."

Will was taken aback. He hunted around and managed to come up with that much money. Then hurried to his car and was again on his way. He had time to think it over and the more he thought about it, the madder he got. When he got to Arrowhead Springs he was an hour late. He was still boiling and spent the first ten minutes telling what had happened to him in Azusa. The veterans were mad, too. In fact, everybody was mad — Will the maddest of all.

When the show was over, he called the publicity man aside and said, "I want you to send this to the papers and to say that I will appear in Azusa and put on a talk free of charge — that is, for the poor people of the town. But not for the judge and the cops. I'm sure they're well-heeled."

The next morning the publicity man reported and said that he was ready to send out the story. Will said, "Listen, I'm over my mad spell. I got here and I made the boys laugh. It's worth being fined a hundred dollars to hear 'em laugh and to feel I was doin' 'em a little good. Don't send out the story. I'm sorry I ever got mad." And that was the end of that. He had, when he did get mad, a hasty temper, but no one in the world was quicker to forgive and forget.

An unusual situation arose. He was to go to Washington, D. C., to do some of the scenes in the story, and there, in due time, he arrived. He was to ride a horse down one of the streets. The director became cautious and said that Will would have to have a double to ride for him. A chauffeur was engaged and made the ride. Will never quite got over it.

Hal Roach's pictures were more successful than Goldwyn's but were not outstanding. Roach was a capable director with a fine sense of comedy, but the medium was not suited to Will.

For Hal Roach he made the following pictures (in addition to the one mentioned):

Hustlin' Hank, The Cowboy Sheik, The Cake Eater, Going to Congress, Our Congressman, Big Moments from Little Pictures, Just Passin' Through, Gee Whiz, Genevieve, Highbrow Stuff, No Parking Here, A Truthful Liar.

In all, Will had made twenty-four silent pictures.

CHAPTER 16

Will Becomes a Writer

WILL MADE a speech in the Town Hall, New York, advocating the election to Congress of Ogden L. Mills, who was an aristocrat, the last word in social grace, a bluestocking — in fact, just about everything Will wasn't. Will's talk will have to go down as about the most remarkable campaign speech ever made. It was reported in the *New York Times,* October 27, 1922, page 19, column 5. The reason the *Times* covered it was that Louis Wiley of that paper had heard Will at a banquet and had sent a reporter to get a story. He got one, indeed. When Will ambled out on the stage he announced that he didn't know the candidate an' didn't want to; he said that was the reason he had been chosen to talk about the candidate — that if a speaker knew him he couldn't say anything favorable. But he did have one advantage, declared Will; he was the only candidate who could enter a Fifth Avenue home without delivering something. He said that Mills was running on the platform of a living wage for bootleggers, and free eye examinations for those who had tasted the stuff. He said that Mills was 100 per cent for the ticket speculators and for everything in his district, good or bad. Also he said that Mills was the only candidate one could accept a gift cigar from without worrying about it. The audience didn't know what to make of such a speech. But it was entertaining. As a matter of fact the speech did more for Mills than a platitudinous one saying that he was the only man who could save the country. In fact, the speech was so extraordinary, in an age of political stuffiness, it started a series of events that Will never dreamed of.

A Scotsman (by descent) with the unusual name of V. V. Mc-Nitt read the paper and was impressed. He was the founder-proprietor of the McNaught Newspaper Syndicate, which was as close to McNitt as he thought the public would go, with offices in the old *New York Times* building. He dictated a letter to Will, telling him he wanted to see him about writing a weekly series of humorous articles. It was promptly not answered.

McNitt was a bit surprised there was no answer, for people were fighting in the street to write for McNaught's. Days passed and naught happened to McNaught. Then McNitt discovered by the vast underground that seems to connect all newspaper syndicates that Charles M. Lincoln, managing editor of the *New York Herald*, had a hook in the water. McNitt seems to have bounded into the middle of Times Square. He got Rube Goldberg, one of his slaves, to take him to Will's dressing room in the New Amsterdam Theater.

"Yep," said Will, "I been foolin' around with a man on the *Herald*. He read about that speech of mine, and I've been writin' some stuff for him about an old cowhand, Powder River Powell, and his talks with a barber called Soapy. But we've kinda run into a ditch. What papers do you sell to?"

McNitt had a daring inspiration. "Would you be interested if we could place your articles in the *New York Times*?" This was a bit risky, as the *Times* never before had used a syndicated feature regularly, but McNitt had previously sold Carr V. Van Anda, its managing editor, special correspondence on national conventions, and was willing to take the chance.

Will's ears stood up. "I guess anybody'd be interested in that."

But there was a catch. The enthusiastic Lincoln had queried the editors over the country by wire; they took it calmly, and Lincoln had offered Will a thousand dollars a week.

McNitt persuaded Will to visit the McNaught offices where McNitt, Charles V. McAdam and Frank Murphy, all syndicate people, explained how easy it was to write humor. Will listened carefully, for he wanted to learn about humor. Finally, he said he would try. The meeting broke up. Will went hopefully into the hurly-burly of Times Square and the McNaught magnates to the calm of their private offices.

It was not long until Will turned in the most depressing example of humor ever offered a major syndicate. The brand of Mr. Dooley was still on every man who tried to write topical humor; the format was for two quaint characters to discuss to-day's topics in a humorous way. Or what was meant to be humorous.

And so Will came forth with two quaint characters talkin' in their keen, penetrating way about what was goin' on in the world. One was a cowpuncher named Powder River Powell; the other was a barber named, not at all strangely, Soapy. Thank God, the piece was never published.

But here it is, published for the first time. No one can read it without wondering why Will (with his remarkable gift of humor) could ever have thought it was amusing:

Powder River Powell was a ridin' into town on his old buzzard headed horse, a keepin' away over to one side of the road so these modern ranchman's fenders wouldn't rake him over a cut bank down into the gulch. He was a middle aged waddie, kind of old-fashioned like, bein' still interested in live stock, politics and his first wife.

He was a goin' to town to-day because a Woman's Journal had strayed away from the home range and drifted into his wife's clutches. In it was an article by some old Maid who said husbands should not be allowed to neglect their personal appearance. So his wife was a goin' to try out this receipt by making Old Powder River go to town every Saturday to get a shave.

This was not such bad medicine to take, as he knew while

he was in the Barber shop a gettin' the buffalo grass ampu-
tated from his mug, that he would also get all the latest from
his old friend, an ex-cowpuncher, who, when he quit
punchin' cows, took to the Butcher business, and naturally
drifted from that into the Barber trade.

But don't you go gettin' it into your head that old Soapy's
shop was of the regulation *Police Gazette* Variety, No siree
old Soapy's Whisker dividends didn't all go for overhead
or Hair Oil. It went for subscriptions for all the latest
papers. While old Soapy might just be movin' and movin'
around and around a barber chair and never gettin' any
where in particular, he sure wanted to know in which direction the rest of the World was headed.

So it was on this Saturday that old Powder rides up to this
Death-on-Whiskers Emporium. Steps off his horse kinder
slow, bein' long of statue, while old Soapy was of the short,
bow-legged variety. He takes the toe of his boot and rakes
a couple of Fords under the porch out of the way, so he
could tie his old Crow Bait by the bridle reins to the barber
pole, Soapy's sole advertising medium, which also doubled as
a hitch rack.

"Hello, Soapy, how's business?"

"Why, Hello, Powder River; I sure am glad to see you,
things sure is slow, been no rain to speak of, and I never saw
hair and beard grow as slow in my life. If things keep on
like this I am going to have to put in one of them mess-
sauges things."

"What is a mess-sauge?"

"Well, a Mess-sauge is a sort of a Solution they have in
the east, where if a man can't wash his own face and keep
it clean why the barber laundries it for him."

"Soapy, don't you ever let my wife hear of it or she would
send and get one and make me take a whole bottle of it. Already she says I have to come in here every saturday, and
get shaved, whether I need it or not. So it looks like if my
wife don't get over this rash she's in now that I will be about

your most constant customer. But say, Soapy, what's the World been a doin' since I was in last?"

"Well, Powder, there's a terrible lot of news. Then agin there's a terrible lot in them daily Pamphlets that ain't news. You see, it takes me days sometimes to round up all them columns. The plum latest is Clemenceau is here. You remember we used to talk about him during Wilson's and Col. House's invasion of Europe."

POWDER: "What did he tell us, Soapy?"

SOAPY: "Oh, he balled us all out and told us just what he thought. He must be the Senator Borah of France. He said we left Europe too soon."

POWDER: "Maby he means we didn't leave Europe ENOUGH."

SOAPY: "No, he says we didn't stay long enough after the War."

SOAPY: "And say, Powder, what do you think he done while he was here? He got up every mornin' at 4 o'clock and had Onion Soup for breakfast."

POWDER: "Say, I'll bet that stopped a lot of them Society Women from imatating, didn't it? But say, Soapy, don't you ever let my Wife hear of that either. She is gettin' awful high-fangled. She wants to move where she can get in one of those Women's Clubs. I can get up at 4 o'clock, but my own Mother couldn't make me gnaw into Onion Soup that early in the mornin'. Besides, Soapy, it's a sort of a Frogs dish anyway, ain't it? As a food I don't think it has any standing among Civilized Nations. Over here we have always considered it more as an Odor than as a Delicacy."

SOAPY: "And say, that ain't half of it. He would eat six and Eight soft boiled eggs for breakfast, too."

POWDER: "You say you don't know what he come after? Why from what you say he must have come after eggs. You know France never has got their hens back to normalcy since the War. You know what it is, Soapy, to try to get things back to normalcy. Look at Warren, in Washington.

You know that Normalcy has just about been the Ruination of him."

SOAPY: "Newberry, he resigned from the Senate. I wonder what he will do now."

POWDER: "Why, he will about go back home and turn honest. You know that may be just the makin' of that man, to catch him before he gets too deep into Politics. You can save 'em sometimes if you get 'em early enough. Course where I blame him is buyin' a seat in that body of men. That's like payin' admission to go in a jail. Who did they put in to take his place?"

The McNaught men told Will that they-had enjoyed-it-immensely-but-unfortunately it was not exactly what the papers were buying at present. This was the first time that Will had ever encountered the suffering that editors experience when they have something too good for the fool public. Will took his quaint characters and crept away, leaving the McNaught people alone in their grief.

Later, McNitt had heady news. Carr Van Anda of the *New York Times* had promised to buy a weekly article by Will at $150 if Will would keep on the heels of the news.

About two years after Will had started his weekly humorous articles, he asked the McNaught Syndicate whether he could produce, in addition, a short daily feature. Irvin S. Cobb then was doing a daily series entitled "My Favorite Story." So it wasn't long before Will came back with an idea for a series to be called "The Worst Story I've Heard Today." The McNaught people listened with the seriousness with which all humorous ideas must be considered, and told him to try his hand. After a time Will returned with the following:

When the Prince of Wales was over here he pulled some stories on me, and in return for his courtesy in laughing at some of mine, I had to pretend to laugh at his. One that he told me I will repeat as being the worst from him that day.

He had just been to the Polo Grounds to see a ball game and like everybody that tells stories, he thought it would be a good time to tell his baseball story. In fact, I think he went to the game just to get an excuse to tell me the story. He related it as follows:

An Englishman over in America (as they generally are) was persuaded to see a game of baseball. During the duration of the encounter he chanced to turn his profile to the game for just the merest instant. A foul tip caught him and rendered him entirely senseless for several minutes. On regaining his mental equilibrium, he interrogated faintly, "What was it hit me?"

"A foul," his American friend remarked.

"Good heavens! I thought it was a mule."

We parted friends, the Prince and I, but it was on account of his other good qualities.

Now how is a mule going to be in a ball grounds? So you see the story has no sense to it. A mule would be just as much out of place at a ball game as an Englishman would.

Will took up one notable after another, recounting their witticisms, often much to the surprise of the notables. But they didn't complain. It was nice to be considered wise and witty.

After a time he ran out of fun-loving notables and began to pin his stories on lesser lights, who proved to be just as wise and witty as their superiors. Example:

My wife comes from Rogers, Ark., where they raise the prettiest girls and the best apples in the world. They have in the town a man I think is one of the greatest humorists in America. His name is Tom P. Morgan, and there is not one of you that havent read his stuff somewhere. He has contributed to *Puck, Judge* for some years and lately to the *Country Gentleman* and lots of the funny sayings to the Sunbeam column in the *Kansas City Star*, one of the best newspapers in America and one of the best columns. I have tried to get him to New York, but he says "I would be so busy dodging that I wouldnt have time to think of anything funny." The Curtis people brought him to Philadelphia to do some work for them, he saw their *Saturday Evening Post* Building, got scared and went home without going in to see them. Here's one of Tom's —

It was potato bug time in Arkansas and a bunch of farmers were talking it over at the store. One of them said, "These bugs et up my whole potato crop in two weeks."

"They et up mine in two days," said another, "then waited in the trees to see if I was going to plant any more."

"That aint anything," said the storekeeper. "I caught a couple of them examining my books a week before planting time to see who had ordered seed."

And still Tom wont leave Arkansas. Why, Tom is a big enough liar to get along even in New York.

The McNaught people again called him in. They said they had laughed heartily at his droll stories . . . but wouldn't it be better if he was just himself and wrote about something current? Will was doubtful, but remembered how, almost by accident, he had become a comedian by being natural. Again he said he would try, and set forth to the galleys that all writers know.

When he returned he had a piece, in form and substance like the one he had written for the *Kansas City Star* three years earlier. McNaughts liked it and so did the public.

This is the list of the papers taking the weekly articles and the rates they paid a few weeks after the beginning of the feature in December, 1922:

New York Times $150
Chicago News $50
St. Louis Post-Dispatch $35
Pittsburgh Press $25
Washington Post $20
Detroit News $15
Buffalo Times $15
Springfield Union (Massachu-
   setts) $5
Youngstown Vindicator $5
Lexington Herald (Kentucky)
   $3

Wichita Falls Times (Texas)
   $3
Boston Globe $50
Kansas City Star $25
Cleveland Plain Dealer $20
Baltimore Sun $20
Atlanta Journal $15
Portland Oregonian $10
Los Angeles Examiner $10
Fort Worth Star-Telegram
   $7.50
Sharon Herald $4

Galveston Tribune $3

Will was being paid $500 a week. Later he was offered $800 a week by another syndicate. He came in to see Charles V. McAdam to ask for more money. Before he could speak, McAdam completely astonished him by telling him that McNitt was going to pay him $1000 a week. This was the link that fastened Will to this syndicate as long as he lived. Some years later he was offered $3500 a week by a rival syndicate, but chose to remain with McNaught at a thousand dollars a week less. "We're gettin' along purty good," he said.

In 1926 his itching feet again wanted to be on the move; he turned them toward Europe. Before he left he happened to drop in at the *New York Times*. Adolph S. Ochs, the publisher, also had heard Will at a banquet, and was his admirer; as they talked, he said, "If you run across anything worth while, cable it to us. We'll pay the tolls." Casual as this suggestion was, it was a milepost.

While he was in England Will was entertained by Lady Astor. His first cable concerned her and appeared in the *New York Times*, July 29, 1926, in a box on the first page of the second section:

Nancy Astor, which is the nom de plume of Lady Astor, is arriving on your side about now. She is the best friend America has here. Please ask my friend Jimmie Walker to have New York take good care of her. She is the only one here that don't throw rocks at American tourists.

Yours respectfully,
WILL ROGERS

Larry Winship, then feature editor of the *Boston Globe*, saw the first of the cabled dispatches in the *New York Times* and telephoned the syndicate in New York to ask whether the *Globe* could use them also. Frank Murphy, the syndicate's treasurer, took the call and at once telephoned the *Times*. The reply was No to the *Globe;* the *Times* held these short cables to be its own, exclusively.

McNitt was in London with his family at the time, and Murphy wrote him that it would be a good idea to talk with Will, then concluding some stage and screen engagements, to propose that a short daily wire dispatch be substituted for the Worst Stories, which had become exactly that. NcNitt tried to find Will to promote this idea, but Will was elusive, as he was apt to be. The best McNitt could do was to elaborate the idea in a letter. Both men were soon homeward bound. Will cabled the syndicate office in New York that he liked the plan set forth in the letter, and the result was the early beginning of the daily feature. Not the *New York Times* alone, but all the papers in the United States that wished, began publishing about October 15, 1926.

Will had been impressed by Larry Winship's unsatisfied desire to publish the earlier cables, and was pleased when Larry was first to order the new dispatches. The feature opened up with 92 papers. And now, to his astonishment, Will was a recognized daily columnist — if 125 to 150 words may be called a column.

Powder River Powell and Soapy were lost forever in the sage-brush.

Soon came the problem of editing; the dispatches arrived in New York in the evening after the syndicate offices were closed; it was necessary to get them on the wires to client newspapers immediately. The problem, however, was small, for the syndicate always had agreed with Will that his personal style must stand. "That's the way I write it," Will said, "and that's the way I want it to lay." For, by now, he was completely convinced that he had made one of the most important discoveries of his life back in 1922; this was to be himself and to imitate no one. It had succeeded on the vaudeville stage; it had succeeded in the *Follies* ... he would be himself in this new medium.

It was arranged that he would send his daily dispatches not to the syndicate — but to the branch office of the Western Union in the *Times* building, New York. This branch had a list of the papers to be supplied, and immediately after arrival the dispatch was on its way again. A copy of it was carried to one of the *Times*'s editorial desks. Indeed, the syndicate people did not see the dispatch until the next morning when they turned to page one of the second section, just as all other *Times* readers were doing.

But the ninety-two papers were not all, for the syndicate arranged that smaller subscribing papers over the country should copy the piece from the big papers in their sections and run it the same day. The number of small papers began going up until nearly four hundred were buying.

One of the legends is that Will never missed a single day. This does not quite stand up under inspection. He missed five days when he was sending to the *New York Times*, before he joined the syndicate. (He was not paid by this paper when he was sending these daily telegrams.) Once he missed filing when he was crossing Siberia by rail and once in India. The syndicate took care of this by piecing parts of two or three old personal telegrams together.

His faithfulness to his column is touching. Once when he was to be operated on for gallstones, the last thing he did before they wheeled him off was to dictate three "telegrams" in advance. And the first thing he did, when he had partly recovered, was to write in trembling longhand his day's message.

The syndicate had one experience at editing. Will, at his Santa Monica ranch, sent a telegram that read something like this: "Flo Ziegfeld is opening his *Follies* tonight. I wont be there, so it ought to be good. I want everybody who reads this to go."

Western Union saw this blatant advertising and called up Frank Murphy and read the telegram. Murphy was afraid the papers would growl at giving the *Follies* so much advertising, so composed a telegram to Will telling him that it would never do to print the piece and asking him to rush a substitute. The message arrived at Santa Monica at two in the morning. Will — always a heavy sleeper — blinked through it, tried to think of another but couldn't, then went sleepily back to bed. The dispatch went out as written. Not a yell.

In 1932 Will went to Chicago to attend the Republican Convention; also he wanted to attend a polo game. So, with a friend who managed the Sherman House, he went off to the game. The game continued; time came to send the telegram which must be filed by a certain hour. Will left his friend, who was lost in the game, and went to get a taxi. But there were none. Finally he hitchhiked to a streetcar, and when that went no farther, he walked. At last he found a telegraph office; the day was saved.

One widespread legend is that he read his telegram to his wife and was guided by what she said; if she didn't like it, out it went forthwith. This is hardly true. She saw not more than one in ten. He wrote his squibs anywhere; sometimes on a plane, sometimes at a little table in a telegraph office, at his beloved chili restaurant. He did like to read them to somebody and would watch the person's reactions. If the person did not seem to like it, often he would rephrase it, or, sometimes, try a new idea. His car was his office. The back seat was a welter of newspapers. He would come sometimes to the car and pick up the papers without an idea in his head. He would scurry through them, a frown on his face, licking his thumb and turning the pages. Abruptly he would pause and, with a stub lead pencil, mark an item. Then start turning through again. Back and forth he would go. Suddenly he would cradle his typewriter on his lap, stare off into space a moment, then begin to peck, always in CAPITAL LETTERS. Now and then the pecking would stop and he would look at what he had written; then start again. At last the thing would be done. The typewriter would return to the back seat, he would lock the door, and his editorial duties would be over.

From time to time he would drop in at the syndicate; felt at home there, he said. "He wouldn't sit still," said Charles V. Mc-Adam. "He would be in and out of his chair; he would look out the window, then come and sit on a corner of my desk, talking all the time. And chewing. Sometimes it would be a piece of string, or rubber bands. One time, just for a joke, I asked him what he was chewing today. It was a rubber sealing ring from a Mason jar. Once something came up and I had to see him about a matter of business. I started down Broadway from our office and there, sure enough, at Thirty-ninth Street, I ran into him and we began to talk business. Will propped his foot on a fire hydrant still talking; then, becoming more and more absorbed in what we were talking about, he sat down on the water plug and wrapped his feet grotesquely around it, hanging on with one hand, still talking. People, hearing the familiar voice and seeing who it was, stopped to stare, but that made no difference to him. He talked and gestured as best he could, clinging to the water plug, utterly oblivious to them. When we had settled our business, he untangled himself and shuffled off down the street as if this was an everyday way of conducting a business discussion."

The syndicate was afraid that Will's unedited comments would cause trouble. One day his piece was about the European war debts due us; it expressed the opinion that we should never have lent such a huge amount. Immediately the *New York Times* was flooded with letters and telegrams of protest. The paper half apologized in an editorial in which it said that Rogers's opinions were his own and were not to be construed as the editorial policy of the paper.

Will, now that he was coming into prominence, began to show a side of his character that had not been evidenced; and this was how sensitive he was to criticism. His feathers had been ruffled.

I would like to state to the readers of the *New York Times* that I am in no way responsible for the editorial policy of this paper. I allow them free reign as to their opinion, so long as its within the bounds of good subscription gathering. But I want it distinctly understood that their policy may be in direct contrast to mine. Their editorials may be put in purely for humor, or just to fill space. Every paper must have its various entertaining features and not always to be taken seriously, and never to be construed as my policy.

Yours,
WILL ROGERS

After Charles A. Lindbergh's flight to Paris in 1927 he made a good-will tour by air of several Latin-American countries, Mexico among them. Will was in Mexico City when Lindbergh arrived there for a great reception, and two editors had precisely the same idea as to what Will might do about it. Larry Winship wired the McNaught Syndicate from Boston, suggesting that Will be asked to lengthen his dispatch for once to 500 words. The *New York Times* wired its correspondent in Mexico City to ask Will to send an exclusive dispatch of 500 words for the *Times*. Will received both messages and decided that 500 words for his full list of papers would please Larry Winship and satisfy the *Times* editors.

When the long dispatch arrived in the Western Union offices in the *Times* building, an editor took it to be the exclusive dispatch requested, and instructed Western Union to send it to no other papers. The dispatch was sent, however, to all the leased wire clients of the *Times*. The result was that Larry Winship received nothing at all for the *Boston Globe*, and was saddened next morning to find the story he had requested well displayed in the *Boston Herald*, a leased wire client of the *New York Times*. All over the country Will's regular clients went hungry, and several of them shared Larry Winship's pain in reading their own story in rival newspapers. It was all a misunderstanding on the part of someone on the *Times's* night staff, in which none of the chiefs had any part. The McNaught Syndicate decided, however, to have Will's dispatches handled thereafter through the Western Union office on Broadway near Forty-second Street, to avoid further mistakes. The *Times* took the move in good part.

Will's unorthodox style of writing offended the sensibilities of many purists. One day, at a lecture, a woman rose up and said she had been reading what he had been writing, and asserted that he would do better if he followed the laws of syntax. He was flabbergasted for a moment. But he was rarely buried so deep he couldn't get out.

"Syntax?" he repeated, trying to think his way through a word which plainly was a stranger. "It must be bad, havin' both sin and tax in it."

The woman persisted. "It means bad grammar and that's what you employ."

"I don't do it on purpose, ma'am," he said earnestly. "I write like I talk and if I use bad grammar it's because I don't know any better."

CHAPTER 17

Will Becomes a Lecturer

THE MORE one studies Will the more one is impressed by his humility. He never recognized his own vast potentialities. Each time a chance was offered in a field that he considered above him, he hesitated; he would say, earnestly and sincerely, that he didn't amount to anything and that the matter was too much for him. He was surprised that he could walk out in front of an audience with a rope and make them laugh. Even after he had succeeded, he lacked confidence in himself and kept his "laugher" planted in the audience. When he was proposed for the *Follies,* he hesitated. His stuff wouldn't go in a high-class show. He was surprised when he was approached to write for the newspapers. Yet in all these means of self-expression he made a complete success. His nature was strange: he did not have an inferiority complex, but he did — and this seems to be the very core of his being — have humility.

Another trait was that he was hard to deal with when he was talking terms with the money men. He always felt they were trying to get the better of him, and that he must be on the alert; and he was indeed, as many of the businessmen found. But after an agreement had been made and he had shaken hands, then the tussle was over. Never a word of complaint. But there was always that watchful preliminary scuffle with fast footwork.

At this time Charles L. Wagner was the best-known lecture manager in America. He had handled some of the greatest and had booked them successfully from one end of the country to the other, always in the most important cities and in the best and most imposing concert halls. He had been privately weighing Will; he could do wonders with him, he decided. So he wrote Will that he would like to send him on a lecture tour, with a background of music; he offered him $1000 a night. Not only this, but he would pay his traveling expenses and guarantee six concerts a week. It was a Santa Claus letter.

But he didn't hear from Will. If he had written anyone else in America, the man would have come as fast as a taxi could get him there. Finally Wagner saw Kelcey Allen, a well-known Broadway figure, and told him what had happened. "I'll tell him to come and see you," said Allen.

In a few days Will came to the box office at the Henry Miller Theater, where Wagner was presenting Helen Hayes and Sidney Blackmer in *Quarantine*. Wagner opened the side door and let Will in. Will was ill at ease and said, "You'll have to excuse me, Mr. Wagner, but I didn't know your letter was on the level. There's a bartender at the Friars named Charlie Wagner and I thought the boys were trying to pull a joke on me."

It was arranged for Wagner to go backstage at the *Follies* and talk with Will in his dressing room. Will asked him again, as if he could not believe that the $1000 offer was real, then said, "Shucks, Mr. Wagner, I couldn't do it. I'm not a lecturer an' I don't know nothing about it."

Wagner outlined the way it could be done, but Will still hesitated. "I want to talk it over with someone," he said, always his way of announcing that he wanted to consult Betty.

At last it was arranged. Will was to try an entirely new field, but he was to be backed up with a singing group — the de Reszke Singers. They were American-born students of Jean de Reszke and, in honor of their teacher, took his name.

Wagner chose Elmira, New York, as the opening place, October 1, 1925. Elmira had been the home of Mark Twain and he was buried there. The people there would appreciate humor.

But what Wagner did not think of was that their idea of a humorist was the sleek Mark Twain. The "lecture" was held in a church, which gave the already half-doomed affair a sober atmosphere. The singers came on; when they finished, Will wandered out with his gum and rope. The rope he carefully placed to one side, this to give suspense. "I was hangin' around the *Follies* so long, I decided I ought to dig up a new audience which hadn't heard all my wheezes, so that's why I'm here tonight." The audience regarded him coldly and he began to flounder. Soon he had the depressing feeling he had lost his audience. "The manager tells me this is a select audience and I can see it is. The riff-raff has gone to Florida." Not any too funny. He tried other things that had been a great success at the *Follies*, but there was no response. At last he got off and the singers came on again; the audience liked them. And then Will had to go back. . . . The depressing evening wore on.

Other bookings had been made and had to be filled. For the first sixteen days, Wagner lost money. Will became more and more depressed. He should never got into this, he said.

A woman wrote a letter to Wagner saying she had heard Rogers and that his *Follies* chatter did not interest her. Why couldn't he talk about more important things? she asked. Wagner passed this along to Will, who was impressed and began talking about national and international affairs.

This was the turning point. He no longer talked about rich men marrying the girls in the *Follies*, but about the disarmament conference and peace treaties and whether they amounted to anything. The lecture began to build. The group was out for eleven weeks and for this Wagner paid Rogers $82,000 — $71,000 more than he would have made in the *Follies*.

He began to like lecturing. He was meeting the plain people; he was having, each night, a wonderful time. He was so successful that Charles L. Wagner came to him with the good news that he had booked him at Carnegie Hall. Again Will was all humility. Carnegie Hall was far beyond him. He was so concerned that he offered Wagner one thousand dollars to let him out of the engagement.

"You can make a success of it," said Wagner. "Besides it's too late. You've got to appear."

Will was resentful and moody and held the whole thing against Wagner. Just another trick of them money men. At last the night came — a two-hour show with Will and his rope and the singers, not a girl, not a backbone.

It was an outstanding success. But Will wouldn't admit his success. "We just happened to draw a good audience," he said grudgingly.

Said Charles L. Wagner in summing up his experiences with Rogers: "I managed Rogers three seasons, sent him from one end of the country to the other. He often said to me, 'The greatest personal satisfaction I've ever got was from my concert work.' But I must point out that Will was not all sunshine and jolliness, as so many people have portrayed him. He was the most temperamental, and hardest-to-deal-with star that I ever handled, and I have managed more than fifty of the biggest and most important stars who have ever performed in America. He was money mad. He was a problem to me on the road, after we discontinued the singing group. I never knew where he was. My constituents would wire me to make certain that he would be there, but I didn't know where he was. He would come into a town late, keep out of sight of people running the concert, then turn up at the last moment. Sometimes they would have a locally important person to introduce him; this would be a big event for the person and he would prepare for it at great pains. But Will would dart out on the stage and begin to talk without any introduction. One time it had been arranged for Governor Ross S. Sterling, of Texas, to introduce Will. But instead of that, Will rushed on the stage ahead and introduced the Governor! Will caused me, by long odds, more worries and anxieties than anybody I ever managed. He was a great man, but from a lecture manager's point of view he was a problem.

"After his successes Rogers became even more difficult to manage. He loved money; he cut my commission down to only 5 per cent, then failed to fill the engagements. When he wanted to join the Fred Stone show, he failed to consult me. I had to cancel sixty-two contracts for personal appearances, calling for dates up to Christmas. My loss was about $30,000. The best settlement I could get out of him was $3000 for office expenses.

"In 1931 I had him booked through Texas, Arkansas, Oklahoma and in other states in the Midwest and South. That spring the second Mississippi flood disaster occurred and again the Red Cross needed money. Once more his eye was keen to self-advertising and again, without consulting me, he volunteered his services for a tour arranged through Amon G. Carter and other newspaper friends in Texas, with the receipts to go to the Red Cross. Announcement of these plans played havoc with the concert-tour bookings I had made in the South.

"It was impossible to hold him to a contract, for there was no contract. Rogers made promises orally, did not write letters and when he sent a telegram he signed it 'Will.' I wanted to sue him but my lawyer said, 'If Rogers goes on the stand, what chance would anyone have before a jury?' "

It is surprising to know that Wagner paid Will more money than Ziegfeld in all the time Will worked for him.

Again Will's sensitiveness to criticism became apparent. In Boston, H. T. Parker, high-brow critic, said Will's diction was poor and his jokes worse and added that he did not come up to the standard set in Symphony Hall. Will was hurt and moody. In his Sunday's article, January 3, 1926, he wrote:

"Last week I was away up in Boston. Can you imagine me appearing in Symphony Hall? From the Stock Yards of Claremore, Oklahoma, to Symphony Hall, Boston. We had had 75 nights all over the country and everybody had been wonderful to us, hadn't received an adverse notice, so this was our last night of the tour. Well, this old Soul is a Musical Critic. Now, can you imagine yourself raising your son to be a Male Musical Critic? His name is Parker. Having a trained musical ear, my jokes were Off Key. My diction was poor, he says. My 'selections' were extremely bad. He thought my High Register was on the bum and my Low Registered Notes had no roundness to them. Dramatic critics review my part of the show. But this man was a Musical Critic. It would be like sending an artist to look at a Rembrandt, then at the last moment asking him to stop on the way back and look at Farmer Jones' yearlings and tell how much they were worth. But you unconsciously paid me a Bear of a Compliment when you said, 'He is a small town Actor.' You bet your life I am small town. I am smaller than that. I am NO town at all and, listen, that is what I am going to stay. Bless your old soul, Parker, I bet if I met you we would like each other. Because in your own heart you couldn't blame an old Country Boy for wanting to finally get into the Symphony Hall. It's your pet, your life work. You want to see only the best in it. You have high ideals for it, and I don't blame you. Now when I come back up there next year, you are the first man I am going to look up, and I bet we have a good dinner and we will kill that old Indigestion of yours and you will be feeling good. But give me credit for one thing, Parker. Wasn't that English of mine the Worst ever spoken in that Hall?"

It is one facet of his character that he — who handed out so much criticism — should have been at all concerned over this.

Bruce Quisenberry, Will's nephew, gave me a vivid description of Will's barnstorming days. He is, as I write, an administration officer of the Signal Corps, in the Pentagon Building,

Washington, D. C. He traveled with Will as his company manager for three seasons. On the trains he slept in the same room; in hotels they had separate rooms; so he saw him in his good moods and in his bad ones. Said Bruce:

"After J. Erwyn Mutch left us, my chief duty was to get my hands on the money. While Will was lecturing I would check the house with the local manager and then we would proceed to divide the money — Will getting 75 per cent. In all the time I was with Will, he never asked to see the books, or for me to give an accounting. I arranged all transportation, train and plane, sometimes a private car. One season we spent seventy-five successive nights in a sleeper. When we had to travel by car it was my duty to have the car tucked away some place near, so that the moment Will came off the stage we could leap into it and start traveling.

"I never saw such amazing energy. He never seemed to be tired. Sometimes, when I was utterly exhausted, he would say, 'Boy, what you so draggy about? You slept till six this mornin'.' Always, after a lecture, he wanted to eat. He dearly loved chili con carne, but this wasn't so bad — he also loved onion sandwiches. On the train we slept in the same compartment. . . . Of a morning, when we were in a hotel, he would be the first person up; he would grab the newspapers and go in to breakfast. We didn't dare talk to him, then.

"Getting his newspaper dispatch off was always a dramatic moment. It had to be filed by half-past one. He would watch the time, then, at the last possible moment, he would put his portable on his knees, stare into space a few moments, then begin to peck. His hands — so amazingly skillful with a rope — were all thumbs when he tackled a typewriter. *Peck-peck-peck!* Sometimes he would stop, turn up the page and scowl at it for a minute. Then peck-peck-peck! If, by some chance, he finished early, he would read it to us — the singers and me — and ask what we thought.

If we didn't get the point readily, he might slip the sheet back into the typewriter and start pecking again. When the telegram was finally ready, I would hop off at the first stop and file it. Sometimes I would have to run like mad to catch the train. When I would finally get on he would say, 'I'll bet we lose you some day.'

"This was his working plan for a lecture. When we would get to the town, he would go to see some person he knew. If he didn't know anybody, he would go to the newspaper and get what he called 'the dope.' He would ask about the paving, street lights, traffic, the city council, the police, the bond issue, boot-legging. 'I hear in this county everybody votes dry, but drinks wet.' 'I hear you got a train that runs down the middle of the street and never whistles during the day when there are people to be run over, but whistles at night when everybody is in bed.' Another question he always asked was, 'What about the mayor? What's he doin' now?' In every town there was always a mayor ruckus, Will said, and this just about proved true. Another question was, 'Who's the richest man in town?' Will said that anything you said about him always went over big. Another question was, 'What's goin' on in the schools? Who's your superintendent?' He would write down the names on the backs of envelopes, or whatever he had in his pockets. When he left the newspaper office he would be loaded with local stuff. Before time to go on, he would pull the notes out of his pocket and look at the names; sometimes he would repeat them aloud to get them firmly in his mind. But after he went on, he never looked at his notes.

"He had three general divisions in his lecture: the local references; these came first. Second, he would take up the state things, such as the governor and politics. Third, would be his national or international material. Always in his second and third categories he had what he called his 'sure-fire stuff.' It was big and important and was the bedrock of his lecture. How long he talked depended on how well his lecture went. He disobeyed all rules of lecturing. Instead of standing still, as all lecturers believed a person had to do, he would walk up and down the platform, lean on the piano, or sit on the piano stool. At the end, if the lecture had gone well, he would come to the edge of the platform, sit down and dangle his legs over. By this time he would have the audience so completely under his spell that he could have hopped across the stage on one foot and the audience would have liked it. The last thing was his ropes. He would bring them out and begin to spin them. His big rope — made out of special Kentucky hemp — was heavy and the handling of it was exceedingly demanding. When he would leave the stage, his shirt would be wet.

"Our worst town was Waxahatchie, Texas. Another bad one was East Liverpool, Ohio. I still shudder when I think of them. One of our best was Ann Arbor, Michigan. The lecture here was held in the University auditorium where he had a college audience. The more intelligent an audience, he felt, the better his talk was received; this, he believed, was because he dealt with ideas.

"He loved audiences who loved him. He would stay with them until the last possible moment. One time the Musicians Club in Wichita Falls, Texas, sponsored him. The tickets ranged from $3.50 down — at that time a top price. Every seat in the auditorium was taken. When he finished, the audience gathered around him on the platform and in the aisle in as splendid a testimonial as he ever had. I had a car tucked away to take us to Waurika, Oklahoma, where we were to get a train to Wichita, Kansas. Finally we got into the car and made a dash for Waurika. Everything was fine — except the train had gone and there we were, far, far from our next lecture date. Elaborate preparations had been made for him in Wichita, Kansas. There was one thing he would not do, and that was to disappoint people who had come to see him. He was plainly stumped. He made inquiries of the station agent who telegraphed to headquarters. Will found that a 'stub' train could be sent from Wichita, Kansas, to pick him up and take him there, but that he would have to pay for it out of his own pocket — $1100. 'Tell 'em to saddle her up,' he told the station agent, and this was done. So we had a private train from Waurika, Oklahoma, to Wichita, Kansas. Will paid for it without a grumble. It was better than disappointing his audience.

"As I look back on those weeks and months with Will, it seems to me the most remarkable thing about him was that he never worried. Another quality that I now marvel at was his ability to work under pressure, and to do so without nervousness. And how well he slept! Also how early he got up. Another point — he never bore a grudge against anybody.

"Oh, I must tell you about the ropes! The situation was like the boy who wanted to get a free ticket to the circus, all he had to do was to bathe the snakes. We bleached the ropes so they would show up on the stage. After Will had done an act they would have been all over the floor and would be dirty. When we got back to the hotel, my job was to scrub them with brush, soap and water. There they would be in the bathtub and there I would squat like a Hindu with his bag of squirming cobras. After scrubbing them, I would drape them on the shower rail, or string them over the chairs and furniture till the bedroom looked like a hangman's workshop. Sometimes at night the ropes wouldn't have time to dry before a show the next morning — thank goodness! this wasn't often. Then I would have to take them into my bed, or berth if on a train, and sleep with the darlings."

Once, when Will was lecturing in Durham, North Carolina, the audience sat like girls in a sideshow frozen in a cake of ice.

He tried and tried, but could not move them. He saw, as he weighed the audience, that it had more women than men. Finally he turned from politics and international affairs and said: "Now I'm goin' to talk just to the ladies and I'm goin' to ask every man with any self-respect to close his ears. Ladies, let's talk about our operations. I'll tell you about mine, but I won't show you the scar." He launched into his "operation routine." The lecture turned out to be a success.

Children made a deep appeal. In a way he was an overgrown child himself. This may have been the bond between him and all children. Once he was on a tour raising money for the drought sufferers. He was in a car with the manager of the fund for that section; they were bowling along at a lively clip. They came to a small town in Arkansas which had a canvas sign hanging over the road. The sign said, WELCOME WILL ROGERS. Twenty or thirty children had gathered to see him pass. "Stop," said Will. "They may have been here all morning." The manager said they were late and must press on, but Will insisted that he must at least speak to them. Getting out, he took one of his ropes and did a few tricks for the delighted children. Then he got back in and the car sped on.

A glimpse of his life on the road was given me by Jack C. York, of Ironton, Ohio.

"I was a newspaperman in Birmingham, Alabama, when he was scheduled to lecture in nearby Florence, Alabama. I was sent to Florence to interview him for our paper and took him to Muscle Shoals, Alabama, and thus we got acquainted. That night, after his lecture, I was waiting backstage. When he saw me, he said, 'Come on before the people catch me. I gotta eat. Take me to a chili parlor.' He tossed his ropes to his nephew and we hurried down a back alley as fast as we could clop. I took him to the nearest chili parlor, which happened to be a one-counter, five-stool joint. I felt ashamed of it and heartily wished we'd had time to go to a better place. Behind the counter was the owner, in an apron that I am confident had once been white.

"Will mounted a stool. 'Two bowls and make 'em big.'

"Soon the proprietor clunked two bowls on the counter and placed beside them two cups of coffee, saucerless. Will ate like a range pony getting a taste of alfalfa. Finally he pushed his empty bowl aside and said with heartfelt appreciation, 'I'm always goin' to remember Florence, Alabama, for its wonderful chili.'

"I glanced at him, thinking it must be a joke, then I saw he meant it. I kept quiet and let him have his high opinion of Florence."

Now that he was getting to be famous and was known to be prosperous, friends of his vaudeville days came to him with extended hands and hard-luck stories. It can be said, I think, that he gave to them all. And to street beggars who came sidling up, wanting a dime. He always gave . . . was it the memory of what had happened in Buffalo? But also he was beginning to give on a far more extensive scale — to such organizations as the Red Cross, the Salvation Army and other relief agencies.

CHAPTER 18

Will Goes to Europe.   Meets Lady Astor and Mussolini

In April 1926, Will lectured in Philadelphia and was invited to lunch by George Horace Lorimer, editor of the *Saturday Evening Post*. Will was immensely pleased; that was getting up in the world. During the lunch, Lorimer said that he wanted Will to go to Europe and write a series of articles to be entitled "Letters of a Self-Made Diplomat to His President," a variant of "Letters of a Self-Made Merchant to His Son." Again Will was all humility. He wasn't big enough for the job; it was quite a different trick from writing for the newspapers. What if he failed? It would hurt him with the papers.

As he thought it over, he decided to try. He would take young Will with him; they would have themselves a good time.

Preparations began. He had been abroad many times, but never had he had a passport; he dived into that troublesome matter.

More and more he was developing the idea of meeting "big people." It was nice to think of himself, an Injun boy, running with the great and mighty. But this ego-satisfaction was not all: he could get copy from them. How would he go about it? This would be quite a different matter from making a person in the audience stand up and be chattered about, or making him come up on the stage. Europe! They didn't know him there. The bigwigs, how could he see them? Letters of introduction! He scurried here and there, getting them. Among the people who gave them were Charles G. Dawes, who was just then very much in the headlines, Congressman Sol Bloom and Alice Roosevelt Long-worth. And from Mrs. Charles Dana Gibson a letter to her sister. He had met the Prince of Wales in New York. Would he be able to see him over there? Sometimes people were friendly when they were in another country; but that didn't mean they wanted to keep it up when they got home.

He and young Will sailed on the *Leviathan* at 11:30 at night on the last day of April, 1926. Immediately Will got seasick; he wrote as part of his *Post* article, "Dear Mr. President: Will you kindly find out for me through our Intelligence department who is the fellow that said that a Big Boat didn't rock? Hold him till I return. Yours, feebly but devotedly, Willrog, code name for Will Rogers."

On shipboard he met other Americans — Garet Garrett and Isaac F. Marcosson, both writers, who gave him more letters of introduction. By the time he reached London he had eighteen letters guaranteed to open any door.

A general strike was on, but he managed to get to the Hotel Savoy; in a flash he was around at Parliament. He liked the House of Commons better; he said, after he'd viewed them, that they lived up to their name. The session opened with prayer. He wrote: "A man who was engaged for that business prayed. He mentioned the King more than he did the subjects. That struck me as kinder odd, because from what I had seen of the King and the house he was living in, I thought he was doin' pretty well and dident need any help. At least, to be fair, I thought the Subjects should have an even break."

When he was in the gallery of the House of Commons, the Prince of Wales came in and took a seat four rows in front. The big-name hunter was electrified. He thought of sending a note to the Prince, but held back; maybe this wouldn't be correct. Will — who usually didn't worry about what was correct and what wasn't — delayed, trying to think how to manage it. Abruptly the Prince got up and scooted out, leaving Will nothing to watch but the House of Commons.

Word was passed and eight days later an invitation arrived for Will to call on the Prince of Wales at York House. He went like a boy to see Santa Claus. He described the rooms in York House he had to walk through and told how he finally came to a closed door. Will, with his guide — no less than a general — paused; suddenly the door opened and there was the Prince. Will described at length how he looked and what he wore, even his shoes, in words that were not far from awe. He described the paintings on the walls and the photographs on the tables, all in a most impressed way. He stayed an hour, and when he left he was as awed as when he had come. One sentence stands out: "Just between you and I, Calvin, he don't care any more about being King than you would about going back to being Vice President."

He angled just as carefully to meet Lady Astor. He had thoughtfully arrived in Parliament with Mrs. Charles Dana Gibson's letter in his pocket, did this strange and inexplicable Will. He sent it to her and, after a decent lapse of time, she came to the room where he was waiting. Seemingly she had not known who he was. Her first comment was, "Where did you get that Southern accent? It sounds like home." His impressed manner remained with him. Yes, Injun boy was gettin' up in the world. It developed she was entertaining some English sailors in chambers and asked if he would talk to them. Indeed he would and, when the time came, he told in extravagant terms what a wonderful woman she was — just one lone woman, he said, among 600 men, hardly news to the sailors. Lady Astor was not displeased.

It was not long before he was invited to a dinner she gave in the House of Parliament. "She," he wrote, "was good enough to invite me." He told what a wonderful dinner it was and what a delightful and charming person his hostess was. There is no evidence this rubbed her the wrong way.

The strange hunt continued. He bagged some big names. Lord Dewar, the whiskey king, was, he said, "the greatest after-dinner speaker in England." He met Sir James M. Barrie and told at length what a great man he was (he hadn't read a line that Barrie had written), and he managed to meet Sir Thomas Lipton, Sir Harry Lauder, Lord Derby, and George Bernard Shaw, who seems to have impressed him least of all. His only comment on Shaw was, "We've got a good deal in Common. Both of us know the world is wrong, but we don't know what's the matter with it." He got many scalps. He continued to hunt. But the big one he wanted was Mussolini. He had started preparing for this before he had left home and now he was drawing nearer. He would soon bag him.

Will wanted to go to Paris. Young Will suggested they fly; in California he had flown over their house in Beverly Hills. Will, the father, hesitated; he was not keen about this new business, but liked to do what his children wanted. They drove to a suburb of London and got on a French plane. (At this time Europe was far ahead of the United States in air travel.) Will was nervous. In his own words: "Just as I would start to enjoy a wonderful old castle down below, somebody would take the air out from under us and down our plane would go like an elevator." But, on the whole, he liked it. It was a speedy way to get around; this fitted in with the trait that was so deep in him — his desire of wanting to go somewhere. It had taken him to South America, South Africa, and on a trip around the world. This passion to be on the move was deep and constant and unwavering. And now that he was writing for both a magazine and newspapers, he wanted more than ever to go to different places.

He went to Spain where he met the Duke of Alba. He pointed out with pride that the Duke was more royal than the King —

got it from both sides of the house, Will said. The Duke invited him to the palace. Will did not deflate it, as one might think, but told how wonderful it was and how out of place he himself felt in it. The Duke said there was to be a polo game the next day and that if Will would come he would introduce him to the King. Will found it convenient to go. When he was introduced to the King, he took off his hat and held it in his hand like a servant in a play. The King told him to put it back on; when Will wrote about him he said that the King was democratic.

At last Will left Spain.

It was during this time that Lady Astor sailed for the United States and he sent his first cablegram to the *New York Times* (July 29). He was paying her back for her kindnesses, as he considered them.

But it wasn't all travel and lion hunting, for he had been signed to make a motion picture with Dorothy Gish. Betty Rogers, with Mary and Jimmy, came over and the family went to Switzerland. They were in the mountains and, for five days, Will was not able to send his daily telegram to the *Times*.

Will pressed on to Rome to see Mussolini; "the greatest man in Europe," he called him. Will found that even with the American Ambassador arranging it, he would have to wait six days. But that was all right. Lots of things to see and do in Rome; and he and young Will proceeded to do them.

Mussolini had agreed grudgingly to see Will and he made the stipulation that Ambassador Fletcher must be along to add dignity to the occasion. In addition, Mussolini made it clear that the interview must be brief and that Rogers was not to treat it lightly.

Finally the big day arrived. Will was to go in at twelve, and, exactly at twelve, word was brought out that Will, accompanied by the Ambassador, was to enter. When Will wrote of this moment, he said in most sycophantic terms: "I was headed for the most talked of, the most discussed — the man that has done more for one race of people in three years than any living man ever did; a Napoleon, but with peace."

The office proved to be huge; one had to travel a long way to arrive at Mussolini's desk. Mussolini kept his eyes on his papers with a pretense of being busy. Suddenly he looked up and surveyed the intruder with condescension, trying to impress Will even before he spoke. Then, as Will drew closer over the vast space of the office, Mussolini abruptly got up, came around from behind his ponderous desk, and suddenly shot his arm out in the Fascist salute. As he did so, Rogers threw up both hands in surrender and cried out, "Don't shoot!"

Mussolini was not amused. There was a coldness for some moments.

Then Mussolini asked if Rogers wanted an interview. Will said No; he just wanted to see if Mussolini was a regular guy.

Mussolini said he was a regular guy. Also he said that he did not want to look mad and sour like Napoleon, who probably was not a regular guy. Mussolini said that at heart he was gay and liked to laugh and have a good time. Then he smiled to show how happy-go-lucky he was.

After they had talked a few moments, Will asked, as delicately as he could, what would happen if Mussolini died . . . who would take over and run the country? Mussolini stuck out his chest, told Will to feel his arm, then said, "Mussolini feel pretty good yet." This was the end of the health examination.

Mussolini did not ask him to sit down, but conducted the affair standing. During it he told Will how successfully he was running the country and pointed out what was wrong with France and England. Having settled France and England, he said that he had just had some photographs made that morning and that he would give a print to Will. He sent for them and gave one to Will. It showed Mussolini on horseback making an impressive jump. He autographed it — "not only that," said the awed Will, "but put my name on it." Will examined the picture and said that the face was so small that it did not show up well. Mussolini solved this deplorable situation by autographing another picture which showed his regular-guy face. Said Will: "I was mighty proud to get them, especially as I hadent asked for them."

Then the incredible interview was over (it lasted half an hour) and Will left with his trophies.

When he wrote up this exciting event, he got out his choicest adjectives: "Everybody is so enthusiastic about his system that I don't see how it can collapse overnight." "If he died tomorrow, Italy would be indebted to him for practically four years of peace and prosperity. Not a bad record to die on at that; but this Guy keeps on getting better all the time. He is the only idealist that ever could make it work. . . . You never saw a man where as many people and as many classes of people were for him as they are for this fellow. Of course he has opposition, but it is of such a small percentage that it wouldent have a chance to get anywhere, even if they would let it pop its head up."

When he got back to the American Embassy he was still excited over the interview and kept telling how nice Mussolini had been. He had reached the high point on his trip, he said; everywhere else would be slumming.

Thrilled with his successes, he left for Russia to interview the great Trotsky. But this was something different. He was just another nosey American. On the other hand, he was not followed and, seemingly, was able to go where he wished. He wandered the streets alone, seeing what he could. He had a guide only once and this was when he asked for one to show him through the Kremlin.

At this time Trotsky was not popular with the clique that was running the government, and Will was not able to see him. But he did have a good quip: "Over here Trotsky is called a conservative. A conservative, among communists, is a man with only one bomb. A radical is what you might call a Two-Bomb Man." Some of his comments are enlightening even today: "It seems the whole idea of communism is based on propaganda and blood. Their whole life and thought is to convince somebody else they're right."

Much of his observation was on the surface. In Moscow he went to the river where he saw people bathing without the formality of suits. He seized on this: "I want to state that while I did not get to see all of Russia, I got to see all of some Russians." Later he wrote a book entitled *There's Not a Bathing Suit in Russia*. It is his most superficial book.

At last he left without having seen any of the important government officials. It was his first defeat of the trip.

He returned to London where he made the motion picture with Dorothy Gish. *Tip Toes* dealt with three American vaudeville players touring England and not doing so well. Will's comment on this: "I've been in vaudeville and know how to play a vaudeville actor who's not very good. All I have to do is to be natural."

As if this wasn't enough for one mortal, what should he do but agree to appear in six travelogue films; and he did, this astonishing man. The films were produced by Carl Clancey and dealt with six European countries. Will also wrote the witticisms that were flashed on the screen. Samples: "The chateau you see on the right is the Café de la Paix — and if you're an American you'll pay. . . . These saloons are so full that half the people can't get in, so they set on the sidewalk. . . . On your right is the French Opera House. If it was in America it would be a movie house. . . . These here are the Tuileries, the most beautiful gardens in the world. The thing spouting is a fountain. If a thing was spouting at home, it would be a Senator."

Will's energy was almost incredible. Not only did he take part in the picture, but having nothing to do at night (as he put it) he agreed to appear in a musical review by Charles B. Cochran, whom Will called "the British Ziegfeld." He was nervous opening night, as he always was; before he went on, he knocked on wood, as he always did. He opened with an attention arrester: "They won't let me work in Hollywood now. They say I haven't got any sex appeal. But I've got a good face — not handsome but it's practical."

The amazing man was not only playing in a film and appearing in a musical, but also writing a Sunday piece of a thousand words for American newspapers, and sending a daily squib to the *New York Times*. In addition, all sorts and kinds of American visitors piled around to see him — "just for a minute." He saw them all; it was not his nature to dodge. How in the world he got it all done, I don't know, and it depresses me to think of it. Someone might say it was because he organized his time. This was hardly true, for no one was less organized than Will. He never made any plans in advance; he would not even agree to keep a date at some future time. His attack on how to get things done was extremely simple: when he wanted to do something, he did it then and there. As soon as it was over, he was ready for something else.

On top of all this, he appeared on the wireless, August 17, 1926, for the highest fee ever given up to that time. (He turned the money over to a hospital.) You would think no one could do more; no one could, I'm sure, except Will Rogers. His energies were inexhaustible. There was a theater fire in a small town in Ireland, Dromcolliher, in which forty-eight people died tragically. Will wired the mayor of Dublin he would come and put on a benefit, if the mayor wished. The mayor wished, for by now Will was becoming an international figure. The benefit was an outstanding success. Aside to the *New York Times*: "I am bringing family greetings from Dublin to every man on the force."

At last the summer was over. What a busy one it had been! How much he had done in four months. Time to go home, and so Will and his family got ready to go back on the ship he had come over on. The story now becomes personal, for I, too, was on the *Leviathan*.

Things had not been going well for me in Forest Hills. I had written a novel entitled *They Had to See Paris*. It had helped mightily. I thought I would go to London, taking with me the same set of characters, and write a book about England. It was a wonderful idea. The publishers thought so well of it that they advanced me money — always the acid test. I had gone frisking off with the intention of sitting down in the heart of London and rattling off a fine story. Soon I was in London at 61 Queensborough Terrace, in a "board residence," and soon I was rattling. Everything went well. I had more background and atmosphere than Dickens. Pretty soon it was all atmosphere and no human beings. I mired down . . . a situation to bring cold sweat to any writer who has ever gone through it . . . and what writer hasn't? The story got worse and worse; it fought me in the streets, on the beaches and in the hedgerows. I speak of it lightly, but it was not so funny then.

Meantime I was using up my money, always an easy matter. Again I tackled the jolly story of Americans in bonny England. Finally I had to give it up. I arose — in this bitter moment — and went straight to a booking office and engaged passage home. I was so low financially — and emotionally — that I had to go steerage. The very word shocked me, when I saw I must do this. However it was not long before I was on the ship and found that steerage wasn't bad at all. I met interesting people. I read a great deal. In fact, I enjoyed myself more than I had ever dreamed possible.

Will Rogers was on the ship. It had been nine years since I had seen my neighbor. He had gone far; indeed he had become a world figure. I had watched him climb with fascinated interest. How could one do so well? I asked myself. But he had done it all himself and in a fine way. It should serve as an inspiration to all Americans. That's the way I felt about him then; it's the way I feel about him now.

There had been a destructive storm in Florida, and a benefit was arranged to raise money for the victims. One of the passengers was Charles Evans Hughes, Secretary of State; later he missed by a narrow squeak becoming President of the United States. Rogers had never met him, but with his interest in notables he sought him out and proposed that the two speak at the ship's concert. It was, so the reports came to us, a most successful appeal.

The next night the two spoke in the second class; more money was raised.

Then word was brought to us that on the third night they would speak to the steerage passengers. The doorway opened and there was my former neighbor. (It seems to me that Will Rogers, Junior, was along.) Almost without realizing what I was doing, I got out of Will's sight, ashamed that he might recognize me. He talked to us standing up, for our quarters were cramped. I listened as he spoke, envying him his remarkable ability. Charles Evans Hughes spoke, and with a dry humor that I had not expected. When the "entertainment" was over, there was no collection.

Will disappeared up the companionway and the matter was over. Forty thousand dollars was raised.

At last the ship reached New York and I was home again. I went to my publishers and told them I had failed. It was not pleasant.

He Becomes a Mayor. Has His "Operation." Again Tries His Hand at a Silent Picture

WILL NEVER let up an instant in those days. He was back only a short time when he started on another lecture tour accompanied by the de Reszke Singers. Every night — six nights a week — he was in a different town. Not only this but he was writing a daily squib and a Sunday article. He was always on exhibit. When he arrived to lecture, people pounced on him. Or he would slip away to the newspaper offices and interview the reporters or editors on What Is the Mayor Up To Now? Or on What Are the Boys Down at the City Hall Doing?

He opened one night in Memphis. The Scopes evolution trial was still in the minds of the public. When the moment came, he shuffled out on the platform, stood awkwardly a moment, then said, "I'm here to give a physical demonstration that Darwin was right." It was the method he was using all the time now of startling his audience with his opening shot.

Usually he made capital of any personal connection he had with a town, but strangely enough he did not mention that Memphis was where he had started his show career — that is, outside of home ropings. It was here, as we have seen, that he had his first failure, and it was here that his name appeared in print for the first time, outside of Rogers County. But there was one catch; the Memphis paper had merely called him Rogers. No Mister, no Will. And he was lumped in with three others.

But the paper did call them "Messers.," a touch of the chivalry, no doubt, of the old South.

He was hopping over the country like a cricket on a griddle. At San Antonio, Texas, the Old Cattle Drivers Association gave him a chuck-wagon party. They had son-of-gun (to be the real thing it has to be made from stolen beef), "free holies," Dutch biscuits prepared by a trail cook; the fire was fed by "chips," as in early days. Best of all, from Will's point of view, was that Johnny Blocker was there. He was now an elderly gentleman, but showed how he threw the Johnny Blocker Loop which he had given the roping world. Will hovered around him, treating him with great respect, for he was the grand old man of rodeo and ranked along with Bill Pickett. Some of them, in memory of early days, called Will "the Cherokee Kid." It was a wonderfully satisfying evening.

Two nights later he was in Fort Gibson, Oklahoma, Cherokee Bill's home town. Cherokee Bill was the worst bandit who ever roamed Oklahoma, as made clear in *He Hanged Them High*, a book no library should be without.

The contrasts in the things that Will did are sharp; not only that, but some are becoming historic. November 15, 1927, Charles L. Wagner booked Will and Mary Garden to broadcast for the National Broadcasting Company. This was the first time this company ever broadcast. Mary Garden was in its studio in Chicago; Will was on the stage in Memorial Hall, Independence, Kansas. They each received $2500, which turned out to be $250 a minute. Manual work wasn't in it.

Everything that Will touched now was successful; this was in contrast to the days when success came not at all and failure walked at his side. His fame was increasing. And his personal popularity. And so was his generosity. Hardly ever did he go out on the street in New York, or even in California, that some individual did not slink up with a tale of misfortune and defeat.

His hand went into his pocket . . . was it that Buffalo experience? And in bigger ways, too. Benefits. No one was more willing to run to a fire than Will.

In spite of the fact that he was away much of the time, Will was becoming, more and more, a member of the film colony. But he was strangely different. No swimming pool; the same wife. No pretense. And he was accessible. Almost anyone could see him who wanted to. And plenty wanted. It was only the people calling him on the telephone eager to let him in on a wonderful business opportunity that he dodged. Sometimes they got him on the telephone. Then he would say, "All right, tell me about it." Usually the person would say he would have to do that in person. Will would say, "If it's too involved to be told over the telephone, I don't want anything to do with it." Then he would be off the telephone.

Much of the time he wore his ranch clothes. When he wanted to dress up he put on his faithful old blue serge. He also had a gray suit with stripes. These suits he had got off the shelves. He had never had a tailor make him a suit.

As to clothes, Charles V. McAdam of the McNaught Syndicate told me this story. Will was in New York and suddenly wanted to go to Europe (he always decided everything suddenly) but must have a new suit of clothes, an understandable bit of male vanity. The two started down Seventh Avenue, late in the evening. Most of the shops were closed, but finally they found one that was still open. Will scrutinized two or three suits, then said he wanted this one. He was going to Europe tomorrow, he explained to the man, and wanted to take it with him. But when he got into the trousers they were too long. He said they must be shortened. The tailor explained that his repair man had left for the day and that there was no way to have them shortened. Will said firmly he wasn't goin' to wear no trousers too long for him. The tailor had a bright idea; down the block was a nonunion tailor who had a small repair shop. Maybe he could do the job. McAdam took over the trousers and asked the tailor. Will, with his own trousers off, sat down out of sight behind a stack of clothes and began calmly to read the paper. After a time the trousers were back; they fitted to a king's taste. Will gave his old suit to the tailor, told him to pass it along to somebody who needed it, and went out wearing his new suit, his shopping completed. He had another suit at the hotel, he said, but one shouldn't ever go to Europe with just one suit.

Another clothes story: Will liked to rope calves on Sunday. He really liked to rope 'em every day, but Sunday was an especially good time to get in some ropin'. He asked Douglas Fairbanks to rope with him. Will told him he would come after him in his own car and they would toss their ropes around. Will arrived in his roping clothes.

Pickfair had a butler named Albert and there was a "second man" who was, it seems, a very dignified individual. When he opened the door this cheery morning he saw somebody his master and mistress would distinctly not welcome. Will said he wanted to see Mr. Fairbanks. The second man narrowed the crack and said that Mr. Fairbanks was not up. Will said that was all right, he would come in and wait. The second man said that this could not be done and closed the door.

The second man went to Albert and told him of the impossible situation.

Albert hurried to the door, looked out — and then opened the door with profuse apologies, and took Will to the breakfast room where Douglas Fairbanks and Mary Pickford were, presumably, deep in their orange juice.

When Albert told what had happened, Douglas Fairbanks was indignant; the second man had taken too much responsibility. Will put in a plea for the man and asked Doug not to discharge him. Finally Doug agreed and once more the sun was shining on the orange groves of California.

His perfervid pace began to make its demands; he complained about having the stomach-ache. He even tried the heroic measure of giving up chili. But his stomach trouble continued; sometimes, when he came off the platform, he would have to sit down and rest, something almost unknown to Will. "I don't think I can give tomorrow's show," he would say. But he gave it. The swinging of the heavy ropes tired him more than ever. But he swung and the audience laughed.

It edged up to December. Will decided to knock off lecturing and go home for the holiday season. The serious thinkers of Beverly Hills, discovering this, went into executive session and came out with smiling faces. Beverly Hills was the home of many movie people who were not uncontrollably opposed to publicity; the real estate board did some thinking on the subject and announced they couldn't see any valid objection. The point of all this unusual activity was that Beverly Hills had no mayor and that it would be fine publicity to appoint Will Rogers mayor. With Beverly Hills citizens, to think is to act. And so a committee had a meeting and appointed Will mayor. Just as the thinkers had forecast, it got the town a wealth of publicity. The reason that a mayor could be arrived at in such an offhand manner was that Beverly Hills was a sixth-class town. (This point was one the progressive citizens passed over quickly.) When Will got back for the holidays he was met at the railroad station with the thrilling news that he was mayor of Beverly Hills. He took it in his stride.

There was a great to-do for the installation. Will was living at 925 North Beverly Drive and a stand was erected nearby. People paraded carrying banners and, when the time came, gathered at the stand immediately in front of the photographers. Will was given a scroll as big as a buffalo hide. The photographers came closer to get a picture of the dignitaries presenting Will with the document. There were so many of them that only by a bit of luck did the document get in at all.

Will had a good opener: "They say I'll be a comedy mayor. Well, I won't be the only one. I never saw a mayor yet who wasn't comical. I'm for the common people, and as Beverly Hills has no common people I won't have to pass out any favors. This town is different from other towns. It's got two swimmin' pools to every Bible. People here would rather see Duke Kahanamaku than Moses." (The Hawaiian was, just then, very much in the news as a champion swimmer.)

In a way he did take the matter seriously, for out of his own pocket he furnished a gymnasium for the police department and paid for the building of a handball court.

The California State Legislature, which seems to have been comfortably dozing, leaped to action and passed a law which proclaimed that in a city of the sixth class, the president of the board of trustees was constitutionally the mayor. So Mayor Rogers was "deposed." He stood up well under the shock. "I ain't the first mayor that's been kicked out. If I'd knowed Beverly Hills was a sixth class town I wouldn't made the race. I hereby notify the world that Beverly Hills has left my bed and board, and I will not be responsible for any debts contracted by said municipality."

The real estate board stood up under it well, too. The town'd got about all the publicity it could get.

Will went back on the road. He complained more and more about his "stummick-ache." Giving up chili hadn't been a magic cure. The people mustn't be disappointed. He'd put on tonight's show, and maybe tomorrow he'd feel more perky.

Finally he came to Bluefield, West Virginia. This is what he wrote later: "I hit a town called Bluefield, West Virginia. Now ordinarily when a pain hits you in the stomach in Bluefield, West

Virginia, it would be a gunshot wound, but this pain was something else."

He hurried to California. On the train he had a sharper attack. When he got home, the family doctor was called. "You'll have to be operated on." Will could hardly believe it. Why, he'd never known a day's sickness, at least not many. He'd had his arm broke, once; and he'd had some spills from horses, but that wasn't sickness; that was just normal life. "It's gallstones," said the doctor. Soon he was in the hospital and from his bed dictated his syndicate dispatches to Betty. When the news was released, the country followed the papers eagerly. Nothing must happen to Will Rogers. It was not until three days after the operation that he had sufficient strength to dictate his telegram to Betty, who took it down at his bedside. It proved to be the shortest he ever sent: "California Hospital, Los Angeles, June 19 — Relax, lay perfectly still, just relax."

For days he had a temperature, but wrote his pieces. At last he was out and back home. That was news in almost every paper in the United States.

Will's first instinct was to do as somebody else had done. He had tried it with his Mr. Dooley imitation; he had tried it with his Worst Story; now he tried it again. Irvin S. Cobb had written a book entitled *Speaking of Operations;* and now Will wrote a book entitled *Ether and Me.* It was not as good as Cobb's, but he paid for his operation many times over by telling about it in his lectures. It became one of his most amusing spots; when an audience sat with glassy eyes, he always fell back on it. If the operation couldn't bring 'em out, nothing could.

Also he thought he would again try his luck in the movies, and he made *The Texas Steer* for Sam E. Rork. Douglas Fairbanks, Jr., played the juvenile. The story dealt with a Texas rancher who is elected to Congress and comes to Washington and bucks in the political corral. The picture was only a mild success. In fact, so far Will distinctly had not done well in motion pictures.

He flew to Oklahoma to see the old ranch. His enthusiasm for flying was growing. That was the prime way to get around. Flying ought to be encouraged. He'd boost it in his lectures and in his telegrams. People ought to know what a wonderful institution flying was.

While in Oklahoma this incident happened. He went to the depot on the Frisco Railroad in Ravia, Oklahoma, to file his daily dispatch. The telegraph operator was sitting inside playing a guitar and singing. Will listened . . . was he thinking of the time when he went to a railroad station to claim a guitar? . . and then asked the operator if he had ever played professionally. The operator said he had, a few times at churches and the Rotary club. Will suggested that he try to get into radio; the young operator went to Chicago, made the try, and succeeded. The operator was Gene Autry. He says that if Will had not aroused his ambition he might never have got into the entertainment field.

Will's love of the soil, especially of his own ranch, was deep. The ranch was being managed by Herb McSpadden, his nephew. So whenever he had a day off, or could find the time, Will hastened to the ranch and walked delightedly out across it. Nearly every acre brought up a memory. Here was where he had built the log cabin with Spi Trent. Here, in the family cemetery not far away, was where his mother had been buried. And his brother and sisters. Here was where the horse had killed Clint Lipe. Here, in sight, was where he had smoked a cigar and set the prairies on fire. Here, in the yard, was where they'd held the stomp dances and where Betty had shaken a foot. Whatever had become of Kate Ellis? How long ago that was! Why, some of the people were dying off. Was it possible he was getting along in age, himself? Why! it was right along here he'd rode in the old buckboard, after he blowed out the gas in Frisco. John

Smith was the name of the boy who'd drove him. Wasn't he in Collinsville now? Where were Aunt Babe and Uncle Dan Walker? And Clem Rogers, the colored boy who'd been named for Papa? And here — lots of places for this — his father had bawled him out for always tryin' to get out of work. Well, he himself must have more understandin' for his own outlaws.

A letter to the author from Kate Ellis, who became Mrs. Robert W. Lewis, 800 North Ninth Street, Independence, Kansas:

"Your letter has gone unanswered for one reason only — I do not want to contribute any information about my years of friendship with Will Rogers. I feel there have been books and stories written of his life, Betty's book, among others. Since they are both gone, I feel it bad taste on my part to add my bit of the years I knew him. It is their story — Will's life, not mine — and I'm sorry but can't see it any other way. I have refused before."

CHAPTER 20

Will Meets Lindbergh

WHILE WILL was working on *The Texas Steer*, in Burbank, word came that Charles A. Lindbergh was to arrive there. Will had never met him; now was his chance. He was so pleased by the prospect that he put this in his telegram to his papers: "Lindbergh is coming here tomorrow. He is the one man in the world that I would stand on a soap box on the corner to get a peek at." He was also pleased by something else that happened. He was invited to speak at a dinner for Lindbergh to be held in San Diego. He'd sure nuf do that.

But when Lindbergh landed, Will was in the midst of a scene in the studio and could not go to the flying field. A disappointment, there. However that afternoon a reception was given at Hotel Ambassador by the movie people. Will managed to free himself from the clutches of the studio and hastened to the reception. The place was running over with executives and big-wigs from the movie studios. It was depressing in other ways, too. These inflated egos pushed up to get a look at Lindbergh, then stood around so that the public could also have the pleasure of seeing them. Will wiggled through and spoke to Lindbergh, but it was only for a moment, for a phalanx of well-meaning people bore down on the bedeviled young man. The thing that impressed Will was that the movie stars were doing exactly what was done to them every time they poked their noses out: thrusting sheets of paper at Lindbergh and demanding autographs. In his telegram the next day, Will described the scene and added, "I'll bet Lindbergh curses the day he learned to write." After a time, Will left. But Lindbergh couldn't. He had to stay and be admired by the elite of Hollywood. His face looked drawn.

Will and Betty went to San Diego by train and the next morning Will was out early at the flying field to watch Lindbergh land. Lindbergh's arrival was a big event, for it was from San Diego that he had started on his flight in *The Spirit of St. Louis*. Will noticed that the first thing Lindbergh did when he landed was to shake hands with the mechanics who had worked on his plane.

It was not long before the harassed Lindbergh was in the stadium, packed with all the people of southern California. He was presented with a parachute. Will, who was sitting next to him on the platform when the parachute was brought up, whispered, "I guess they'll expect you to go up and give a demonstration of how it works."

Of course, that night there had to be a banquet put on by the well-meaning people of southern California. Lindbergh, who was beginning to tire of banquets, came like Sidney Carton to the scaffold. Speaker after speaker got up and told what a wonderful person he was; the place dripped with honey and adjectives. Then Will was called on. He liked to come toward the end of a program so that he could pick up material from the preceding speakers. He arose and waited a moment, as he always did, then looked up and down the tables of guests.

"Colonel, they've been tellin' you what an inspiration you are to American boys. I've got a couple of American boys and you ain't no inspiration a-tall. What the people've been sayin' is applesauce." Lindbergh was startled. He didn't know Rogers well; this was the first time he had ever heard him speak and he knew nothing about his way of starting with a shocker. "It's a lot of applesauce because if our boys tried to follow you they'd be in the middle of the Atlantic Ocean. I don't want my boys tryin' to do the stunts you've been pullin' off."

Lindbergh blinked, still not knowing what to think.

"The speakers have been tellin' about the wonderful record you made. But they ain't mentioned the one record that will remain unsurpassed and go unbroken and down through the ages. This is that you are the only man who ever took a ham sandwich to Paris."

Lindbergh laughed now. He was beginning to understand Will a little better.

The next day Lindbergh started to fly in a trimotored Ford plane, furnished by the Lincoln dealer Jack Maddux, from San Diego to Los Angeles, with eleven passengers, two of whom were Will and Betty. Now a personal note: in an interview Lindbergh remembered the incident and told me, "It was an all-metal plane and I was proud to be handling it. Will came up for a while with me in the cockpit. Finally he got out and I was alone. Some time after he left the cockpit, I noticed the plane was getting tail-heavy and realized that I was making excessive stabilizer adjustment to compensate for this condition. I passed some pretty uneasy moments after I reached the limit of the stabilizer adjustment and then had to keep pushing harder and harder on the stick to keep the nose of the plane in a normal flight position. In my years of flying I had never encountered anything like it. At that point, naturally, I looked back into the cabin. The cause of the trouble was apparent enough. All passengers but one (who was focussing a camera) had jammed back into the tail of the plane with Will Rogers to have their photographs taken. Y'see, I've encountered problems with photographers in more ways than one! When I saw this was the explanation of the trouble, I was no longer concerned. Today, in a modern plane, the hostess would keep the passenger weight distributed."

Will himself told the following incident of the flight (this happened while he was still in the cockpit). He used it to show that Lindbergh had a sense of humor. Will said, "How can you tell where to land when you don't know which way the wind is blowing?"

Lindbergh pointed to a washing of clothes flapping on a line. "That tells me," he said.

"Suppose it ain't Monday?" said Will.

"I just wait till it is," said Lindbergh, and Will laughed.

Before the plane had taken off, word had been brought to Lindbergh that a huge crowd was going to be at the airport in Los Angeles to see him. He had been handled roughly by crowds and didn't look forward to another free-for-all. So he asked the passengers if they would mind if he landed at the new Mines Airfield. The passengers agreed; any old where with Lindbergh would be all right with them. But when the landing was made it was rough; the field hadn't been leveled off and the people in the plane were tossed about like popcorn in a skillet. Lindbergh was most apologetic, when it was over, asking if anyone was hurt. No one had been. Will was impressed by this. "He took as good care of us as if we were settin' eggs," he said.

At about this time Will received an invitation from Dwight Morrow, Ambassador to Mexico, to visit him and to meet the president of Mexico. Mexico was Will's favorite country. His boyhood trip to South America had started his interest in Spanish American countries, so he readily agreed.

Morrow was earnest in trying to bring about better relations between the two countries, so he had invited Will and also had arranged for a Lindbergh Day.

It was not long before Will was in Mexico and was taken to meet President Calles. Three candidates for president had just been assassinated and the country was as nervous as a jumping bean. When Will advanced to meet President Calles he held up his hands in surrender and called out, "I ain't any rival. I'm not a political candidate for anything."

This was translated to Calles, who laughed and escorted Will aboard the presidential train in which he was to "do" Mexico.

Will was seeing the interior of Mexico — its power dams, its co-operatives, its agricultural development — and he was hearing about governmental loans to small landowners. At one place where the presidential train stopped for a few hours, a rodeo had been arranged on the Parbellon Ranch in honor of President Calles. Will borrowed a lariat, stepped out before the crowd and did some trick roping. Morrow was delighted. Here was really a good-will ambassador! Morrow had strong feelings on the best way to bring a proper understanding between the two countries; this informal way was better than all the state dinners in the world.

One morning Will went to the front end of the train to talk to the soldiers who were guarding it. When he got to the dining car he was late for breakfast. President Calles and a gaggle of Mexican officials were impatiently waiting. Calles smiled and chided through the interpreter, "Mr. Rogers, you've committed a breach of etiquette. You should have been here waiting when I arrived."

Will, with his quick wit, took care of that. "I'm awfully sorry, Mr. President. I've been in Mexico only four days but I'm getting an idea about it and the government. From what I see so far, it's better to stand in with the soldiers than with the president."

These were high days for Will. He called himself "Guillermo Rodriguez." He had conquered Europe; and now Mexico was his. But an embarrassing incident occurred. One night he was entertained at dinner by General Obregon, who once had been president of Mexico and who had made enemies. After dinner the men went into another room where the guests sat smoking (all except Will). General Obregon was a good storyteller and began to tell how, a few days previous, a man had stolen up and thrown a bomb at him. The bomb had gone off so close that Obregon had barely escaped with his life. Will sat close beside

General Obregon, listening raptly; the bombing of presidents was not in his line of thinking and he was all ears. Just at this moment, by chance, the lights at the uncertain power plant went out. General Obregon, knowing the habits of the power plant, remarked humorously, "They're getting ready to throw another bomb." Will caught the word bomb.

The lights were off a few seconds, then came back on and when they did, Will was on the other side of the room hiding behind a chair. The men twitted him. He was embarrassed and ill at ease and tried to joke his way out of his unheroic action, but did not do very well. This was one time the joke was on him. He was always sensitive about this, and rarely ever mentioned it.

Will visited the Chamber of Deputies where he found that the members were permitted to carry pistols. One of the men attached to the American Embassy asked him what he thought about this.

"Maybe it's a good idea. Maybe our congressmen ought to carry 'em. Then they wouldn't call each other liar so often. Why! in Washington that's gettin' to be the accepted form of greetin'."

Lindbergh arrived, twenty-seven and one-half hours in the air from Washington, D. C. The people went wild. Morrow's expectations were fully justified. He now had two good-will ambassadors.

When Lindbergh was brought to the Embassy, Will offered to give up his room and go to a hotel, but Morrow said Will was to stay and that he would give Lindbergh his own room. It came out a little different in his dispatch. "I offered to give up my room to Lindbergh, but Morrow said mine wasn't good enough and gave him his own."

The next day as Will was going into the Embassy he met Lindbergh coming out. Will asked Lindbergh where he was going and Lindbergh said he was going to take a short flight.

Will — seeing what he thought was a rare opportunity — asked if he could go along.

Soon they were at the airfield. Will looked at the plane; it was unusual. But that was all right, and soon the two were inside. When they got down, Will asked what kind of a plane it was. "Oh," said Lindbergh, "it's an old antiquated French plane used in the first part of the World War. I wanted to see if it would still fly." Will blinked. When he wrote of it afterward he said, "My only chance of ever bein' remembered after I'm gone would be to fall with Lindbergh."

Finally came that bane of civilization — the Ambassadorial dinner, which was held in the University Club. The evening droned along, then came the most depressing part of all — the speeches of good fellowship. These went on and on until the fellows were ready to fly at each other's throats. Poor Lindbergh sat there, looking as if he wished he were far out over the Atlantic. Finally Will was called on. He opened with his shocker: "I didn't come here to tell you that we look on you as brothers. Nope, not at all. We look on you as a lot of bandits. And you look on us as one big bandit." He paused, as he always did after such an opening, then continued, "So now we understand each other and don't have to depend on diplomacy. That's the only way people can get along together — when they are honest and tell what they think and get to understand each other." He continued in his humorous, truth-probing way: "A diplomat tells you what he don't believe himself, and the man he's tellin' it to don't believe him, so it balances. Diplomats meet and eat, then rush out and wire their Govament they've completely fooled the other fella. The reason I speak so freely about diplomats is that there is none here. America has none and you all down here haven't. Over in Europe is where they take 'em seriously, they breed 'em over there, that's the reason they have so many wars. Morrow he's different. He just represents the will of the people; he knows we don't hate you and that you don't hate us."

He continued to shock, flatter and cajole. Never did his listeners know one sentence ahead what he was going to say. Abruptly he paused, looked up and down the table and seemed to be studying the people. "Say, listen, we're in the University Club." He pointed accusingly at one of the guests. "Where's your sheepskin? You ain't got one and you know it. You're here under false pretenses. The best you can do is a score card at the golf club." He turned to another guest and demanded, "Where's your diploma? All you've got is a score card from your bridge club."

He went up and down the table, calling one person after another by name and telling what the person could do — dance, play polo, nothing of any educational stature.

He fixed his eye on Mrs. Morrow. "There at the head table is Mrs. Morrow. She's the only one who ought to be here. She got a degree at Smith. Then one day she went slumming to Amherst and got herself a husband."

Will went back to Los Angeles. He got two things out of his good-will trip. One was the need to keep Mexico as a friendly neighbor; the other was the importance of flying. In a Sunday article addressed to President Coolidge he wrote: "Keep after this air stuff, Calvin. Let's get all the planes we can, do all the commercial aviation we can to keep the boys in training, and get our navy fleet the biggest there is. If America has all these things, then we can just sit here and take care of our own business. You can bet nobody is goin' to come over and pounce on us."

Will Runs for President

As WILL GREW OLDER his dominant traits became more and more pronounced. One was that he was, first and last, a showman. He liked audiences; big or little, he must have an audience. If an audience responded, he would give it his great talents. And he would work as hard for a little audience as for a big one. For him there was an intoxication in standing before an audience and in seeing what he could "do" with it. Audiences were not limited to those who paid money to see him. To him an audience was any group that would listen. He liked to have an audience even at a chili counter, or on a train, or at an airport. It so happened, sometimes, that another person wanted the attention of the audience, too. Then there would be a contest. If the other person won, Will would abruptly stump off and leave the people. He loved audiences so much that when he attended a meeting at which he was not a speaker, he was unhappy until he could find an excuse to get out in front. Sometimes, when a speaker finished, Will would be discovered and would be called on. Then he was happy. He had his audience.

His attitude toward notables was changing. The year he had gone to Europe — the year he had admired Mussolini so extravagantly — he had been awed by foreign dignitaries. Now he was beginning to take them in his stride. He was no longer tremendously impressed. In fact, he began to deal with them almost casually. Sometimes his offhand manner startled them. Then they would laugh. It was just his American way. But Will, on his own side, was using them either in his lectures, or in his writings. They were all grist for his mill. For the most part, he liked them and they liked him. Indeed it would be hard to think of anyone not liking him. But some didn't. He had enemies. It was always a shock to him to find that someone didn't like him, but he didn't worry about it. His way of dealing with a person he didn't like was simple: he just kept out of the person's way.

He had discovered the audience appeal of an epitaph and often quoted one in his lectures. Each time he changed the phrasing as if unconsciously seeking exactly the right words. In Iowa City, Iowa, he said, "I've selected my epitaph. Here it is: 'Here lies Will Rogers. He joked about every prominent man of his time, but he never met one he disliked.'"

His great zest for life continued. And his amazing energy continued. When he wasn't working, he was resting. He frequently fell asleep while reading the papers. If the paper slipped from his hand and fell to the floor, he would look around self-consciously to see if anyone had noticed. If someone twitted him, he would say that the paper wasn't worth reading.

He was extremely proud of his teeth. They were white, strong and well-formed; he sometimes said he had never had toothache in his life. And he was proud of his eyes — "Injun eyes," he called them. But as he grew older his eyes began to give him trouble. He would have to hold the paper almost at arm's length. Sometimes he would stop and rub his eyes. He solved the problem in his own way. He went to a ten-cent store and to their box of spectacles, and tried them on, one after another, until he found a pair that suited him. Woolworth's were his first opticians. He developed an odd trait with the use and management of his glasses. When he was talking to someone, he would take them off and swing them around and around in his hand. Then he would put the ends of the frontals in his mouth and gnaw them. When the ends became twisted and out of shape, he would go back to Woolworth's and lay in a fresh supply. Once a count showed that he had eighteen pairs of gnawed spectacles in the drawer of his desk.

His love of money also continued. But after he got it he would treat it almost casually. He would spend large sums with, seemingly, hardly a moment's weighing. On top of this, his donations to charities were exceedingly generous. Not only would he "play" a benefit, but also he would put his hand in his pocket. In truth, no other figure in the American theater was so generous with his time and money.

Lesser traits stood out. One was that he would not kill an animal. The biggest game he had ever hunted was a rabbit, and this when a boy. He did not care to fish; outside of wetting a few lines in the Verdigris he had never caught a fish. He had no interest in golf; never played it, although, later, he had a four-hole course on his ranch. He had only a slight interest in baseball; this came chiefly through his acquaintance with some of the players; as an example, Mike Donlin whom he had known in vaudeville. But polo! That was something else. Rodeos, trail-drivers' meetings, chuck-wagon parties, roundups — Ah! that was living. He never grew tired of them.

His great pleasures were his family, travel, roping calves, going visiting. If he found a congenial group he would stay up till late at night, talking and reminiscing, "swapping stories." Sometimes at these little groups he was at his best, better than on the stage. He dominated every group; he was the funniest and the sunniest. His voice always could be heard over everybody else's.

Another trait that is hard to understand is that he did not realize his own great importance. He knew he was an international figure, but he didn't take it seriously. It just happened to work out that way, that was his attitude. And, strangely enough, the people around him and who worked with him every day did not realize his greatness. "Oh! That's just Will Rogers."

He took umbrage more and more easily. Although a world figure he would worry about a flea bite.

His unique talent was to be able to walk out in front of an audience, with no props at all, and bring that audience up to where it was shouting for more. By the sheer magic of his personality he could hold them, not just for an hour but for two hours, yea! for two and one-half hours. There has never been anything else like it in America.

He enjoyed his fame, and was always testing it out. On a train, on a plane, even as he walked down the street, he watched to see how many people recognized him. At night he liked to drop into a chili stronghold, sit down on a stool and see if the counterman recognized him. If he wasn't recognized he would lead the conversation around to where he could get the man to express himself on Will Rogers. If the man said something uncomplimentary (seldom) Will was delighted. Sometimes Will would leave without revealing who he was. If Will had a friend with him and the chili purveyor said something uncomplimentary about Will, then that was the end of a perfect day. But it was quite a different matter if someone said in print something uncomplimentary to Will. In spite of his repeating time after time that he was "just an ol', igerant cowboy," Will thought that his opinions should not be challenged.

So great was America's faith in him that people began to say he would make a good President. Every morning at a million breakfast tables he was putting into words what the average man was thinking. More and more the idea gained ground. Will himself didn't take it seriously. "There was a piece in the paper this morning that somebody was seriously proposing me for President. When that is done as a joke its all right, but when its done seriously then its just pathetic. This country hasn't quite got down to where it wants a professional comedian for President."

Will was a Democrat, but he had never voted and did not mess with politics. But politics had always been a deep and unwavering interest. His father, during the latter years of his life, had been a politician.

In spite of Will's disclaimer, interest in the idea grew. Among the thinking it could not be anything but a joke, but many people were completely serious. At this time Robert E. Sherwood was editing *Life* — not the present *Life* but the original *Life*, an out-and-out comic weekly, for the alleged humorous weekly was still flourishing: *Life*, *Puck*, *Judge*. They were all frisky colts kicking up their heels in the comedy field. Sherwood seized on the idea for his magazine. His letter:

"I certainly did run Will Rogers for President, in 1928, when I was still editor of *Life*. (Shortly after election day I was fired. That, thank God! marked the end of my editorial career.) The Rogers for President idea was hatched up by Fred Cooper, the artist, and me. I went to see Will in his room in, as I remember, the Hotel Astor, and talked him into it. He named it 'The Anti-Bunk Party.' He agreed to write several hundred words a week, giving his platform and campaign speeches. It is my recollection, possibly fallible, that we paid him $500 a week, which was a lot of money for *Life*, but peanuts to Will. We distributed thousands of campaign buttons with Will's picture and the party slogan, 'He Chews to Run' (an obvious pun on the Coolidge statement that he did not choose to run). We were given time on a local radio station for weekly broadcasts and had a lot of fun with this, getting such guest stars as Eddie Cantor, Leon Errol, Bob Benchley and Amelia Earhart. Will himself never appeared, as he had other radio commitments.

"Will didn't take much interest in the campaign and we had a time getting copy out of him. When he did get his copy in, it was very sketchy and never nearly enough to fill the space. So I filled it out, imitating Will's style as best I could. This had the unfortunate effect of convincing him that he need write practically nothing. I think, as a matter of fact, there were one or two weeks when he supplied nothing at all and I had to write the whole piece. He never complained about my work. The only allusion he ever made was once when he said with a slight grin, 'That was a pretty good piece I wrote for you last week. I think I ought to have a raise.' He and I were good friends and he asked me to write some stuff for him for the show that he did that fall in which he substituted for Fred Stone. I did this for no charge and continued to do it for weeks after the show opened in New York. But it was trifling stuff and far below the Rogers standard.

"I was told there was a large write-in vote for Will Rogers all over the country, but it was impossible to check the figures. In the issue that came out just after the election we claimed that Rogers carried the District of Columbia overwhelmingly; we explained that this was particularly significant, since the people of the District are the ones who have to live with the guy for the next four years.

"This is a little beside the point, but I do want to add it. I once saw Will give a show which must be unique in theatrical history. It was a Sunday night 'charity' with a very high society audience. Will was the whole show. He came out on the bare stage, with no props other than his gum. He started at 8:40 and, with one ten-minute intermission, talked until half-past eleven. He had them in stitches all the time. I doubt if there ever was any other man in the world who could have done that. He was truly a great man."

As nomination time approached, Will decided he would fly to the Republican Convention in Kansas City, take that in, then go to Houston where the Democrats were to have their high jinks. It didn't work out quite that way. At Las Vegas, New Mexico, the plane ran out of gas and the pilot had to come down in a hurry. In fact he came down in such a hurry that the plane landed on its back. Will was shaken up and was still dazed when he was helped out. But even in this condition his ability to twist a quip out of a situation did not desert him. "I'm the first candidate to land on his head and, bein' a candidate, it didn't hurt me." The severe shake-up didn't dampen his enthusiasm for flying. He still believed as he had when he had written, "Keep after the air stuff, Calvin."

When the Democrats opened in Houston, Will was on hand; and with his quips, too. When a reporter asked him if he were a candidate he said, "I sure am an' I ought to make a good one. No one knows how I stand." He wrote: "It took the chairman twenty minutes of steady hammering with his gavel to get the convention to listen to a prayer — then the preacher read it, endin' up with the Lord's prayer. He read this, too. I'm goin' to keep goin' to these conventions till I find a preacher who can pray from memory." When the band played "Dixie" he said, "In Texas that's as sure fire as a flask."

The weather was hot. The convention dragged on. It became deadlocked. One night when the weary delegates were slumped in their chairs half asleep, votes were cast for Will Rogers. There were no banners, no placards, no parades, as so ambitiously shown in the motion picture supposedly of his life. There were hand cheers and applause, but that was all.

In 1932 the same thing was, in a way, repeated. The Democratic convention dragged on. The hour grew late. Finally Governor "Alfalfa Bill" Murray got to his feet and cast all of Oklahoma's twenty-two votes for Will Rogers. Will, who was in a doze, came to. His eyes fluttered in that delicious stage between sleep and wakefulness, then completely closed and he was asleep again, thus becoming, so far as is known, the only candidate who ever slept through roll call for nomination to the great office of President of the United States.

CHAPTER 22

Will Makes His First Talking Picture. The Stock Market Crash

THINGS HAD NOT BEEN going too well with me. Then one day I had a telephone call from Al Lewis, eastern story editor of Twentieth Century-Fox, at 1776 Broadway, New York, to come in and see him about an "idea." I got in so quickly he must have thought I was downstairs.

He said he had heard of me and maybe sometime his company could utilize my services. I tried to look agreeable. Then he said that Winfield R. Sheehan was coming East from Hollywood and had asked him to round up for inspection a number of possible stories and that Mr. Sheehan was going to get off the train at Hutchinson, Kansas, and telephone and ask if he had found anything halfway presentable. Then Al Lewis said it had occurred to him that maybe he should include *They Had To See Paris* in this list.

My heart leaped like a fish at sunset.

This book had been up and down like a pump handle. Movie editors were always walking out with it but none had ever asked it to be a bride. Once Paramount had offered me $18,000 for this story for W. C. Fields and I had walked home on air. Then another of those heartbreaking silences. I had waited at the church, too proud to ask what had happened to the groom. Finally, swallowing my pride, I went in to see Paramount. Well, they'd just had a salesmen's convention at Atlantic City and Fields's picture *The Old Army Game* had not been favorably previewed, and they were not going ahead with Fields as they had planned. I went home by Long Island Railroad.

I told Al Lewis that I thought it would be nice to include *They Had To See Paris* in this list. He said the best thing to do would be to draw up a five-day option; nothing would come of this but it would show his boss that he was on the job. I said that I wanted to help him out with his boss. He said that maybe sometime I could go to Hollywood and work for his company. I explained that I was very busy but that I would consider it. He pondered and said that he would make out the five-day option for the nominal sum of $5000. I was pleased; soon I would be in Hollywood on the payroll at a fat figure. And so, on yellow paper, the option was drawn up.

Four days later the telephone rang. Would I kindly come in? When I got in, Al Lewis looked uncomfortable. A most surprising thing had happened; it was, he announced, typical of Hollywood. Mr. Sheehan had decided to take up the option on my story.

I was pleased. Well, at last! A little meat in the pot was better than none at all.

The story, I thought, was for Chic Sale. Well, that was fine. He was really a great artist. Maybe I would be asked to work on the scenario.

One day, Glendon Allvine (an old *Kansas City Star* boy) called up from the publicity department of Twentieth Century-Fox and said, "Do you know who is going to play your story?"

"Chic Sale."

"Will Rogers is going to play it."

I was wholly and completely astonished. My old neighbor! The great, the wonderful, the magic Will Rogers. A few days later the wonderful telephone rang again. Would I come in and meet Will Rogers who was going to play my story? I said I would.

It was a moment for me when I came in. Present were Al Lewis, who was so importantly figuring in my life, Owen Davis and Will Rogers. Will Rogers looked at me curiously. "Say, don't I know you?"

"I live in Forest Hills. I guess that's where you saw me."

"Sure it is! Of course that's it. Do you know Fred Stone?"

I had to tell him I didn't.

I tried to talk to Owen Davis, but did not get very far, for he is not a man to throw words around just to be jolly. Then I kept quiet.

Later Al Lewis said he would take us to lunch and we all started down the street together. Will had a peculiar way of talking to you and, at the same time, looking to see if people recognized him. Two men who were partly back in a doorway saw him and called out, "Hello, Will!" He was visibly pleased. I expected at lunch that Will and the others would talk about the picture that Will was to be in, but they hardly mentioned it.

After lunch Will and I walked together a short distance, me very proud indeed. He asked me where I was from. I told him, but the town was so small he had never heard of it. He asked me why, since I wasn't from Oklahoma, I had written a story about the state. I had to tell him that I had got the idea of a family striking oil and taking the daughter to France to marry her to a count, and that I had located the story in Oklahoma because it sounded real.

It was not until later that I found out why my story had been selected. It wasn't quite as flattering as I had thought. When Will had returned from abroad, Winfield R. Sheehan approached him to do a talking picture, but Will said, "I've had my bellyful of pictures." Sheehan urged him, pointing out how well others were doing in pictures. Will still hesitated and was self-distrustful, as he always was about anything new that was proposed. He hadn't done well in silent pictures; was there any reason to believe he would prosper in talking pictures? At last he gave in a little, but would say neither Yes nor No, which was a characteristic when important decisions were being arrived at.

At last he said he would be willing to take a whack at talking pictures if he could play *The County Chairman*. This was a play by George Ade, in which Macklyn Arbuckle was appearing. Al Lewis and Sheehan were delighted; it would fit him like the wallpaper, they said. But when they went to buy the talking rights they found a dog at the door; the story had once been made as a silent picture and had briars all over it. They did buy the talking rights for $20,000, but it had so many whereases they decided not to go ahead with it.

Meantime, Owen Davis had read my book and suggested it. And now the people who had taken Will on had to unsell him on *The County Chairman* and talk up my story as the one they had hoped to get all along. Will regarded this with sour suspicion. A copy of the book was given him. He didn't read it, but Betty reported on it favorably. He trusted her judgment and said he would play the story. Thus it was that my telephone rang. There had not been quite the popular clamor for my story that I had thought. But it had been sold. I was to be the author of the first talking picture for Will Rogers. I would get to know him.

One day the telephone rang again; I sped to it with the dispatch that a writer has for any legitimate break in his work. It was Will Rogers. Wouldn't I like to come in that night to see *Three Cheers?* I said I would.

This was the musical play attracting attention at the time because of the dramatic set of circumstances back of it. Fred Stone was to play the lead, but had broken both legs in an airplane accident in Connecticut when he was trying to pilot the plane himself. When Will heard of it he was on a lecture tour, but immediately wired Fred that he would try to take his place, as he put it. This would mean the cancellation of his lecture dates, but Will was prepared to do this. And soon he was in the play and soon it opened. The press agent seized on the combination of circumstances and made endless publicity for the play by announcing that Charles B. Dillingham, the producer, each week gave Will a blank signed check and told him to fill it in for whatever he thought was fair and just. It was a pretty story but not quite accurate, for Dillingham paid Will $5000 a week. There is reason to believe that Will shared some of this with Fred. It is worth pausing here to tell how the amount paid was discovered. John Chapman, drama critic of the *New York Daily News*, was looking around for a news item and went to William and Harry Brandt, the movie-chain operators, who had bought the old Globe Theater and taken over the Dillingham offices. In the office was an ancient safe which John Chapman seems to have approached with the unerring instinct of a reporter. When he tried the door, lo and behold! it opened. The place was a pack rat's nest of old papers and there, in the welter, he found a bundle of canceled checks made out to Will Rogers, signed by Dillingham and marked "weekly. *Three Cheers*." If properly approached, Mr. Chapman will show you one of these checks, with Will's signature on the back. Use my name.

That night I sat up in front, a pleasant novelty. I thought it was the best musical comedy I had ever seen. I laughed like Fred Tejan. Then suddenly came something I wasn't expecting. Will edged out and peered over the audience. I straightened up slightly and sho' nuff he asked me to stand. I obliged him.

"Folks, you see that long, lanky fella standin' there? Well, that's Homer Croy who wrote the book called *They Had to See Paris*. I've just signed a contract to make a movie of it and it'll be my first talkin' picture. Homer, who is that lady you got with you?"

I mumbled something about my wife.

"How did you ever fool her into marryin' you? Listen, Mrs.

Homer, if you come out to Hollywood, you watch him. I've got the same wife I took to Hollywood but that's so unusual they stand around on street corners and talk about it. Homer, you know Dorothy." I said I didn't. "Well, you ought to. You're neighbors. And there, settin' near you, Homer is — hey! stand up, Doc. Folks, this is Dr. P. G. White. He ripped out my gallstones."

This was about all. It was nice to be introduced in a Broadway theater by Will Rogers. I liked it.

The play was a substantial success; after it closed its New York run it went out on the road. Will continued to introduce people from the audience just as he had done in the *Follies*. On the opening night in Boston, Babe Ruth was in the audience, and with him his bride. Sitting near Babe was the new Secretary of the Navy, Charles Francis Adams. Will introduced Babe Ruth and talked about him a few moments, then introduced Adams and talked about him; then he introduced the two men to each other. Babe plumped over and shook the hands of the Secretary and all was well.

There was a pause. "Now, folks," began Will, "I've got somebody else in the audience I want to introduce to you." Then he addressed Babe Ruth and the Secretary. "I've got to tell you two men that the man I'm goin' to introduce is bigger than either of you; in fact, he's bigger than the two of you put together." There was a pained silence. The two men looked at each other, not knowing what to think or do. But Will knew what he was doing. "That's what I mean — he's bigger than the two of you together. He's the giant from the Ringling Circus. Stand up, son."

The giant who had been sitting quietly in a box now rose. It was one of the biggest laughs that Will ever got in the theater.

The show finally closed in Pittsburgh, June 1, 1929. It had been a success.

At this time something on a national scale haunted Will, and this was a growing uneasiness that all was not well with our country. People were making money and not having to work. Too many silk shirts, too few callused hands. He mentioned this in his daily piece and in his Sunday articles, each time with increasing apprehension. But no one paid any attention. Money grew on trees and under the trees were baskets. "Things are goin' just fine in this country, if you want to look at it that way. We don't have no economic problem. If we want a thing, all we have to do is to buy it on credit."

One night Will went to Dinty Moore's for dinner, as he often did. At one of the tables was Eddie Cantor and Will sat down with him. Eddie was glowing. He was telling how he was getting rich playing the stock market. "Why, I've made more in one month than I did in two years on the stage!" Turning to Will he said, "Are you getting yours?"

Will shook his head. "I'm getting some by workin'."

Eddie looked at him pityingly; then very earnestly began to tell Will he should put every dollar he could scrape up in Wall Street. "I'll give you the name of my man at the Manufacturers' Trust Company and he will fix things up for you. This is the time to clean up, Will. I know because I'm doing it. You're a fool if you don't get in on this."

Will was obdurate. "I've always had to work for mine. When I get a little money I put it in land or life insurance."

"Do you mean to tell me you haven't *any* money in Wall Street?" asked Eddie incredulously.

"No, not a penny."

For some time Cantor sat there, punching Will on the arm and advising him to dip from the golden stream, but Will was not persuaded. "There's something wrong with all this, Eddie. I'm going to keep on working for a livin'."

The end came quicker than even Will — who was especially

prescient on current and national affairs — realized. The stock market crash of 1929! Eddie Cantor was wiped out. Will did not lose a cent.

He saw how serious the national situation was and felt that he must do what he could to help keep up the morale of the country and so started to joke about conditions. "Why, in New York they are havin' to stand in line to get a window to jump out of. Speculators are sellin' space for bodies in the East River. This winter Prosperity is goin' to be enjoyed by everybody lucky enough to get a place in the poorhouse."

Conditions grew worse. The more serious they grew, the more he joked. In fact, conditions were so serious that Eddie Cantor started a newspaper column, thinking that was a soft way to make money. In almost no time at all the column failed and Eddie was back on the stage earning it the easy way.

Meantime the motion picture was moving forward and I was walking around so people could see me. At last came the great day: the picture was completed. We were to have a private preview; that great day my wife and I and Mr. and Mrs. Owen Davis went to a little, stuffy private viewing room on Tenth Avenue, New York. I was silent and nervous . . . what if it was no good? Suddenly a shaft of light shot out and there it was! Will was talking. Talking my very words . . . out of Owen Davis. But the very words I had set down in the book. He had no make-up and he did not seem to be acting. Why, anybody could do what he was doing! An actor should act. Then I began to get the effect of the story and the way it was presented. During the whole run-off I didn't chirp a word. Finally it was over out in the great warehouse of a place. I didn't know what I thought. Only one impression was uppermost: the picture wasn't as good as it should be.

We escaped to the street and there Owen Davis spoke for the first time. "It has a great sense of reality," he said.

He said a few more things as we stood in front of that barn, then climbed into a taxicab, and my wife and I walked to the subway. I felt down.

Out in Hollywood, Will was having his troubles. During the making of the picture he had been self-distrustful. He would be repeating his silent-movie history. He was a director's delight; he would do exactly as told. Finally, after three months, the picture was done. It was to be given a Hollywood preview. Seats were to be sold at an extravagant price; notables would be as thick as crab grass. As the time approached and the plans for the preview matured, he became more and more nervous and more and more apprehensive. Suddenly he astonished the studio people by announcing that he would have to go back to Oklahoma. He couldn't do that, the studio executive said. He had business to attend to, he said, and mounted a plane and was soon in Tulsa. But he was not his gay, bantering self. He was dispirited and refused to have his picture taken — a bit of history in itself. N. G. Henthorne, of the *Tulsa World*, arranged a luncheon. Suddenly, at the luncheon, Will's mood changed and he became a torrent of words — they poured out, no one else could wedge in a sentence. He talked exceedingly well, as he always did, for he was the greatest table conversationalist in America. He brought up his father, anxious to see what the others thought of him. They thought well, for he had been a power and influence in the developing of early-day Oklahoma. Will was pleased and, from time to time, called him "Papa."

The next day he received a telegram from Betty. "The picture has opened and you can come home now."

He didn't go home immediately. He would have a little fun, typical Will Rogers fun — the fun of a man who never hunted, fished, or played golf. He'd run down to Texas and see Jim Minnick — Jim Minnick who had been the first one to ride a running horse on the stage for him. Jim was prosperous now; he had been dealing in polo ponies and had, in addition, a big horse ranch in the mountains. The two talked far into the night, but were up shortly after dawn and started to drive from Amarillo, Texas, to Cimarron, New Mexico — quite a jump. They drove half the night, tackled it again the next morning and drove all day, just looking and talking. Jim's horse ranch was above timberline. The two went as far as they could by car, then mounted horses and for two days they rode, just the two of them, talking and yarning and enjoying life. Then Will told Jim he would have to lope back to California. Soon Will was back in California; he'd had a wonderful time.

He went to see the picture and was pleased with it. It was getting fine praise and Hollywood was now talking of him as a new movie star.

And I, in New York, was truly astonished by the success of the picture. All my early doubts and fears were gone. How could I have ever doubted, I asked myself. Now and then I thought of the price. . . . In the meantime I found that Will had got $50,000 for making the picture; and, later, I found that the company had made a profit on it of half a million dollars. But that was part of the business of trying to write.

Soon afterward, out of a clear sky, I had the chance to go to Hollywood.

CHAPTER 23

Will in Hollywood.
Stands by His Old Friends

WILL THE GREAT celebrity had exactly the same traits and characteristics he had had when he was a child. But now they were more marked. One was his ceaseless physical energy. Another was his friendliness. Another his interest in political affairs. Another was his honesty and integrity. And now, to these, was added his love of his family. He had him a nice mess of Cherokee kids an' a mighty good and understanding mother for 'em.

Also to his interests was being added his enthusiasm for flying; it fitted exactly with his nervous, always-on-the-go temperament. By this time he had had two accidents, but he gave them hardly a second thought. In one, he had cracked two ribs and, for weeks, had to go around trussed up like a Christmas goose. But that was all right; didn't amount to nothin'. In almost every speech he made, he extolled air travel; he mentioned it in his Sunday articles and in his daily telegrams. To this he added his belief that if this country had plenty of planes and if we "kept our noses clean" we would never have trouble with any other nation.

Even though he was now fifty-one, his gusto for life was growing instead of waning. He was doing what he wished to do and was enjoying it thoroughly. And his health was good, except now and then when his chili got him down. But in a meal or two he would be all right again and back on his beloved chili. And beans. He loved them, too. Oklahoma beans were best.

Nobody really knew how to cook 'em except the folks back in Oklahoma.

His desire to have a good time was as pronounced as when he had gone to the stomp dances. At any party he was the loudest and most boisterous person present; and the funniest and best-liked. When he came into a room, its tempo shot up. But by many he was considered casual and unreliable; this was his way of putting fun and living ahead of business. "He can't be pinned down," they said. And certainly this was true — at least from a businessman's point of view. He refused to make plans. "I might want to be doin' something else on that day," he would say. Suddenly, out of a clear sky, he would say, "I've got to go to South America," and in just no time at all he would be on his way. The businessman would call up to tell Will that he wanted to see him and would find that Will was God knows where. "When is he coming back?" he would ask the family. The family never knew; no one knew, Will least of all. Then, later, the businessman would be surprised to have Will come sauntering in. Will's method of entering into a contract shook Hollywood till the orange trees bent over as if in a great wind. The lawyers went to work on a contract between Will and the Twentieth Century-Fox, and at last came forth with an impressive document. "What does it say?" Will asked Winfield R. Sheehan, just then the sun. Sheehan explained in detail, then gave the papers to Will. Will picked up a pen and wrote across the outside of the contract, "I ain't read this but Winnie Sheehan says its all right and thats good enough for me. Will Rogers." Hollywood heard this and blinked; what kind of duck had come among them, anyway?

But the duck wasn't to be sneezed at; in one picture he had become a star and had the promise of making real money. This latter, alone, was enough to make Hollywood cross itself. But he was not a part of Hollywood. He did not go to its parties, he did not take part in its activities, unless it was for some benefit.

From early days he had talked of buying a ranch; after he had been married it had been of buying a ranch, settling down and giving up vaudeville. And now, since he felt he would be in Hollywood for some time, he bought a ranch at Santa Monica, the first he had ever owned. It became his passion. He gave it far more thought and effort than he did his motion-picture career. Indeed, his motion-picture career seemed to be a sideline. Sometimes, when one was with him, he would go a whole evening without speaking of pictures. His ranch — his boyhood days in Oklahoma — his days in South America and South Africa — his experiences in vaudeville — these were the things he talked about.

At about this time I had my first letter from him. Here it is, just as he wrote it, spelling and punctuation, no date. He never messed with periods:

My Dear Mr. Croy,
    Say why havent you been around to see me, I couldent tell you whre to come for I never know whre I will be but we have one of the Bungalows at the Beverley Hills Hotel,
    We are still unsettled on a story, I am trying my best to get "So this is London", They want me to do some little concocted thing they made up on the lot, sort of a "Story of your life affair, I want to do somebody elses life I have done mine pretty thoroughly already. I would like to see you and have a chat, call up, Regards to you and the Lady
                                                                WILL ROGERS

He had his way and they put him in *So This Is London* (price $60,000) and used the same basic story elements that had appeared in the first one: Will thrown up against a foreign background in which he was humble, but packed with good, sound sense. And he had to solve a young love affair. In his silent pictures he had played romantic parts but Romance no longer rode the range with him. So now he had to fix it up for the Young Things who got all snarled up in its toils. *So This Is London* was a success.

The studio weighed the future. Will must be brought back to America; he couldn't forever loiter on foreign shores making sage remarks and settling tangled skeins, so Owen Davis and I were teamed together to write a picture patriotically to be called *See America First*. This was the day when tourist camps were a novelty; some had platforms for entertainers. The headlights of the cars were turned on the improvised stage and there the travelers would skip and hop and have their fun. The film was to tell the story of the tourist camps, almost from coast to coast, with Will doing a great deal of skipping and hopping and solving the love situation that had so completely baffled everybody else. Owen Davis and I flew into it. Every day or two Will would come around and ask how the story was getting along. We told him how extremely good it was; it would be as good as *They Had to See Paris*, I said modestly.

We worked two months, then turned it in. In a few days "the front office" called up and said they liked it tremendously.

"That's ominous," said Owen Davis.

This seemed to me an absurd point of view. I knew the story was good, Owen Davis liked it and the front office was enthusiastic. What else could one want? Owen still shook his head. "I don't like the looks of things," he muttered.

Time soon revealed he had underestimated the story's chances, for the office suddenly changed its plans for Will; the story was put on the shelf and, for all I know, is still there gathering smog.

The film company began to realize what a big fish had swum into its net and wanted to do everything humanly possible for its new star. They built a Spanish bungalow on the lot for him. It was magnificent; it looked like something from Granada improved by American imagination. It had a shower bath, a fireplace where one could dream of the dons, and an office that must have taken days of planning and preparation and in which no man in his right mind would want to stay longer than to make a telephone call. The bungalow was next door to John McCormack's — the very John McCormack Will had heard sing at the St. Louis World's Fair.

The gesture of the Spanish bungalow was well meant, but Will had always had the simplest of dressing rooms; the one in the old days at the New Amsterdam theater was an example. And now he was the occupant of a magnificent bungalow. He shunned it as one would quicksand. Once I went in with him and all that he had in it was a pair of boots and a bootjack. There was a couch to rest his weary bones. I asked him if he didn't, at least, use the couch.

"No. I go out to the car and curl up there."

Another reason, I found on questioning him further, was that if he lay down on the couch somebody was sure to peek through the door and he would have to get up and be host. So he stayed away from the bungalow with a simple determination that could not be shaken. The bigwigs could not understand it; the publicity men were baffled. Will wouldn't co-operate, they said; he didn't understand the picture business.

Meanwhile he went on being completely and wholly himself.

One of his problems was to keep from seeing all the people who wanted to see him. He had met so many people in all parts of the world that it was hard to keep them straight. Some way or other, all these people seemed to get to California and into the studio and onto the sound stage. He was extraordinarily generous about giving up his time to them, but sometimes — especially when he wanted to get out to the ranch — he got a little more than he wanted. One day he indicated a man who was standing beyond the visitors' line on the sound stage and said, "Do you know who he is?"

I looked and saw a shortish man with an up-and-coming beard. I did not know who he was.

"That bird has sent word that he knows me and wants to see me. I want you to find out who he is and come and tell me."

I edged over as circumspectly as I could. Of all things — it was Jo Davidson, the sculptor!

They had met at the Savoy, in London and, it seems to me, some other place.

I then led Jo Davidson up to Will, who was glad to see him. Jo reminded Will that, in London, he had asked Will to pose for him and that Will had said, "You lay off me, you ol' head hunter."

Will's amazing physical activity continued. He was writing his Sunday feature and his daily squib. The tourist problem was a trying one. Every visitor to Southern California wanted to see him. Will would always put on an entertainment. The executives had callers they wanted to impress and would herd them straight to Will who was never too tired, or too disinterested, to put on a show. He would talk to them and make them laugh. And then, after a busy day at the studio, he would go home to his ranch — not to rest but to rope. In no time at all he would be on a horse and a rope would be over Will's head like a halo.

Another trait was his intense loyalty to his boyhood friends; anyone from Oklahoma had him by the ear. And he was just as loyal to the Negroes with whom he had grown up as he was to the whites. Aunt Babe and Uncle Dan Walker have been mentioned. Uncle Dan, it will be remembered, was the first person to teach him how to rope. Always, when Will came home, he went to see his two black friends.

And now, for a moment, the story leaves Hollywood and goes to Joe Galbreath, a rancher who lives near Talala, Oklahoma.

He knew Will and he had known Aunt Babe and Uncle Dan since he was a child.

One day, in 1933, Aunt Babe came to Joe, greatly perturbed. She had written four letters to Mr. Willie in Hollywood, and hadn't heard from him. Had Mr. Willie forgotten her? It was hard to believe, but he was now a great man and sometimes big people forget little people.

Her boy Eli was in trouble, she said; he'd fell out with his wife and had taken a shot at her when she was fleeing down the street. He shouldn't have done this, but it had been did and he was now in jail in Bartlesville, and the law was tryin' to send him to the pen. "An' Mister Willie don't pay no attention to my letters."

"I'll see what I can do," said Joe and sent off a telegram. There was no response. Well, maybe it was as Aunt Babe had said. . . .

And then one day a telegram came from Will to Joe from Kansas City telling him to meet the two o'clock plane at the Tulsa Municipal Airport. Joe thought that Will wanted to buy some land, for Joe was a land appraiser. When Joe got to the airport, he found six or seven bigwigs, among them he remembers Waite Phillips, Joe Hoge and Charles W. Short, Junior. They were a kind of reception committee. They surged forward, shouting and waving their welcome, leaving Joe in the backwash. When Will came out he glanced over the men, and shot a glance at Joe. There was much hand-shaking and laughter. Several minutes passed. Then the men started into the building. As Will passed Joe, he shook hands with him; when Joe opened his hand a note was in it, a note that Will had written on the plane.

"Meet me in 10 minutes in the men's lounge so we can talk alone."

Joe, being a son of the rolling prairie and not used to the baffling ways of the city, thought the men's lounge was a place where they drank cocktails. He inquired and was told that there was no men's lounge at the airport. He went to the colored porter and asked him what was the best thing to do.

"You go to the men's room; that's what he means."

In a few minutes Will came in. "Hi there, Joe. Is this the place where you entertain your friends?"

There was (in Joe's words) some tomfoolishness for a few moments, then Will said, "Say, what is this about Aunt Babe's boy gettin' himself into trouble? I got your telegram and asked around and found that Aunt Babe had wrote me, but Sandy Blake had thought it was just another person wantin' help and had put the thing in the back lot."

As Joe told him the situation, Will grew serious, then finally said, "I want to do all I can for Aunt Babe and Uncle Dan. I want you to go to Bartlesville and get Eli out of jail. Here's some working capital." He wrote a check on his knee. "You go an' see a fellow named Bill Hurt and tell him to get Eli out of jail. He's a lawyer. I think he'll remember me."

Joe stuffed the lawyer's name into one pocket of his ranch shirt, and the check into another; soon he was bounding toward Bartlesville. When he got there he reached into his pocket for the lawyer's name, but he had lost it and could not remember it. He went to the courthouse and to an office marked prosecuting attorney. He asked the man if he could tell him the names of the lawyers in Bartlesville; he would recognize the one he wanted. "That's a pretty big job," said the prosecuting attorney; picking up a list he read the names — twenty-seven in all. But the name he wanted was not there.

"I've given you all the names except my own which is "William F. Hurt."

Joe jumped. "You're the man I want."

Then Joe told him that he had come to see about getting a colored boy out of trouble — Eli Walker by name. "You're a little late," said Mr. Hurt. "He's been sentenced and will go off to McAlester Monday morning."

Joe was put down. Then he said that he was there at the behest of Will Rogers and that Will had told him to come to Mr. Hurt. The man stared. "You mean Will Rogers, the comedian?"

"Yes."

The man was delighted. "Does he remember me? I met him only once and that was years ago."

They discussed the situation. Finally the man said, "If Will Rogers says that Eli Walker is a good boy, we've got to do something about it."

The two went to the jail and there, indeed, was Eli, his head down, his spirits even lower. "We've come to get you out. Will Rogers wants you let out."

Eli's face lighted up. "I knew he would. My mother wrote me a note in a biscuit and said she had sent word to Will Rogers an' I knew he would do it."

After the unfathomable ways of lawyers, there was a new trial. This was held after dark, yet a large crowd was in attendance. One of Will's boyhood friends was there — Hamp Scudder, a rancher and county commissioner. Eli was freed on the ground of insufficient evidence. He is alive and kicking today and, as I write this, is running a barbecue stand in Bartlesville, Oklahoma, where he is delighted to tell the story of how Mister Willie helped him get his feet from the second floor of the jail onto (as he puts it) solid ground.

Will's old friends came to him more frequently than ever. He could not resist their appeals. Ed Echols told me how Will helped him . . . only it didn't turn out quite that way.

Ed Echols is, as I write, a famous figure in Arizona, "the last of the old-time cowboys."

Ed is the real article. He was born and "brung up" in San Antonio, Texas, and has a drawl that makes you wish you had a recording tape. In 1912, Calgary, Canada, put on its first "Calgary Stampede." Ed walked off with cash prizes amounting to $1500 and the title of World's Champion Steer Roper.

During the summer of 1901, he roped with Will at San Antonio; he found that he was just three days older than Will. Will entered the steer-roping contest and when the steer came out of the gate and into the arena, Will and his pony lit out after it and soon overtook it, says Ed. Will swung his rope as purty as you please and landed, but the steer jerked Will's horse down, instead of the other way 'round. Will cleared himself of leather and hoss flesh with not a watch-tick to spare.

Johnny Blocker (one of the judges) came up to Will and said, "Will, the next time the steer throws your horse, you go right ahead and tie the horse and we'll give you 'time' on it."

Will could laugh at what Johnny Blocker had said. Will was, says Ed, a fella who could take a joke on himself.

Ed Echols saw Will from time to time. In 1930, Ed decided to take a whirl at politics. He was living in Pima County, Arizona, on a ranch, but his post office address was Benson, Cochise County, which was a horse of another color. He wanted to be elected sheriff of Pima County, but knew it would be tough going. So he bethought himself of Will. Ed speaking:

"I didn't tarry but hit out for L. A. where Will was makin' pictures for some studio or other. I finally got to his ranch an' he says, 'I'm saddled with some Texas oil men. You set on the porch till they leave,' which I done. When they were gone, I told him what I wanted and we gassed a while. Then he said, 'Come out to the stables and I'll show you my things.' My eyes were big as full moons, so many trophies did he have. As we walked here and there he had a rope in his hand and would spin it, now and then tossin' it over a post or any object it would encompass. Finally he says, 'What's on your mind, Ed?'

" 'I'm out for sheriff,' I says, 'and I need your help.'

" 'Money?'

" 'No, I need you to make a speech in my favor. Mostly they're cattle people and they'll do about anything you say. You can elect me, if you'll do it, Will.'

"He looked at me kind of funny, tucking his chin down and lookin' at me from under his eyebrows, which was his manner of doin'. 'Sure, I'll do it, Ed' he says hearty. 'You say the election is in about two months. Sometime between now and then I have to fly to Mexico City. I'll stop off long enough to give the voters a sales talk on you. I won't tell 'em the truth, I'll just tell 'em favorable things.' He roped another post. 'I won't know more'n a day or two ahead. I'll wire the mayor, the chamber of commerce and the newspapers, an' maybe they can turn out a crowd. I won't mention your name so the hoss thief runnin' against you won't know anything about it and start up a rival attraction. Is that all right, Ed?'

" 'It shore is, Will. I appreciate it and I'm reasonable certain it'll turn the election.'

"Will grinned. 'Us ole cowpokes have got to stick together.'

"Well, Will sent the telegrams just like he said he would. I reckon he never made a promise he didn't fulfill. I wasn't there, bein' in Tucson, an' didn't know anything about the speakin'. Half the town was down to welcome him and, after some preliminaries, took him out to the park where there was a band and a speaker's platform. He made a wonderful speech. Amongst other things he said, 'I've known Ed Echols half my life. He was raised up in San Antone where they raise the best sheriffs in the world. A man down there who don't aspire to be sheriff is considered a suspicious character, maybe with outlaw leanin's.' Suddenly, as he talked, a wind sprung up. Will was quick on the trigger. 'Don't be alarmed about that wind, folks. The Legislature is in session.'

"He went on speakin', from time to time insertin' that I was a deservin' man. Finally he finished and went back to the airport where the plane was waitin' and flew off, no doubt goin' to Mexico City.

"Well, that was just mighty fine and I appreciated it. I don't know any other man who would gone to that much trouble. But there was a slight mistake. Will, as I found later, had looked at the map and saw that Douglas was the largest town in Cochise County and, since I was gettin' my mail at Benson, he thought that was where I was runnin' from. In other words he got the two counties mixed up and made my campaign speech in the county where I wasn't runnin'. It nearly broke my heart, when I found out about it. I lost the election by 480. If Will had spoke in the right county, I would won by 4800. That's what I figger."

It worked out all right later for Ed Echols, for in 1936 he was elected sheriff of Pima County and was re-elected four times, thus serving ten years, a record. He is, as I write, a constable in Pima County — emphatically not Cochise County. He says Will was a great speechmaker. He would have loved to have heard him.

Will's success as a picture player made the business office hop in all directions at once. He was money and they meant to keep him working. But there was the matter of material. Finally the business office came forth with the idea that Will should do a sequel to *They Had to See Paris*, using, in main, the same set of characters, but laid in the United States. I worked out an idea along this line. One day, when I was at the ranch, Will said, "Have you got a story idea for me yet?"

I said I had and took from my pocketbook a crumpled sheet of blue paper on which I had typed an outline: "An American family in the Midwest has been living high. Suddenly a depression comes along and impoverishes them. They are defeated for the time being, but pluck up their courage and make a success of a new life in a small and unpretentious home under new conditions."

He stood in the patio, holding it in his hand and reading it. "I think there might be something to it. Let me show it to the bosses."

It was not long until I was called in to "develop" the idea. This meant writing off a "treatment" of five thousand words, outlining the action.

Then followed the mysterious and baffling silence all studios have when you give them your heart. Finally word came "it might do," but for me to develop it still further. I turned in a still more extended outline — then happy day! It was accepted — so far as I know the shortest story idea ever submitted in Hollywood.

An item is worth noting. Fifi Dorsay was the French girl in the story. I brought her to Oklahoma and gave her a number of scenes. Suddenly, from the bosses, came word to "write her out." Her agent wanted too much, and out went poor Fifi. (And out went some of the story value, too.) Eddie Burke and I started to write the screenplay. He was an old hand at the business, with a string of successes as long as a pasture fence.

Finally *Down to Earth* was done — the only sequel Will ever played and the only "original." It was a minor picture and was not a real success. I worked eleven weeks and was paid a thousand dollars a week. From the picture one thing important in Will's life did come and this was the idea to use only "tested material"; that is, to appear only in stories that had proved themselves in other fields, such as book form, or stage plays. After this he never deviated from this principle.

There is one small item I must put in and here, I suppose, is as good a place as any. After I was on the staff of the film company, I became acquainted with Quinn Martin in the scenario department. We were discussing *They Had to See Paris*, a situation

I never objected to. "Did you ever know how much we allowed in our budget to pay you for that story?"

"No."

Reaching into his desk he pulled out a sheet of paper and there it was — $35,000.

I was bitter for a time, after I left him. And then I put it aside. Life has to go forward, not back.

Will Works in the Sound Studios.
Tries to Be Funny with Women's Hats

I WAS WORKING for Twentieth Century-Fox adapting a stage play by Owen Davis called *Lazybones*. I had got Robert Morris Yost, the scenario editor, to agree to let me work at home, the Tamarind Apartments, Carlos Avenue, Hollywood. This is an ideal that all scenario writers aspire to. I was enjoying my outings and excursions thoroughly and really getting acquainted with the charm and beauties of southern California.

One day, when I got back from a delightful drive, my mother-in-law told me that the studio had been trying to get me all day and that I was to come to the scenario department as fast as I could. My conscience dug me like a rooster's spurs. I certainly would never make that mistake again, if I ever got on another payroll. After all, a studio did have certain rights.

When I got to the lot it was five, and, seemingly, the hour that had been set, for I saw a number of other scenario writers trudging toward the story section. It was strange, I thought, that so many of them should be on the lot today. And it wasn't pay day. Soon I saw they were all going down the passageway to the room given over to writers.

We gathered around the council fire, no one quite daring to ask what it was all about. Finally there were a round dozen present. They talked about horse racing, a subject which has so many devoted students in writing circles in Hollywood. But all were privately trying to figure out why we were there. I felt immensely relieved when I saw the other men there. Surely they wouldn't have mass firings.

Finally Mr. Yost leaned back and said that "the front" had decided to put Will Rogers in *The Connecticut Yankee at King Arthur's Court* and that we were all, every one of us, to turn in a treatment of at least five thousand words. "You will have two weeks to do it in. I'm going to ask you to meet the date. The picture is to be made at once. It's the most important production on the lot and the tracks are to be cleared for it."

I floated out, down the very passageway that I had trod some minutes before with knees not functioning quite right. But now they were in fine shape; I remember, just before the end of the passageway, they gave a little crowhop. In no time at all I was at home where I told my wife that we wouldn't, after all, have to pull in our horns, at least just yet.

Copies of the immortal book had been passed out to us, and I immediately got my nose in mine. I must say, on close reading, I was surprised how old-fashioned and contrived the story seemed, and, I must honestly say, not very amusing. Its eminence was far greater than its excellence.

I gave it the best I had and finished, curiously enough, just at the end of the two weeks. When I went in to deliver my manuscript I saw copies of other manuscripts bound in the yellow covers being used, just then, for treatments, all piled on Mr. Yost's desk. Mine was added and I went back to *Lazybones*. But not too fast. I needed a breathing spell, I told myself, and a chance to get outdoors.

I took up *Lazybones* and his problem of getting a satisfactory wife. Then one day the telephone rang and the scenario editor, in a most friendly voice, asked me if I would come in. My heart gave a thump that would have rattled a drum, and I went in, prepared to look modest.

No other writer was there and I was glad of it, for this would probably hurt the rest of them. I plopped into a leather chair and awaited the good news.

"Well," said Mr. Yost, "we've decided who is to write the scenario."

I nodded understandingly.

"It's —— " and he named one of the men who had been there the first day. "So now you can go back to *Lazybones*," he finished.

I went back to *Lazybones*, heartily wishing that the good-for-nothing had never been born.

And that is all I had to do with *Connecticut Yankee*. Privately I hoped it wouldn't do well, but it turned out to be one of Will's great successes. And so now I'd succeeded twice and had failed twice. But I must say that Will was tremendously friendly, for he looked on me as having given him the story that had established him in talking pictures. I held back, for I knew how many people were running after him, but he was kind and went out of his way to make advances. Little by little we became better acquainted and I began to see him oftener and oftener. He gave me his ranch telephone number, which wasn't listed, and now, as I look back, I realize I used it far too often. Sometimes, when I blithely telephoned, there would be a long wait, for he would be at the stables, or rambling around over the ranch. The telephone had a connection at the stables, so that wasn't quite so bad. Finally he would appear and I would chirp out my message. I hate to think now what he must have thought privately. But I must say he never showed it.

Not only did people seek out his office in Beverly Hills, they also began coming to his ranch — people he had never heard of and people who had no call on him. One night he and Betty came home from a movie and there, in the drive, was a sight-seeing bus with a guide telling 'em all about it. This was too much for Betty. Tourists must be kept out. It was three quarters of a mile from the highway to the ranch house, up and around a hill. She said that a gate must be placed at the highway. Will hesitated. Wasn't neighborly, they'd never had a gate in Oklahoma. But she prevailed and a gate was put up. There were two cement posts, each with an ornamental iron top. The iron top on the right-hand side could be lifted off; under it Will kept the key to the gate. He told a few of his friends. I guess I abused this privilege. I liked to take a friend out to the ranch and, with an important manner, hop out, insert the key, open the gate and sweep in. However, it wasn't quite as bad as it seems, for many times Will wasn't there. After showing off the place I would take my friend back to Hollywood, feeling good that I had shown him how I could hobnob with the great.

One day I went out to the ranch to see him on some studio business. He wasn't at the house, but Emil Sandmier, the butler, said he might be at the stables. I found "Sandy" Blake, his brother-in-law, who was in charge of the stables and the horses; he said that Will wasn't at the stables but might be in the calf pen. And there through the cracks I saw him, roping calves all by himself. A fence ran up to the pen and I climbed up on this so that I could see over. I called to him and in a moment he came riding up.

"What are you doing?" I asked.

"Learnin' to rope." He went on to say that he had been down in Mexico on William Randolph Hearst's ranch where he had seen a Mexican roper who could do things with a rope Will had never seen before. "He had one throw that seemed to be mostly from the wrist. This is the third day I've been tryin' and I ain't as good as I was when I started. I'd give a thousand dollars if I could do what that hombre could."

He gave his answer on the matter I had come out to see him about and when I left he started back to the calf pen. I think I am safe in saying that these were his happiest hours — roping.

Sometimes he had his sons with him; sometimes one of his cowboy friends; it was his royal way of entertaining. But he would just as soon be by himself. He was never lonesome when he was on a horse with a rope in his hand.

When Will first started in talking pictures, he dressed fairly well; that is, the faithful blue serge, or a gray-striped suit that he favored — bought from the shelf. But as he continued in pictures and as he became more and more an international figure, he became progressively a more casual dresser. He wore blue overalls with brass rivets, a cowboy shirt, a handkerchief around his neck, boots and spurs. He never wore a ten-gallon hat. Instead he had the authentic small cowboy Stetson, almost white in color, with a little rain-crease in front. When visitors saw him they always gave a start of surprise. "Is that really Will Rogers?" they would gasp. It really was. No one was ever more thoroughly and completely himself than Will was. That was the way he wanted to dress — it was natural — and it was the way he meant to dress come high-ho.

He drove his own car to the studio. The back seat looked like a cuckoo's nest — newspapers, ropes, old clothes, boots, telegraph blanks, a portable typewriter, horn-rimmed spectacles sprawled on the rear window shelf. If the car had been abandoned and left beside the road, a highway patrol officer, coming along and inspecting it, would have thought it belonged to a sharecropper on his way to town to buy the family groceries.

Will was always at the studio on time and would come in with a bundle of papers under his arm. He was the most popular person on the lot and everybody would call out Good Morning. The electricians and grips would be going about their preparations; the actors would be studying their parts, but Will wouldn't; he never studied. In fact he never knew his part. He would sit down and begin to read his newspapers with fierce concentration. The director would be rushing here and there in a fever of last-minute preparations. There would be a call for lights and Will would be summoned to do his scene.

"If I could act what would I be supposed to do?"

The director would explain it and the script girl would read the lines. "That's goin' to take a lot of high-class actin', ain't it? Say, did I ever tell you about W. C. Fields in Pittsburgh?"

A pale, ghostly smile would form on the director's face. He was working on a budget — the set would be costing $5000 a day — and every minute was precious.

"No. What about W. C. Fields in Pittsburgh?" the director would ask patiently.

Will would tell about W. C. Fields in Pittsburgh.

When he finished he would laugh delightedly.

The director would also laugh. "Very, very funny, Will. Now let's get ahead. It's half-past ten and we haven't got a thing in the can."

"All right," Will would say earnestly. "Let's dig into it." Lights would go up, spots would be tried out, workmen would rush here and there. Will would amble over to the director, laughing and chuckling to himself. "Guess who I saw last night. A fella I rode with at the St. Louis World's Fair. Let me tell you what happened to him on The Pike. Oh boy!"

He would tell the amusing story of what had happened on The Pike.

The director would laugh politely, then remind him that time was slipping away. "Will, this is the scene where you tell your son he is about to be trapped by the designing girl."

Will would become serious. "All right. Read it to me again." And now he would really pay attention.

At last the scene would begin. He would change the lines from what we had written, but usually for the better; at least they would be more natural for him to speak.

At noon he would sing out, "Lunchee! Lunchee!" And pretty

soon would be on his way to the Café de Paris, admirers following behind him like a tail on a kite. It was high jinks the moment he entered the restaurant. Everybody was in good humor. Visitors wanted to see him; sometimes they would be brought up; he would be pleased to see them, but it was to his old friends he wanted to talk. He always sat at the same table. "Did you save me back some chili?" he would ask the waitress. "I cain't act unless I got some chili under my belt. I've got an awful difficult scene this afternoon, so bring me a double helpin'. Chili is the secret of good actin'."

There was more laughter at his than at any other table; and highest and loudest of all would be his voice. People at other tables would look at his table enviously.

When the meal was over, he would take up all the checks. "I'll put 'em on my expense account." Then he would pause. "I've got to write my telegram. Good land! I just about forgot it."

In a few minutes he would be in his car and would begin running through the papers, with a stub of a lead pencil in his hand; now and then he would make a dab at something. Then he would open the door, sit down in the front seat, with his feet on the running board, the typewriter on his lap, stare off into space a moment, then begin to peck. He would take what he had written back to the studio; the help knew he was coming and would gather around expectantly. He would read it aloud, watching the effect. If they didn't quite comprehend what he meant, he would change it then and there. A messenger would be called and the telegram would be on its way. Then Will would disappear. But not far, for he would be in his car sound asleep. The director would wait and, after a time, Will would show up with a flurry and bluster — where had the director been? He'd been huntin' everywhere for him.

The director didn't like it, but there was nothing he could do about it; also he knew that Will hadn't made a talking picture yet that wasn't a big money maker.

He would work faithfully through the afternoon; and he would do something almost unheard of in acting — help the other person. His showmanship was uncanny; he would stand watching the other person, then go up and quietly say, "I don't want to butt in, but it might be a good idea to try it this way," and would make a suggestion. Sometimes it would be a change in words, or in the way the line was read. If it was comedy, he usually was right, for his instinct for that was uncanny, too.

When five o'clock came, he would go to the director and begin making circular motions with his hands as if managing a lariat. The director — and everybody else for that matter — knew what this meant: time to get out to the calves. And that is exactly what he would do. He would climb into his littered car and in no time would be at the ranch and on a horse, and a rope would be looping in the air.

Will was exactly what he was. Never in all the world, I repeat, was there ever a person so wholly and completely himself. Once a scene called for him to kiss his wife, Irene Rich. But he kept putting it off. Finally the director told him he had "shot around him" and could delay the taking of the scene no longer. But still Will would not go through with it. The director got Irene Rich off to one side and told her to take command of the scene and give Will a good whacking kiss, herself. The rehearsal began again; when this part came, Irene Rich grabbed him and gave him a kiss that made the lights blink. Will was so flabbergasted that he hardly knew, for a moment, what he was doing. When the scene was over, he was still a little dazed. He pulled at his lock of hair and rubbed his chin, as he did when embarrassment was upon him, and said, "Good land! I feel as if I'd been unfaithful to my wife."

Some kinds of comedy he could not do. Once a "special effects comedy director" arrived at the studio to do a "laugh sequence." This proved to be a scene in which Will put on and took off women's hats. The hats were carried on and the special director started in to show Will how to be funny. Will was eager to learn, just as he had been when the newspaper syndicate people had told him how to be humorous. He put the hats on his head and he took them off. The scene was depressing. The director told him to do it faster. Will did it faster. The scene was even more depressing. Finally Will stopped and said, "I can't be funny with 'props.' I can only be funny with ideas. If you want a comedy sequence here, get W. C. Fields with his pool table. He'll make them howl."

The scene was not made. But what Will said then, it has always seemed to me, was the very bedrock of his comedy. He could be funny only with ideas.

One of his remarkable gifts was to be funny at any time, completely without preparation. Example: One night Hal Roach was having an elaborate birthday party at Hotel Commodore, New York. It was being held in a room completely enclosed with drapes. Toward the end of the party Will happened to start through this room, heard a chatter of voices, peeked through the curtain and saw his old friend. Will — always eager for fun — thrust his head through the curtains and called out a cheerful hello to the people at the table. Then, with only his head sticking out, Will kept talking and quipping for half an hour. Then his head disappeared like a turtle's and Will was gone. Hal Roach said it was as fine a bit of impromptu entertaining as he ever saw in his life. No other comedian in America could have done it without going into a prepared routine. In such things as this, Will was extraordinary.

He liked to talk of show people; especially he liked to talk about Eddie Cantor and W. C. Fields. He admired Fields tremendously and was generous in his praise. But Fields was a jealous, bitter soul. He had been a success while Will was still unknown. He had watched Will's rise with growing uneasiness and rarely ever said a good word for Will. Fields fell ill and was taken to Las Encinas Sanitarium, Pasadena. When Will heard that Fields was there he immediately went to see him, but at the gate in the wall which surrounded the grounds he was told that no one was allowed in to see Fields. Will pretended to start back to his car, but as soon as he was out of sight of the gateman, he climbed over the wall, dodged through the shrubbery, asked here and there and finally attained Fields's room. Will cheered Fields up, but finally had to go. After he had gone, the nurse said that Will was the funniest man she had ever seen.

Immediately Fields took umbrage. "He's a fake," he said sharply. "I'll bet when he's at home he talks just like anybody else."

On the other hand, Fields always praised Tom Mix. He was a real cowboy, he said. (Was it because there was no competition?)

Once I said to him, "Will, I've got an idea for a story for you."

"Is it one where I've got to make love?"

"Yes, it's got that in it."

He looked at the ground thoughtfully for some moments, then made a mark in the dirt with the toe of his boot, as he sometimes did. "I don't want any truck with it. Hollywood park benches are filled with ex-actors who didn't know they were too old to make love."

One effect his pictures had was their reality. He used no make-up and was so natural that he did not seem to be acting. Even in Los Angeles where people are supposed to be wise, at least to pictures, his pictures carried a sense of conviction. Noel Kaho, previously mentioned, told me this story. He was at the Los Angeles Airport when Will's plane landed. A newsboy recognized Will and ran gleefully forward. "Hello, Mr. Rogers," he called. "Have you still got that hotel?"

Will was puzzled. "What hotel, son?"

"The one you had in *Lightnin'*," said the boy, who apparently believed that the hotel was real and that Will owned it.

His theory of "tested material" worked well, indeed. My weak *Down to Earth* had pointed the way. Picture after picture was coming from the studio and all were successful.

I had a letter from him, pecked off by himself on his portable typewriter, no doubt on his lap, for I was beginning to realize this was the way he wrote:

DEAR HOMER.
Your letter come awhile ago, But you know I been keeled over sick, too much Chili. Now about that David Harum, they seem to think they will do it, so they are trying to get it framed up for late fall Production, and have promised me Borsage to direct it, so you would fit in fine with him, So you write me or come to see me and let me know you are still here, I know they had someone on it, but I also know they think its going to be hard to make it modern, so they will need help, so I think you could sure help us, so drop me a line, we will be starting working in a couple of weeks on another mess, so come out and have lunch with me. Hows Chick Sales, tell him I want to see him, Get him and come out and see me,

                              Good luck to you and the Mrs,

Again he got what he wanted. *David Harum* had been phenomenally successful as a book and as a stage play. The part of the horse-trading deacon would fit Will like a saddle blanket. But there was a burr under the blanket and the story wouldn't shape up. I was called in, and soon I was just as stumped as the others ahead of me had been; it was the scenario writers' La

Brea Tar Pits. Four writers had disappeared from sight in its deceptive depths. It was to be directed by James Cruze, who had given the world the fabulous *The Covered Wagon;* one of his old stand-by writers was to work on it, too. Every day I would go to Jimmy Cruze's in Flintridge and the three of us would tackle the story, usually for a loss. We would talk awhile, then play the game of "darts" which, just then in Hollywood, was the way to encourage the subconscious mind to do creative work. But our subconscious minds balked as firmly as any Missouri mule ever did. Then back to our darts. Then it would be lunch-time. In Hollywood it is an unwritten law not to talk business during lunch; this we obeyed as if a G-man were behind the arras. After lunch we would be slightly sleepy; however, in time this would wear away and we would again start in to think. This period would be brief; then to the faithful darts. There was, after all, a certain magic in the game, for suddenly Jimmie Cruze stopped and said, "I know what's wrong with this cursed thing. The book is made up of half a dozen short stories about the same set of characters, and we've been trying to put the best of every story in the scenario. We've got to decide on just one short story — one idea — and stick to that through thick and thin." As soon as he said this, I realized the truth of it. We selected a young love story which would be resolved by helpful David Harum, and began the actual writing of the scenario. It was a period story, laid in Homerville, New York. The climax was a sulky race in which Will's horse would only run when Will sang to it — a far-fetched situation but acceptable for its comedy value. We wanted a period song. I remembered one we had sung when I was a boy in country school and suggested "Ta-ra-boom-de-ay." When the story was released, many people spoke to me about the film; nearly always they mentioned the song with its meaningless refrain. It made me feel good that I had yipped it as a boy.

During this time I became better acquainted with Will and began to realize he was not the simple personality that most people assumed. He was, as I began to sense him, a remarkably complex person. His easy, boyish, open approach made people feel that he was just what they saw on the surface. In one sense this was true, but beyond this hail-fellow-well-met personality he was vastly reserved; there was a wall that no one went beyond; and there were dark chambers and hidden recesses that he opened to no one.

I was impressed by what a wonderful, natural-born showman he was. And how he must always have an audience. I recall an incident that illustrates this. I was living, part of the time that I was working on *David Harum*, at the Hollywood-Plaza Hotel. At night I would sometimes peck off some of the dialogue, or bits of the scenario. One evening he dropped in and the two of us must have been alone in my room for close upon an hour. When we were alone, I never thought of him as a comedian; he was someone I liked and felt at home with, a lusty, vibrating, appealing personality but not necessarily a comedian. For a while we talked about the story and what were its deepest values, then we talked of whatever flew up. At last I went down with him in the elevator. The boy operating the elevator recognized him and called him by name. He told someone else that Will was there and soon the word spread. Will and I paused on the sidewalk for some last words; in no time a crowd was around him. And now he was a showman. He talked to me but watched the crowd, as he always did, and as he always watched an audience. I laughed, for he was immensely amusing. The crowd laughed; Will was in fine spirits. At last he left and I went upstairs again, still a little astonished at how he could be two such contrasting personalities.

It was the same way on the movie lot. He would start talking to one person; soon the studio help would be around him like bees around a molasses jug. But what I didn't at first realize was that he was trying out his material. He watched acutely to see what "went" and what didn't. There he would stand, talking

seemingly extemporaneously but, in reality, using jokes and ideas
he had been storing up. Sometimes, later, they would appear in
his daily piece or in his Sunday article. But if someone else began to talk and get the attention of the audience, Will would
abruptly turn and walk away.

One day he saw me on the set and said, "What are you goin'
to be doin' Thanksgiving?"

"Nothing special," I told him.

"Now you come out to the ranch and have a gobbler with us."

What a day it was! How vividly I remember it. It was the kind
of day Will liked best — entertaining a few friends at the ranch.
Today, in honor of the occasion, his overalls were off and he had
on his faithful two-piece suit. He was all over the place. He
showed off his prize belongings — his cigar-store Indian, his
stuffed calf, his mechanical street organ, his Indian rugs and the
paintings on the wall. He talked of the big window, command-
ing a view, that Ziegfeld had had installed, and spoke tenderly of
"Mr. Ziegfield."

Time ran along. Emil, the butler, came in with a harmless
cocktail and the time moved along some more. Finally Betty said,
"Dinner is ready."

Will bounded to his feet. "Say, hold back a minute! I've got to
write my telegram."

Betty didn't say anything . . . she must have gone through this
many times.

Will went hurrying off toward his part of the house and I
rested my eyes on the clock. In exactly fifteen minutes he was
back. He didn't read it to us and there was no mention of what it
was about. A messenger took the paper and disappeared.

The dinner went along — stories, laughter, good fellowship.
Could there ever be anything else with Will present?

That afternoon Elliott Roosevelt dropped in and Will began
to entertain as he liked to do. The horses came out; all who

wished could take a whack at the calves; and those who wished could bang around on the four-hole golf course. And those who wanted just to visit could sit around and do that. (Me.)

The next morning in the paper I read the telegram. I was surprised and delighted:

Didn't want to get too enthusiastic about Thanksgiving till I saw how it turned out. My old friend William S. Hart (Bill) showed up at my igloo with a "gobbler" that he had shot with two guns. Now if you will bring everything, I defy anybody to give you a nicer party than I will. Homer Croy, who wrote "They Had to See Paris," was as hungry as an author can be. Mrs. Florence Ziegfeld, looking exactly 25 years old, and not reducing. Then an outlaw dropped in. He was only the Crown Prince's son and the Kaiser's grandson, Prince Louis Ferdinand. While he got no white meat, as in his early childhood, he seemed mighty cheerful, and a fine young chap, and was satisfied with the wings.

I'll never forget the day.

Will Becomes Sensitive About His Age. His Religion

THERE WAS NO MAN in the United States as important as Will Rogers was who conducted his affairs in such a casual, offhand way. He did not have an office in the usual meaning of the word. He transacted most of his business wherever he happened to be — on a street corner, in a car, on horseback. In a way, his office was under his hat. He would conduct a quarter-million-dollar deal propping up a building. There would be a handshake and the matter was closed. But the demands on him grew — mail stacked up — until he had to have a place to receive it. Mail was not delivered at the ranch; it had to be picked up at the post office and toted out. Finally he rented an office in a business building in Beverly Hills (Beverly Hills was still called "the Village.") But it was not a true office. He never took anyone there; he never transacted any business in it. It was a mail depot. He did not have his name on the door, but people discovered he had an office and came there hoping to find him. California, at this time, was a get-rich-quick land; a person who didn't have a scheme to get rich was looked on as suspicious and eccentric. And they all wanted to see Will so as to let him in on something good. They would wait in the halls and on the ground floor ready to pounce on him as he went by. But they didn't get to pounce, for he practically never came to the place. Even if they had got his ear, it would have done little good, as he was putting his money into life insurance and real estate. Never once did he go into one of their "sure things." It, no doubt, saved him millions.

Mrs. Daisy Tyler gave me a glimpse into Will's Alice in Wonderland way of running an office. She was the first public stenographer in Beverly Hills, except for a girl in the Beverly Hills Hotel who did work for the guests. Mrs. Rogers needed help to handle the increasing amount of mail and sent some work to Mrs. Tyler by the chauffeur. Finally Mrs. Rogers sent word for Mrs. Tyler to come to see her. She engaged Mrs. Tyler to act as Will's secretary, if the job could be called that. Mrs. Tyler told me:

"We got the mail in two ways. Mail addressed to him in Beverly Hills was put in a post office box. There was no mail delivery to the ranch, so all the Beverly Hills mail was put in this box. The letters that came to the post office in Beverly Hills were, for the most part, from readers of his daily piece; sometimes they agreed with him; sometimes they attacked him. He always paid more attention to the latter than to the former. In addition there was the studio mail; the amount was surprising. It was my duty to pick this up and take it to the office and thus there would be the accumulation from the two sources. This was also true for the telegrams; they were signed for and came into my hands.

"I would go over the letters and telegrams and pick out the ones I thought he would be interested in, type out a digest of the letter or telegram and pin this to the original. Then I would take all this to the ranch. Week ends when he was home (not too often) he would go over the digests and type the answers himself. He never kept a carbon copy. Or sometimes he would make a notation on my digest and I would expand this into a letter to the person. I was always astonished by the number of letters he could take care of in this way — all pecked off on his little portable with one finger on each hand. He made no choice between the rich and important and the humble in answering his letters, if the subject interested him. That was what he answered, the subject rather than the person. I don't think, in the eight years I was with him, he dictated eight letters. Sometimes I would not glimpse him in two weeks.

"He sent a great many telegrams. Sometimes he would peck them off himself, then send them by messenger to the telegraph office; sometimes, either coming or going to the studio, he would stop at the telegraph office, sit down at the little desk and write his message. He never kept a carbon of this, either.

"Sometimes he would be on the other side of the world; I would then send a digest of the letters to Mrs. Rogers, who would handle them in about the same manner he did. Mr. Rogers never complained or found fault and was easy and pleasant to work for."

From my own personal point of view I can say it is true indeed about the telegrams. He sent me several, but something happened to them; I cannot find even one.

His great physical activity was beginning to tell on Will. He complained about feeling tired, but he kept up the pace. Betty bought him a machete; he was delighted and spent a great deal of time by himself on the back trails of the ranch whacking away at the underbrush. Sometimes he would sit down beside the trail and rest.

One day his family was having dinner in the patio, and all were talking about a polo game they had seen that afternoon. Mary mentioned the name of one of the players and said, "And think — he's forty-two." Will took offense and growled, "That's not old. I can play polo and I'm a lot older'n forty-two. I guess you kids think of me as an old man hangin' around the house and gettin' in people's way." For some minutes he was sulky and would not talk.

He would fall asleep reading his paper. He complained about his jokes; they were not as good as they used to be; didn't have time to work 'em up. Sometimes he spoke of "old actors" and "old days." The actors were better than the ones today; vaudeville had been the greatest training school ever known. But "vaude" was gone. "Where are they goin' to get their training?" he would ask plaintively.

Sometimes he referred to his encroaching age in a wry manner. When the racing scenes for *David Harum* were being made at Riverside, California, he said, "Y'see, they've got me rigged out to drive a trottin' horse to a sulky. I never saw a man under eighty drive a trottin' horse. That's the reason they picked me."

Also he was growing increasingly sensitive to criticism. He did not subscribe to a clipping bureau, but his admirers would cut clippings from their home paper and send them to him. If he found one that was unfavorable, he was indignant. The *Pella Chronicle*, Pella, Iowa, was a small weekly paper. A clipping was sent Will in which the paper criticized Will. Immediately he wrote the paper a hot defense of himself. It was published February 5, 1931. No other international figure would have paid any attention to what the paper said.

He also had a feud with the Bohemian Club of San Francisco, too complicated to go into here.

Will went to Pullman, Washington, to lecture. Two or three days after his lecture, Dr. Claudius O. Johnson spoke before the Parent-Teacher Association; in his talk he said that Will didn't know anything about international affairs. Someone sent Will the clipping from the *Pullman Herald*, January 20, 1933.

He sat down and promptly sent the paper this telegram: "Two or three people been sending me clippings from your paper telling me about some old college professor up there named Claudius O. Something. I don't wonder he put that O after Claudius. Well, he says I don't know anything about international affairs, but that he does. I'll come up there and debate him on anything foreign he can think of, whether its an affair or not. He says he gets all his news out of a Magazine called 'Foreign Affairs.' When a magazine can learn him foreign affairs, I want to tangle with a guy like that."

Even as late as 1933, Will was still an upholder of Mussolini and he would denounce anyone who questioned his (Will's) judgment. February 11, 1933, his daily telegram in the *San Diego Union* contained this paragraph:

"Say, Mussolini could run this country with his eyes shut, in fact that is the way our Congress has been running it. Mussolini with no money, no natural resources, no nothing, has kept his country going while us, with a surplus of everything under the sun, are mangy with representatives and liberty. But we can't digest either of 'em."

Eddy Orcutt, chief editorial writer for the paper, wrote a mild editorial chiding Will for his enthusiasm for Mussolini, pointing out the deplorable state that Italy was in, and twitted Will as a "homespun philosopher" who quite often was wrong. In the editorial he said: "No person who is not a member of Mussolini's party can hold office. No elections are held, even for district or village governments. No opposition newspaper comment is tolerated. Terrorism is an advertised weapon of the minority, and even assassination has been proved against it. Mussolini might offer some improvement in running a country — even with his eyes shut — but the people of our country would have to keep their eyes shut, too."

The editorial got to Will, who was ruffled indeed. He wrote the paper this angry letter (March 14, 1933):

"I want you to publish this, for you had a long winded editorial against me when I said that what we needed was a dictator. Well, Mussolini is an amateur compared to Mr. Roosevelt's power and the whole country is tickled to death. Dictatorship is the best government in the world provided you have the right dictator. So the *San Diego Union* can still run the country by congressmen, but I will take Roosevelt for mine. I am sending one of these to your opposition paper in case you don't use it yourself."

The paper was a bit surprised that Will would say that dictatorship is the best government in the world, provided, etc., but let the matter drop.

He became more and more truculent and was offended more and more easily. November 16 he mentioned in a radio broadcast the new Liberty Memorial to the war dead that the people of Kansas City had just completed. It was their pride and civic joy. He said that it looked like a silo. The people of Kansas City were indignant and demanded that he apologize over the air. He muttered a feeble, half-hearted apology and got away from the subject as fast as he could.

Some of the attacks were bitter. The Socialist paper, the *American Freeman*, Girard, Kansas, said: "Will Rogers likes to pose as 'home folks' but the truth is he's a millionaire. He has never written a word in support of a worker on a strike. He has never spoken a sentence that doubted the divine justice of the capitalism system. Many of his wisecracks reveal a hidden sympathy for the Fascist type of Demagogue. The great Mark Twain was a real humorist who wasn't afraid to utter some bitter truths about the mountebanks of religion, militarism and politics." This must have hurt him deeply, for he never replied.

In some ways, however, he had mellowed. One was in his attitude towards Ziegfeld. He had worked for him, on and off, for ten years. He had started out by not liking him, for Ziegfeld's personality was as cold as a pair of rubber boots on a farmer's back porch. Worst of all was Ziegfeld's lack of a sense of humor. If he had had his own way he would not have had a comedian in the show; just acres of girls. But he knew their value, so in they went. Great showman that he was, he had chinks in his armor and began to lose money. The customers could stand just about so much of glorified girls, then began to think how they would have to cut down the rest of the week. His debts piled up like straw behind a threshing machine. His health began to fail. He went to California and took a house near Will and Will began to see him often. They rode together on the back trails of the ranch, two as assorted individuals as you could scare up. Will who liked everybody within reason, the glib talker, the hearty laugher, dressed like a sharecropper. In contrast was Ziegfeld, immaculately dressed in perfectly fitting riding attire. He couldn't ride well, but he looked the part. And thus, all alone, the two came together in closer understanding than they ever had before in all their lives. Will still called him "Mr. Ziegfield." Ziegfeld called him "Will."

The strain, the worries, the mountain of debts were too much for Ziegfeld and he died July 22, 1932 — bankrupt, without a dollar to his name; in fact, Billie Burke after his death had to work for years to help pay off his debts.

Will spoke at his funeral and wrote feelingly of him in his daily piece and in his Sunday article. But this was not all; he paid his funeral expenses. Through a touching loyalty, Will never spoke of this and few ever knew it.

His fame was growing. He was the most influential private citizen in the world. He was always hopping off on some air trip; when he arrived in any country in the world (except Russia) he was given an ovation. If there was an earthquake or a disaster of any kind, he would fly to the place; the people would receive him with touching acclaim. He could help them. He was their friend. He was America.

His response to flood disasters, earthquakes, and benefits was truly astonishing; he was never too tired or too weary to pack his little brown bag. Not only would he appear as an entertainer, but, as I have said, he himself would contribute, and not merely a casual contribution. As an example, at Managua, in Nicaragua, he contributed $5000.

With the great pressure that was constantly on him, he continued to turn out motion pictures. For the first one, as we have seen, he was paid $50,000. He was now getting $110,000; his new contract called for $125,000 for each picture, plus 50 per cent of the profit. And he was making three a year. This contract was signed, no more handshakes; the explanation Will gave was that "the presidents of this company come and go so fast I don't have time to shake hands with them."

His great motion pictures were: *They Had to See Paris* (you won't catch me leaving this one out); *Connecticut Yankee*, by Mark Twain; *State Fair*, by Phil Stong; *Steamboat 'Round the Bend*, by Ben Lucien Burman.

Phil Stong told me an ancedote about the filming of *State Fair*. Phil, with others, usually sat at Will's table in the Café de Paris. On this day Will sat down at the table with his hand over his mouth, laughing and chortling to himself, so amused that he could hardly talk. Then he got hold of himself. "Say, I've got a good one on Betty!" He was so amused, so delighted he had to stop and laugh. Finally he was able to tell what had happened.

Some days before this he had gone to the Guaranty Trust Company Bank, in Los Angeles, and as he was finishing up his business the manager said, "I think that was a good deal your wife made the other day."

Will was puzzled, for he knew nothing about it. But he didn't let on. "I can't think just what it was."

"That stock she bought."

Will had never owned any stock and now Betty . . .

"Oh yes! Yes, of course. I can't think right now what that stock was."

"The Kreuger & Toll stock. She bought $250,000 worth."

Betty had always worried about their financial future. Things couldn't continue so good. They must prepare for their old age.

So for years she had been carefully saving from her housekeeping budget and by other means all the money that she could, waiting for just the right moment to invest it.

"I didn't say a word," continued Will, "about what I had found out, just kept quiet. She didn't tell me 'cause she was waitin' till we went broke and she would keep us from goin' to the porehouse. Well, yesterday morning we was havin' breakfast in our window and I was plowin' through the Sunday papers when I come across something that gave me a start. '*Hmm!* what's this?' I says and read the headline: IVAR KREUGER KILLS SELF. I pretended I didn't think of him as in any way hooked up with us. Then I read the subheadlines: MATCH KING ENDS ALL WITH BULLET. MAY MEAN END OF MATCH KINGDOM BUILT UP BY WELL-KNOWN FIGURE. STOCKS TUMBLE.

"Still I pretended it didn't concern us, I was just readin' what I saw in front of me. Well, Betty set there, her face growin' whiter and whiter. Suddenly she began to cry." Will paused, stirred by the memory of that moment. "It made me feel miserable. I wouldn't done it for a million dollars if I'd known it was goin' to hurt her."

The point of it all was that he had hurt Betty. The loss of the money was nothing.

During the filming of a picture Will was a cut-up; he was having fun and he wanted everybody else to have fun. The plot of *State Fair* revolved around a prize boar; to make it authentic the film company sent back to Iowa and bought the Grand Champion — Blue Boy himself, who was a mountain of meat. He had huge tusks and was as fast on his feet as a feist. It seemed incredible that an animal so huge and with feet so small could move so quickly. Those sharp, curved tusks meant something. They could, in a few slashes, make a man into a tossed salad.

When the towering, suspicious, semisavage animal arrived, Henry King, the director, told Will to beware of the creature and to keep out of its way. Will said, "Oh! I've always been on friendly terms with hogs. Me and him'll get along all right."

"Not Blue Boy," said King earnestly. "Please keep away from him."

Shooting on this scene was to begin. Henry King got his cast together, in make-up, and started across the lot to where Blue Boy was captive. The call boy had been sent for Will, but couldn't find him; this wasn't too surprising, for Will wandered here and there as he pleased. Finally, Henry King and his actors arrived at the pen — and there, inside, was Blue Boy lying on the ground asleep and there was Will, also inside the pen, stretched out on the ground, with his head propped up on the mighty animal, his hat over his eyes, pretending to be asleep. Will knew more about hogs than King did; he knew that if he did not disturb him and arouse the animal's fighting instinct he would be safe. But when Henry King saw Will he shook like a diaper on a clothesline. When the joke was over, Will climbed out, having had the laugh of the day, and the shooting of the scene began.

Once, later, the scene called for Will to punch the animal and stir him up. Will watched closely, for he knew the signs. The animal became more and more resentful. Suddenly he turned, the skin spread back, the great tusks stood out — and Will went over the side of the pen like a wild turkey. He knew when there was danger, and also he knew when one could pretend to snooze.

When the picture was completed, the business manager of the film company approached Will to buy Blue Boy. He would sell him at a bargain, he said; the animal would keep the family in meat a long time. Will hesitated. "I just cain't do it," he said. "I wouldn't feel right eatin' a fellow actor."

Sometimes his comments on the set were so good that they were incorporated into the story. Dillinger, the robber, had just escaped from jail by whittling out a wooden gun and covering it with tinfoil. The story that Will was making (*Handy Andy*) had a jail scene. Will was standing behind the bars for a close-up when he said to Dave Butler, the director, "Y'know, I could get out of this jail any time I wanted to. I already got my wooden gun whittled out." The comment was so good that it was inserted into the story and was one of the best laughs in the picture.

He rarely ever went to church and took no active interest in religious matters. But he never slurred religion and never took a superior attitude toward anyone who found solace in it. He wanted his children to have religious training and often, at the breakfast table on Sunday morning, would urge them to go to church. When the family was living in Beverly Hills, he found there was no church in the town; this disturbed him. However, he discovered a kind of Sunday School was being held each week in a grammar-school building. Will sent his own children and then pitched in and helped raise money to build a real church; the church still stands and is known today as the Beverly Hills Community Church.

In 1933 the Reverend A. Raymond Grant, pastor of the Simpson Methodist Episcopal Church, in Minneapolis, wrote Will that he was going to preach on him a Sunday or two later and asked Will what his "religion philosophy" was. Will said: "I was raised predominantly a Methodist, but I have traveled so much, mixed with so many people in all parts of the world, that I don't know just what I am. I know I have never been a nonbeliever. But I can honestly tell you that I don't think any one religion is *the* religion. If I am broad-minded in any way (and I hope I am) I know that I am broad-minded in a religious way. Whichever way you serve your God will never get one word of argument, or condemnation, out of me."

His religion might more properly be termed a philosophy, although he always laughed off the word, pretending he didn't even know what it meant. He wrote the following which, it seems to me, sums up his attitude toward the mystery of life: "We are here just for a spell and then pass on. So get a few laughs and do the best you can. Live your life so that whenever you lose, you are ahead." The last sentence has been seized on and is emblazoned on the Memorial, in Claremore; and well it might be, for it is the very core and substance of Will Rogers.

"I Never Met a Man I Didn't Like" — How It Originated. Will Makes His Last Movie

His strange interest in epitaphs continued. He had pronounced his first, as we've seen, at the Molly Pitcher Club, in 1922, and had been quoting epitaphs for himself ever since. He nearly always changed them. It was almost as if he were working to get a perfect one. Always the epitaphs had to do with politicians, for he liked to prod them and then tell them he really loved them. It was his way of taking out the sting; it was successful, for none of the political figures held his digs against him. In 1928 when he spoke in Iowa City, Iowa, he changed it to: "He joked about every prominent man of his time, but he never met one he disliked."

In Los Angeles, at a bar meeting where he was the chief speaker, he turned his epitaph-making to lawyers: "A lot of you lawyers have been squirmin' because I've been pokin' fun at you. Well, that shows you are important. I only poke fun at the big ones. When I die I want this epitaph cut on my tombstone: 'Here lies Will Rogers, a comedian. He never picked on a man when he was down.' "

I had a small experience with him myself in the matter of epitaphs. I got up a book yclept *The Last Word*. It was a collection of real tombstone epitaphs; the last section, however, was devoted to imaginary epitaphs, each supplied by a living person as appropriate for himself. (I thought it was a funny idea; it developed that I stood alone. It is now a Collector's Item, with practically no collectors.) When I approached Will for one, he walked to one side of the set, as he always did when he wanted to arrive at something that took a bit of thinking, plopped his lips and mumbled to himself as he did when he was trying out something, and said when he came back: "Here lies Will Rogers. Politicians turned honest and he starved to death."

He had written or spoken at least twenty epitaphs, no two exactly alike. One, however, had surprising results. The Reverend Dr. J. Whitcomb Brougher, an old family friend, delivered a sermon in the Tremont Temple Baptist Church, in Boston, and, after his address, asked Will Rogers to get up and "say a few words." How many times Will had heard that! Rarely did he ever fail to respond. He said, "I've got my epitaph all worked out. When I'm tucked away in the old graveyard west of Oologah, I hope they will cut this epitaph — or whatever you call them signs they put over gravestones — on it, 'Here lies Will Rogers. He joked about every prominent man in his time, but he never met a man he didn't like.' I'm so proud of that, I can hardly wait till I die so it can be carved and when you come around to my grave, you'll probably find me sittin' there, proudly readin' it." He went on to say that he had never known a man, or a community, that he could not find some good in. He had in mind only politicians and was limiting his statement to them. The story appeared in the *Boston Globe*, June 16, 1930, page 12, column 7.

It was the shot heard around the world. It was taken up by the Associated Press and spread far and wide. No one was more surprised than Will. He had used it many times — or others almost like it — and it hadn't created a ripple. He was delighted; it was another illustration of the wondrous luck that was so often his companion. He was enough of a showman to realize its value and to keep quiet about fine distinctions. It came to be applied in a way that he had not meant at all, for there were plenty of people he didn't like. This line endeared him to the public more than any one thing that had ever come into his life. Sometimes, however, it caused him inconvenience, for, now and then, he would meet a person he did not care for, but he had to pretend that he loved him as a brother.

To be fair it must be said that he liked nearly everybody. He was having such a wonderful time living that he approached another person like a small boy running toward someone he knew he was going to like and who was going to like him.

Will liked to ask advice. One day he told me that Henry Duffy, a play producer, had come to him with the idea of putting on *Ah! Wilderness* by Eugene O'Neill as a stage play in Hollywood, and what did I think?

I told him I didn't believe it was a good idea. What I was thinking was that he could not memorize lines and that he was not an actor, as this is usually thought of, and that he had never done a sustained characterization; he had always been just himself. And now a whole evening. . . . He listened without comment and, I thought, agreed with me and was going to drop the idea. A week or two later I was surprised to see in the paper that he was going to do the play. I was a prophet of gloom. He would suffer defeat. I felt sorry for him.

Henry Duffy told me the story of the opening: "I wanted to do myself proud and had a wonderful lobby display by the late John Decker in which everything was 'Will Rogers in Eugene O'Neill's play *Ah! Wilderness.*' They were 8-sheets and 1-sheets, with a life likeness of Will Rogers and made, I thought, one of the most beautiful lobby displays I had ever seen. Rehearsals were called for ten in the morning. When I arrived at eight, Will was in the lobby in his blue jeans and boots. I called out a cheery 'Good Morning' but he did not answer. He kept looking at the art. I thought he was delighted with it, just as I was. Finally he turned to me and said, 'Boss, how was this show billed in New York?'

"I explained to him that at that time the Theater Guild starred no one and that the billing was 'The Theater Guild Presents Eugene O'Neill's *Ah! Wilderness* with George M. Cohan.'

"'That's what I thought and that is good enough for me. I want you to take all of this stuff out of the lobby and bill me the same way, and I will pay for it. I don't want anybody to think I'm as good an actor as George M. Cohan, 'cause I ain't. I'm just a cowhand gone wrong.'

"We opened in Fresno; then we were to hit San Francisco. In the audience, this opening night in Fresno, was Betty Rogers and with her, as her guest, was Dale Winters. They sat in the rear of the theater. It was really an old-time opening. The house was packed; it was Will's debut as a legitimate actor. When the house lights were lowered for the curtain to go up, Betty Rogers reached across, took Dale Winters's hand and said, 'Oh God! Please take care of my boy tonight.'

"Well, He did. Will was a tremendous success. The day after his funeral I went to the ranch house to talk to Betty, and naturally *Ah! Wilderness* came up. She told me that of all the things that Will had ever done, *Ah! Wilderness* gave him the most pleasure. He played for me ten weeks — and it cost him personally $250,-000, for that is what he lost on his movie contract."

As I look back now, I have a twinge. In my days with him he talked over with me many of his plans and asked what I "thought." So far as I can remember, I never gave him a single bit of advice that was good. Why he kept asking me, I don't know. The only thing in its favor was that I always told him what I thought, poor as it was.

Suddenly, almost unaccountably, Will picked up his family and hopscotched off to Japan. Of course the reporters were down to meet him — all dressed, as Will said later, like ambassadors. And there Will, in his faithful blue serge, was interviewed by the impressive gentlemen. Here is what one of them said. It appears in the *Jiji Shimpo*, August 12, 1934:

"Mr. Will Rogers, comedian of the world's fame, has arrived here by the *Empress of Canada*, accompanied by the members of his family. With that proverbial outburst of laughter, after rubbing his shaved chin as you often see on the screen, he made a statement, 'We are going to stay several days in Tokyo and see places whence as we extend our trip to Soviet Russia. Don't worry, boys, I won't ever be 'Red.' Ha! Ha! Ha!

"Though Mr. Rogers looked older with more gray hairs on the head, he seemed to be the incarnation of youth with his peps. As reported elsewhere in this article, Mr. Rogers brought his two sons with him. The older son is a student of the University of Stanford, while the younger one is a star player of the pole vault of Pamona University. When it came to the talk of his two youngsters, the famous smile broadened all over the old man."

(If Will saw the interview, I wonder what he must have thought about the reference to "the old man," sensitive as he was to encroaching age.)

His old pace continued, but he rested more and slept more. On the set he would sit down in his chair; his head would droop. He would be asleep. When he awoke he seemed to have his old-time energy. The cast liked to work with him, for he gave them more laughs than did any other actor. Example: as he was making *Steamboat 'Round the Bend*, word came that the front office was going to change the title. Will liked the title and asked them not to change it, but, after the inscrutable ways of the business office, they sent word that the title was going to be changed and that was all there was to it, take it or leave it. Will decided to take it. There was a character in the story called "The New Moses." Will was supposed to be on a steamboat going up and down the Mississippi River. Every time the boat docked, in the picture,

Will would come to the rail and call out to the people on the dock, "Have you seen The New Moses? I've got bad news for him. Winnie Sheehan and Sol Wurtzel want to change the title of this picture. Don't let 'em, Moses." Of course this showed up in the "rushes" and was seen by the bosses. It began to have its effect; finally they sent word that the old title would stay. Will was delighted and said to Ben Lucien Burman, "I tell you that New Moses has got power."

The picture was filmed on the Sacramento River, in California, and while it was being made, Buck McKee sent word that he lived nearby at Roseville, and would Will come to see him? Will was delighted. Buck McKee! He found that Buck had a riding academy on the old Whipple Ranch. Buck was stove up and limped; the many falls he had had from horses had begun to tell, for Buck had also been a rider for Pawnee Bill, Miller Brothers' Wild West Show, and for the 101 Ranch, and had had countless falls. The two men had been together for five and one half years, and they talked over old days. Did Will remember the time he had tried to rope the steer in Madison Square Garden, but the steer had got away, dragging Will's rope? Did Will remember the time Teddy had encountered the lather? Did Will remember the time he'd lassoed the fireman in Berlin? Will told Buck what had happened to Teddy; he had sent him back to Oklahoma and had put him on a pension, and there, on the Rogers ranch, he had lived until he died. At last the cheery, laugh-filled evening was over, and Will left Buck in Buck's little cottage near his riding academy, and went back to the hotel where he was staying during the making of the motion picture.

Steamboat 'Round the Bend was the last picture he made. Another picture, all finished and completed, was resting on the shelves awaiting release. Will became concerned with the order in which the two were to be released, for he considered the other picture weak, and said to Burman, "I want them to release *Steam-*

boat first. I'm slipping at the box office. If the other is shown first, I'll be down at the bottom of the list."

He insisted on this and it was finally agreed to by the studio. And now, for the first time since he had gone into talking pictures, he had to worry about his box office. There were now more stars in Hollywood; the glamorous ones were getting the business. In spite of the young and exciting stars, he was still great and powerful. But there were shadows.

CHAPTER 27

The Airplane Crash

WILL WAS OVERLY APPREHENSIVE. There was no slump in his pictures; there might be more glamorous stars in Hollywood, but also America wanted believable, down-to-earth characters. And his newspaper popularity was growing. He wrote for the greatest number of papers of any writer in the world. His pay rose and fell with the papers, but hovered around $2500 a week.

However, he was becoming increasingly careless about his writing; sometimes it was so ambiguous it didn't even make sense. He sat down and pecked it off as fast as he could. He paid little attention to spelling and tossed in a capital letter whenever he felt like it. His favorite punctuation mark was the comma; now and then a period got in, but it always seemed a bit self-conscious. Sometimes when he finished, he didn't even reread the piece; he sent it to the telegraph station or pushed it into the post office. And when they were printed he didn't read them even then, except his daily squib. Sometimes he didn't even see this, for he would be traveling and the paper, in the town where he arrived, wouldn't have it. But it didn't worry him. After he pecked the thing off, he lost all interest in it.

He was growing more serious. Now and then he spoke of "influencing thought in America." This could be done in three ways: in his lectures, his radio talks, and his writing. He was filling fewer lecture engagements; it was more fun to ride over the ranch. And to visit with his family, even if they did talk about a man of forty-two as being old.

One day, outside a studio as the two of us stood alone, he said he had the idea of wanting to become the world's first "flying reporter." I didn't know what he meant until he explained that he wanted to buy a plane, keep it in London, and then post off to wherever there was a hot spot. "When I knock around, my newspaper stuff gets better."

As he finished *Steamboat 'Round the Bend* he became extremely restless. He wanted to go somewhere, but he didn't know where. But he would go by air. That was the only way to travel. It was perfectly safe, too; in all the miles he'd traveled he'd had only a couple of minor mishaps. Why, if he'd walked that far he'd had more'n that!

He thought of going to Rio de Janeiro, catching the German Zeppelin and flying up the coast of Africa; the great ship was, at this time, making scheduled flights. He had never been on a Zeppelin. It'd be fun. The papers'd like it.

Then, by chance, Wiley Post came to Los Angeles. Will had been a great admirer of Wiley Post. Wiley was just about the greatest flier in the world, Will said. Wiley had made two flights around the world; once with Harold Gatty, once alone, and had picked up a hatful of medals. He was twenty years younger than Will. He had been born in Grand Saline, Texas, the son of a farmer. But soon the family had come to Oklahoma and there Wiley had grown up. He looked on himself as an Oklahoman. He got a job in the oil fields at rough labor. One day as he was working with a man who was swinging a sledge, a steel chip flew off and struck Wiley in the left eye. He got a compensation of $1800 and took that and became a flier. His trip around the world was made in the *Winnie Mae*. When he came back, New York gave him a reception and a parade up Broadway that old-timers still talk about. A little research shows that when the street cleaning department swept up the ticker tape and confetti there were 175 tons of it. This was an excellent showing. General Eisenhower suffered by comparison, for when he got back from World War II, only 77 exuberant tons were tossed at him. Admiral Halsey got only 39 tons, a pittance. Captain Henrik Carlsen got 75. The all-time high, according to the New York Department of Sanitation, was the reception for General MacArthur who got 3249 tons of ticker tape, confetti, shredded telephone books, and one girdle. Wiley Post did not get a girdle, although he was a great hero and certainly deserved it.

Post had had a plane built for him at the Union Air Terminal, Los Angeles, after his own ideas. It was his dream plane. It had the fuselage of a Lockheed Orion, a Sirius wing and a Pratt & Whitney Wasp motor which developed 550 horsepower. The propeller was a three-bladed Hamilton Standard; the angles of the blades could be changed by the pilot from the cockpit. In addition it had other fancy touches. It had compensating tanks, one in each wing. The operator was supposed to watch and, when the gasoline got low in one tank, he was to take hold of the handle and move it over so that the gasoline would flow in from the other tank. This, later, became important. But there it was, a fine, new, sleek plane. Wiley was as proud of it as a boy is of a new cowboy suit.

Will was eager to see how it worked and made a flight with Wiley to Waite Phillips's ranch in New Mexico. It was discovered that the plane was nose-heavy. Some scrap iron was wired into the tail, and everything seemed to be all right. Once Will seemed to be concerned, but dismissed it with "If it's good enough for Wiley, it's good enough for me."

Post had been to Alaska and wanted to go back and see if it would be feasible to lay out a mail-and-passenger route between Alaska and Russia which would avoid the long flight over the Pacific. He talked about this to Will. Will had never been in Alaska; maybe he'd better hop north instead of south.

Wiley was going to Seattle to have pontoons put on the plane and some other changes made. No official inspection was made.

Will was still busy on *Steamboat 'Round the Bend* and still hesitated. He told Wiley to call him from Seattle; maybe by that time he'd know what he wanted to do. Wiley called and, on the telephone, Will made his decision. It was part of his nature to make a sudden decision and then plunge into carrying it out.

Betty did not want him to go. He hesitated. What should he do? It would be fine to see the north country; papers'd like it, too. The two on horseback took a ride over the ranch. He pointed out where he wanted to make a new trail; he'd do it as soon as he got back. She tried to persuade him from making the trip, but no, that would throw Wiley out. Besides, he'd be back soon. There was a lot of work on his desk — a passel of unanswered letters. Well, he'd let 'em wait till he got back.

That afternoon he packed two bags — packed them as he always did by just stuffing things in. When they wouldn't hold any more, why, then he had everything he needed. He had on one suit; another was in a bag.

He and Betty went to see the last part of a polo game at the Uplifters Ranch; when he came back, after the game, he went to his beloved calf pen. The calves were getting tame; they'd come up and make faces at you if you didn't rope 'em. Have to get some new calves.

After dinner Will and Betty started to Los Angeles to attend a rodeo in the Gilmore Stadium. On the way Will stopped at the hospital to see Emil, the butler and houseman, who had broken his leg. Then back into the car again and on the way. At the rodeo some of the riders came up and spoke to him. He was gettin' too old to do that stuff any more himself, he said, but he shore liked to watch it. Someone gave him a small trick puzzle; he tried to work it, then put it in his pocket. When the rodeo was over Betty and Will started for the airport, where Will was to take the night plane to San Francisco. He told Betty good-by, then went to the airport newsstand and scooped up a roll of newspapers. The plane taxied down the field, then turned and, as it came back, Will smiled and waved. Then the plane disappeared into the night.

He telephoned the next day from San Francisco. Everything was just fine and don't nobody worry about me. The following day he telephoned from Seattle. Yep, everything was all right; goin' to play a game of polo this afternoon. (The field is now named in his honor.) And here, in Seattle, the plane was loaded. The last thing to go aboard was two cases of chili.

Soon Will and Wiley were in Juneau, Alaska. Will was in high spirits. Now for a holiday without a care, see a new country, have new experiences, get stuff for the papers.

Rex Beach was there — Rex, who had written his first motion picture. The two had a wonderful time talking of old days and old times. Did Will remember the time he had made a running dive and knocked his arm out? Did Will remember how Rex's wife had to bullyrag Will into making a silent picture? Wiley Post sat silently listening. Will saw that Rex had noticed this. "Wiley does the flying and I do the talking; it's about a fifty-fifty job," said Will. However, a serious note came into the talk when Rex asked Will if he wasn't afraid to tackle the North. "Not with ol' Wiley. He's the most careful pilot I ever knew. Amelia Earhart told me she considered him the finest flier in the world."

Rex asked Will his plans.

"Ain't got any. We're just a couple of tourists. Maybe we'll go to Siberia. After that I reckon we'll head for home." He spoke with his old enthusiasm about flying. "Me and Wiley are goin' to take a day off with nothin' to do and go flyin'."

The next morning, before time to take off, he bought a red fox fur, had it boxed and himself took it to the post office and addressed it to Betty.

He was in the same high spirits when they got to Matamuska where a colony was being established. Even before he was out of the plane, there was a crowd around him, standing in weeds almost up to its knees, wanting to laugh. Will never disappointed an audience. "Where you folks from?" he asked as he got out. "Anybody here from Claremore?" It was not long till he was back in the plane; in a few moments he was asleep. Lively and entertaining as he was when there was a crowd, he would fall asleep the moment they were gone. It was getting to be hard work to keep a crowd going.

At last they arrived in Fairbanks, Alaska, where they found Joe Crosson, Alaska's greatest flier. Wiley already knew him. The three went to a hotel and soon were having a fine time, telling stories and swapping flying experiences. But Will — however good a time he was having — was always thinking of his papers. Must get his telegram off.

The two waited here, ready to head for the V of land that thrusts itself out into the polar sea and is called Point Barrow. There is no town called Point Barrow. The town is Barrow, Alaska; it is ten miles south of the tip of Point Barrow and is 327 miles inside the Arctic Circle. Here there was a depot of gasoline. When the fliers left Barrow there would be nothing till they got to Siberia, a long and forbidding stretch of sea and ice.

At Barrow there was a weather station which reported to ships and planes and was the one connection with the outside world. It was as primitive and as remote a place as you could scare up. The town was a fishing village, with a native Eskimo population of 500, and nine white people. Here was located the Presbyterian Mission and Hospital. The latter was under the direction of Dr. Henry W. Greist and his wife, a trained nurse. He was the only doctor in a thousand miles; that is, for five hundred miles on each side of him. He looked after the Eskimos who were hurt when "sealing" or injured in working with their reindeer; and after the few white people. He had a Sunday School; some of the Eskimo women taught classes for him. He liked his work and the people liked him. Now and then, during the very short summer season of six weeks, a boat would stray into Barrow; sometimes an American hunter would come by. Now and then a Russian plane would drone overhead. In the winter nothing happened. If a native got a fishhook in his finger the whole village buzzed.

It is 510 miles by air from Fairbanks to Barrow. To get there one has to pass over the wildest range of mountains on the American continent. If your plane goes down, the jig is up.

In Fairbanks, Will and Wiley became restless. They were having fun but must press on. They radioed to Barrow to ascertain the weather. Stanley R. Morgan, a staff sergeant in the United States Army Signal Corps, was in charge of the government weather station. He sent back word that there was a fog so heavy that no plane could live. The next day the query came again, and this time he was told that the message was for Will Rogers and Wiley Post. Back went word: the fog is impossible.

Wiley grew even more restless. He finally said, "I think we can make it." "If it's good enough for you, it's good enough for me," Will said.

Joe Crosson again counseled against it. There was a notch in the mountains, he said; when they got through they were to turn right and head for the northeast coast. All planes hugged the coastline.

Dr. Henry W. Greist gave me a first-hand account of what happened. I interviewed him at his home, 318 North Tippecanoe Boulevard, Monticello, Indiana. In fact, I stayed overnight with him. His words took me close to the Northland and its stark tragedy.

Dr. Greist:

"I had been in Barrow for seventeen years. I was both a minister and a medical doctor. My wife was with me; she is a trained nurse. We looked after the physical and spiritual welfare of the natives and the few whites in this bleak and barren section. You will understand there were no trees, only tundra grass, Barrow being 350 miles north of the tree line. All lumber is shipped in from Seattle and to get enough wood to build a hut was a demanding job. We got mail four times a year. We were 1125 miles from the North Pole. The people live by fishing, hunting seals, walrus and whales and from the flesh of their reindeer. But I liked the life and I liked the Eskimos. I never learned to talk the language, for we always had interpreters. However, I knew some of their simple words.

"I will reconstruct the scene as we put it together later. Some of it we verified from the Eskimos who were in boats along the coast, some from the hunters. The weather station had told the fliers to come up the west coast of the triangle that constitutes Point Barrow. But Wiley Post, it would seem, when he got through the mountains, turned east as instructed by Joe Crosson. He circled around and around in the impenetrable fog, not knowing where he was, nor what to do. This was established by our hunters. One hunter heard the plane three times; this meant the plane was circling. Meantime the gasoline was going. At last Wiley Post seems to have realized — by what methods I don't know — in which direction Barrow lay. As he headed for it he saw through a rift in the fog a lagoon large enough to make a landing place, and a white tent. This was a tiny spot, not shown on the maps but which we called Walakpa Lagoon, sixteen miles southwest of Barrow. You will understand that Point Barrow itself is a spit of sand sticking out into the polar sea, dotted with a few Eskimo huts.

"Post settled the plane and then he and Will walked out on the pontoons. They were only a few yards from the sealing camp of Claire Okpeaha and his wife. Claire could talk only a few words of English, but his wife was a teacher in my Sunday

School and could talk English fairly well. Wiley asked which direction it was to Barrow and she told him. Will asked what they were fishing for and she told him it was for seals. Then Will and Wiley, still standing on the pontoons, talked together in low voices for a few moments, then Will waved at our little Eskimo family and got into the plane.

"In order to head toward Barrow, Post would have to turn the plane around. Subsequent investigations showed that he made a mistake in handling the plane. There were two tanks for gasoline on the plane, one in each wing. When one tank was exhausted, the other tank was to be turned on by hand control. The pilot had to be alert to know when to do this. It would seem that Wiley Post was tragically low in gas as a result of having gone east 150 miles to the coast and for hours was lost in the fog, and was trying to conserve his supply in order to make sure he could get to Barrow where he knew a supply awaited him. Anyway, when he was about fifty feet up, in trying to 'bank,' he must have heard the misfire of the engine, then frantically turned the hand control. But it was too late for the gasoline to reach the engine and vaporize. The plane came down like a rock, landing on its back, with the pontoons up like a turtle's feet. The water in this little land-locked lagoon was about four feet deep. The ground surrounding it never thaws to a depth of more than a foot. The plane split open and the sand and gravel was shot up into the broken plane with terrific force, as I will show in a minute.

"Claire ran to the plane and shouted, but there was no answer. He consulted his wife, then started to run to Barrow. It was a difficult route, for he had to skirt small lakes and inlets and bogs of land. It took five hours.

"When he arrived he went to the native store and told Bert Panigeo, the owner, what had happened. The storekeeper called Frank J. Daugherty, our schoolteacher, on the telephone. Of course a crash was serious and the loss of life was serious, but it was thought it was a Russian plane, or the private plane of American hunters — who else would be on the west coast?

"Mr. Daugherty, as Government agent, ordered out the boats. Then he asked Sergeant Morgan if he would go along. The natives then rushed over and told Charles D. Brower what had happened. Mr. Brower was United States Commissioner and represented the Territorial courts. He sent his boat down, with his son David as captain. Sergeant Morgan was not at any time in charge of the party.

"Of course all this was proceeding as fast as matters could be managed. Then Claire, who had panted out his news, spoke again, for he had had time to recover and to add a few details. He said in his broken English, helped by the interpreter, something that put an entirely different face on the matter. 'One mans big, have tall boots. Other mans short, have sore eye, rag over eye.' We looked at each other in alarm. Was it possible that Wiley Post and Will Rogers had wandered down the west coast? . . .

"Three motorboats were put into the water. One of them towed a small *oomiak*, which was to be used in getting across the sand bar that enclosed the lagoon. On the three boats there were about thirty Eskimos. I was operating at the hospital and was not a member of the party.

"The plane was bottom up, badly split and wrenched. David Brower cut a hole in the plane and crawled in. Soon he came out and said, 'It's Will Rogers and Wiley Post.' There was a silence among those standing there, then they went in and took out Will's body. A block and tackle had to be used to get out Wiley's, for it was jammed. Wet eiderdown sleeping bags were taken from the plane and the bodies placed in them, then the bodies were lowered into the *oomiak*. Then the three boats started back; the current was flowing westward which slowed progress.

"My first sight of the sad procession was when the boats came in. Dispatches, later, told how the Eskimos were singing a dirge. The Eskimos do not have a dirge, but they do have a plaintive song they sing when the headman in a village dies. They were singing this. Once heard it is never forgotten. The sight of the boats coming in, the little *oomiak* bobbing behind, and the song floating to us . . . I'll never forget it.

"The bodies were carried to the hospital and there my wife and I examined them. I'll not speak of the condition they were in. The impact in the shallow water had been so great that the plane had split open and the sand and gravel had shot up into the clothes of the men. The first thing we did was to take our scissors and cut the clothes off. The clothes were so deeply impregnated with sand and gravel and so blood-stained that we put the garments aside.

"We took out the contents of their pockets. Rogers had about $770 in cash, $2040 in travelers' checks and a trick puzzle. I understood later that he had started with this when he left Los Angeles. And there was a picture, from a newspaper, of his daughter. There were also a pocketknife, spectacles, a reading glass and two watches. Wiley Post had a gold watch. It had stopped at the moment of the crash. But Will had a two-dollar watch, attached to his vest with a string. It was still running. Will's other watch was a large affair and was used as an alarm clock when he was traveling. The pocketknife was not a sleek, dainty affair, but a rough-and-tumble one such as a Boy Scout might use for trading purposes. In all it was a strange assortment.

"It can not be said that the Eskimos were sad, as it has always been reported in the papers, for they had never heard of either of the men. But they did know that we were deeply affected and that something important had happened. About fifteen of them remained through the night, sitting in the hall of the hospital, talking to themselves in low voices. We furnished them coffee.

"There was the matter of clothes. The white people did not

have extra suits they could give for that purpose, so we went to the missionary barrel and got out two old-fashioned long night-gowns that had been sent up from the States, and put the bodies into them. Then they were wrapped in freshly laundered white sheets, taken to the new warehouse and put on the floor under lock and key. It was a long, ghastly night.

"Later we washed out the clothing and returned it to the widows — everything except the cut rubber boots which I threw away. His typewriter and rifle were broken; in fact, everything in the plane was broken except tools of small size.

"The next day Joe Crosson came from Fairbanks by plane and we carried the bodies to his plane and put them in. The natives stood watching and, as the plane rose, they waved a silent fare-well."

He stopped and there was a silence. I had been greatly moved by the story as seen through his eyes.

"Could you tell me the condition the bodies were in?" I asked.

"I've never told that."

I stirred, ill at ease. I told him that I didn't want to pry into anything he didn't wish to tell, but for my own full knowledge I would like to know. He glanced at his wife, called her by name and said, "Shall we tell?"

There was a pause. I could see she was weighing something that must have been on her mind a long time. "We're getting old. It might be well to leave a permanent record."

He sat for some moments looking at his desk. Then glanced at me.

"Once the widow had us to her ranch house for dinner. Three of the children were there. After dinner the two younger went out and Bill and his mother were alone with us. 'I wish you'd tell me the condition Will's body was in,' she said — 'Do not spare me.'

"I didn't know what to do. Should I tell her? Would she be

better off by knowing? Finally I said, 'He was badly broken,' and passed it off the best I could. I never told her and I've never told anyone, as I mentioned." There was another silence. I could see that he was greatly disturbed. "I will tell you," he said abruptly. "I think my wife is right. I am eighty-four. His left arm was broken and his forehead was caved in. Evidently he had been standing up, as we tried to reconstruct it. His head had had a blow from in front — his scalp had been detached and was hanging down in front of his face like a mask. There was a star wound in his right cheek. I made under sutures and restored it as best I could. He had on a pair of high hip boots. The long bone of his right leg had a compound fracture, a section thrust through his trousers and through the boot till it was sticking out several inches, a ghastly sight even to one who has seen many terrible sights."

"What did you do about the bone when you went to dress the body?" I asked.

"I replaced the section broken off — a six-inch piece. My wife and I worked till morning. It took us five hours and I am considered a rapid operator. We rouged and fixed the face as best we could. In the Territory, doctors were not allowed to embalm."

I was touched by this recital which was so simple, yet so moving. When I spoke my voice was strained. "Can I print this?"

He glanced at his wife. "Yes. It will serve as a record."

"Did the widow ever send you anything?" I asked.

He nodded. "Yes. She sent me a hundred dollars, and she sent a hundred dollars to be divided among the Eskimos who had gone on the boats."

There was another silence. "Do many people ask about the crash?"

"People come to see me. A good many high-school students; they get it as a classroom assignment. I tell them about it, but I don't go into details."

The first the outside world knew was when the bodies were

brought to the hospital and Stanley R. Morgan sent a radio message to Seattle. It had to be relayed twice and was about two hours in getting there. The message said, in effect, that an Eskimo runner had brought back word that an airplane crash had taken place, that boats had gone to the scene and that the bodies of Will Rogers and Wiley Post had been discovered. Then he added that Post's watch had stopped at 8:18. But this was misleading, for he had been carrying Oklahoma time. The time, in reality, was 5:18.

Colonel Charles A. Lindbergh was at North Haven, Maine, when the Associated Press called on the telephone and told him what had happened. He was technical adviser to the Pan American Airways and was aware of the difficulties in ground and water transportation in Alaska. He telephoned Juan T. Trippe, president of the company, and suggested that a plane be sent. Soon word came to Joe Crosson, in Fairbanks, to go after the bodies of the two men he had laughed and joked with just a few days before.

When Joe Crosson arrived in Barrow, the fog was still so thick that he had to wait several hours before he could start out again. When the bodies got to Fairbanks, a silent crowd gathered to witness their arrival, a crowd that was in contrast to the one that had laughed and joked when Will and Wiley had left. A hearse arrived and the bodies were put in it. They were embalmed, suits were put on them and again started on their way.

After Will had left on his trip, Betty, with her sister, Theda Blake, went to Skowhegan, Maine, where Mary was appearing in a stage play called *Ceiling Zero*. She was playing the part of a girl whose father is killed in an airplane crash. In the play with her were Humphrey Bogart and Keenan Wynn.

In the colony, living there and taking part in the plays, was Arthur Byron, a well-known actor. Betty and her sister were in the Byron cottage where Betty was telling Arthur Byron how worried she was about Will; they looked out the window and saw a car coming. It stopped in front of the cottage and Grant Mills, the manager of the Lakewood theater, got out. He called to Betty's sister; she came out into the yard and the two walked off to one side. His manner was greatly agitated and he spoke in a low voice. In a few moments Betty's sister came back. Betty saw by her manner that something had happened. Betty's first thought was of Jimmy, who was driving from California in a car with a friend. "Has something happened to Jimmy?"

Her sister put her arm around her and said, "It's not about Jimmy. It's Will. He's had an accident."

After she had composed herself a bit, Betty rode to the theater where Mary was rehearsing and told her the news. Almost unbelievably soon, telephone messages began to pour in. Colonel Lindbergh called and asked to speak to Mrs. Rogers; his was the only call she answered. He said he would fly to her and would take her to Alaska. She thanked him but said she would not go. In a short time the little summer settlement was filled with newspaper correspondents and newsreel cameramen.

Jimmy Rogers, with his cousin, had just arrived; they were at the Gotham Hotel in New York on their way to Maine when Jimmy heard the news. He put through a call to his mother and the two talked together. Young Will was working on an oil tanker in San Diego on which he expected soon to leave for the Philippine Islands. And there the news was told to him.

Wiley Post's body was taken to Oklahoma, Will's to Forest Lawn Cemetery, Los Angeles. His was the most impressive funeral ever given for a private citizen in California. All motion-picture studios were closed; flags flew at half-mast over all government buildings in the state; at two o'clock, by order of the governor, there was a minute of silence. The funeral service took place in the Wee Kirk o' the Heather; it followed no formal denominational rite, for Will belonged to no church. An unusual part of the funeral were the flower arrangements, for the flowers were made into chaps, spurs, lariats and saddles. Most of the great names of Hollywood were there. John Boles sang "Old Faithful," a favorite of Will's — a cowboy's song to his horse. There were two or three unexpected turns. One was that the Soviet Ambassador, in Washington, D. C., sent a huge floral piece. And there were four Cherokee Indians who had driven all the way from Oklahoma in an old and decrepit car. The family had known they were coming and had given them cards that admitted them to the space occupied by relatives and nearest of kin. The first person to arrive was the colored comedian who had worked with Will in several pictures — Stepin Fetchit.

Wiley Post's funeral was held at the same hour in Maysville, Oklahoma, in the Baptist Church.

Personal. One of the striking things about the death of Will Rogers is that nearly everyone can remember where he was when he heard the news and how it affected him. I well remember how it came to me. I was in New York. The telephone rang, and when I answered it was the National Broadcasting Company with the news. For some moments I could say nothing; it seemed to me my ears had tricked me. I felt as if a member of my family had gone.

The next evening there was a memorial broadcast. It was hooked up with different cities in the United States. Others in the New York studio who spoke were George M. Cohan, Gene Buck, Thomas Hitchcock, Eddie Rickenbacker. We had to wait in the studio about twenty minutes before time to go on. We talked among ourselves of different experiences with Will, but George M. Cohan sat through the twenty minutes without speaking to anyone. I never knew whether it was because he was so deeply affected, or whether it was just a chance to rest. Anyway, when he came to the microphone he spoke the most movingly of anyone there.

The story of how the news of the crash affected the people of Oklahoma was told to me by N. G. Henthorne, editor of the *Tulsa World*. He has a farm near Locust Grove, and, on this day, was overseeing half a dozen men who were building a fence. All of the men were part, or fullblood, Cherokee.

An elderly man was seen coming down the dirt road, bumping along in an ancient car. When he got to the men, he stopped the car, came to Mr. Henthorne, and said, "Some bad news has come in to Locust Grove. The operator wrote it down an' asked me to bring it out to you. Comes from your paper."

Mr. Henthorne opened the note, glanced at it, then read it aloud.

The men listened silently and, seemingly, expressionlessly. Some leaned on their spades and some on the posts, and some squatted on their heels; some held nails in their hands and dug into the ground with them. But the men did not speak, so personal, so devastating was the news.

After a long silence the men began to recover; they began to talk among themselves of how they'd known Will, or how he'd done a favor for a brother of theirs. Now and then as they talked they would roll a cigarette, or take a chew of tobacco. Finally one of the men said, "I can't work any more today."

"Me either," said another of the Indians.

Then they piled their shovels, axes and wire-stretchers together and those that had cars got into them; the others started walking across the fields to their shanties so they could tell their wives the news they'd heard about Will.

Will lay buried in Los Angeles for nine years; then his body was brought back to Oklahoma and placed in the crypt in the Will Rogers Memorial, at Claremore, May 22, 1944. Betty died a month later and her body was also put in the crypt; and with the two is Freddie, who died at the age of eighteen months. So inspiring, so somehow beautiful was Will's life that 1200 people a day visit the Memorial. No one can see the Memorial, or stand beside the simple crypt in the memorial garden, without being touched.

For Will Rogers and Wiley Post
by Ada Jackson
Oh Death — how seldom do You get
Courage and Laughter in one net!

The Amount of His Estate. The Building of the Monument at Barrow, Alaska

AS NEARLY as the scene can be reconstructed, Will was standing up in the rear of the plane. Was it because it was nose-heavy? When his little bag and his papers were taken out, the last thing he ever wrote was found. It was water-soaked; it was ironed out and a photostat was made. It has never before been published. It is too long to be printed in its entirety, so I am using the part that has to do with Balto, the famous dog of the North. (Some of my readers may remember when Balto raced across the newspapers of America.) Now to Will's last piece; it is all one long paragraph:

WELL ALL I KNOW ABOUT DOGS IS NOT MUCH, BUT WHEN I WAS UP IN ALASKA THERE IS AN AWFUL LOT OF DEPENDENCE PUT IN DOGS. . . . THEYRS WHOLE EXISTENCE TANGLES AROUND DOGS. OF COURSE THE PLANE HAS DIMINISHED THE DOG TRAVEL A LOT BUT STILL THE BACKBONE OF THE ARCTIC IS A DOGS BACKBONE. I MET UP THERE JUST AS I WAS LEAVING FAIRBANKS THAT FAMOUS "MUSHER" AND DOG RACE WINNER, "SEPPALA." HE BECOME IMMORTAL ON THAT FAMOUS DRIVE WITH THE INFANTILE PARALYSIS SERUM TO NOME. . . . SEPPALA IS AS IDENTIFIED WITH DOGS AS MAY WEST IS WITH BUXOMNESS. . . . HE USED TO WIN MOST ALL THOSE BIG DOG RACES, THE BIGGEST OF WHICH WAS THE "ALASKA SWEEPSTAKES," WHICH HAD PRIZES AS HIGH AS $20.000. HE IS A LITTLE BIT OF A FELLOW, BUT MIGHTY

HUSKY. . . . HE WAS I BELIEVE HE SAID 58 YEARS OLD, KINDER
SAID IT LIKE HE THOUGHT A MAN THAT AGE BETTER BE DYING
OFF, AND IT DIDENT MAKE ME FEEL ANY TOO CHIPPER. ONE OF
THE HARDEST THINGS HE SAID IS TO TRAIN DOG TEAMS TO PASS
ON THE TRAIL AND NOT TO GO TO WAR WITH EACH OTHER.
THEN YOU ARE ALL WINTER SEPERATING EM, TO SAY NOTHIN
OF HOW LONG IT TAKES TO SEPERATE THE DRIVERS. . . . WELL
NOT KNOWING ANYTHING ABOUT IT, I ASKED ABOUT THE DOG
"BALTO". . . . THERE IS A STATUE TOO IN CENTRAL PARK
NEW YORK IN HONOR OF THIS GREAT RACE, AND HE TOLD ME,
"BALTO WAS NOT THE DOG, THE REAL HERO OF THE RACE WAS
"TOGO" MY LEAD DOG. BALTO WAS NOT IN MY TEAM, HE WAS
INTHE TEAM OF THE DRIVER WHO MADE THE LAST LAP OR EN-
TRY INTO NOME, AND HENCE HE RECEIVED ALL THE CREDIT, AND
BALTO WAS NOT EVEN THE LEAD DOG." THE NEWSPAPER MEN
ASKED HIM THE NAMES OF THE DOGS AND THE DRIVER TOLD
THEM THE LEADER WAS "FOX." WELL, HALF THE DOG TEAMS IN
THE NORTH THEY SAID WAS NAMED FOX, SO THEY KEPT ASKING
OTHER DOGS NAMES IN THE TEAM, AND FINALLY HE MENTIONED
"BALTO" SO THEY HOPPED ON THAT. . . . IT HAD HEADLINE POS-
SIBILITYS, AND TODAY I GUESS ALL OVER THE WORLD YOU FIND
IT ON DOG FOOD BOXES. . . . HE SAID HE DIDENT MIND IT FOR
HIMSELF BUT THAT IT WAS HIS WONDERFUL LEAD DOG "FOX"
THAT DID SUCH GREAT WORK AND THEN LOST THE CREDIT. . . .

(This is all that deals with Balto. He now begins to talk about
a dog named Mickey, who belonged to Joe Crosson's partner.
He tells how, when Mickey went out, a bear got after him.
Mickey came back as fast as his legs would take him. Now to
quote Will):

EARNEST [JOE'S PARTNER] HAD TO SHOOT THE BEAR TO KEEP
HIM FROM RUNNING MICKEY UNDER THE BED. THEY SAY THERE
IS MORE FELLOWS BEEN CAUGHT BY A BEAR, JUST THAT WAY,
AN OLD PET DOG . . . JUMPS THE BEAR . . . THE BEAR [CHASES]

AFTER EM, AND THE FIRST THING YOU KNOW YOU GOT A BEAR
IN YOUR LAP, AND A DOG BETWEEN YOUR FEET. SO MICKEY IS A
GREAT BEAR DOG . . . HE CHEWED ALL THE HAIR OFF THE BEAR,
AFTER DEATH.

It will be noted that the last word that Will ever wrote was
"death."

Claire Okpeaha, as I write this, is still living. From Lawrence B.
Williams, already mentioned, I was able to obtain a few details.
His letter:

"Claire was born in 1891 and is still a hunter and fisher. His
Eskimo name was Ok-pe-a-ha which can be thought of as rhym-
ing with Minnehaha — first syllable is pronounced *oak*. Some
time ago the teachers and missionaries insisted that the Eskimos
had to have two names — a first and a last. Until that time (at
least until the missionaries came in) every member of a family
had a different name. This double-name helped the government
to keep the members of the family straight in matter of income
taxes, relief rolls and so on. Claire was given that fancy name
by a missionary.

"He makes a living by hunting, fishing and trapping. He has
six living children. He is very proud of the fact that he was the
only human being who saw the crash and to bring the news to
our village. He poses for pictures for the few tourists that
wander in, not many, for only one ship a year — a freighter —
comes to Barrow.

"Claire is subject to income taxes. I guess you never escape
them. There are two kinds of taxes here: the Federal and the
Territorial. But Claire hasn't edged up high enough for the
Federal to nip him.

"Our town has about one thousand natives, the population
having doubled in the last six years due to government projects.
The natives draw the same wages as the whites, so they're doing

all right. In other words Uncle Sam pays better than seals. The natives who don't work on our government projects do fishing, hunting and 'sealing.'

"So tell your readers that Claire is a great man in this section and very justly, for what he did that day was a notable feat."

Will's great confidence in flying had continued, but Betty had been apprehensive and, to reassure her, he made out a new will three days before he left. It was on one sheet of paper and gave everything to his widow. The following were named as executors: Betty, who was not required to put up bond; Oscar Lawler, the family lawyer; and James K. Blake, Betty's brother, who helped Will in business affairs. The witnesses were: Ewing Halsell, of Vinita, and Eddie Vail, Jaloma Ranch, Santa Barbara County, California.

A rather unusual thing about the estate was the way the money was invested. Will had never owned stocks or bonds. He always said he didn't want to buy something he didn't understand; but there were two things he did understand — life insurance and real estate. He had, as we've seen, sent back money from South Africa when he was the Cherokee Kid to take care of his life insurance. He had never deviated from his faith in life insurance, and had added to the policies during the years.

A report was published that Lloyd's of London had paid the widow $2,500,000. I took up the matter with Swett & Crawford, 3450 Wilshire Boulevard, Los Angeles, who handled the policy. John C. Spencer wrote me: "At the time Will Rogers crashed, the maximum capacity of the Lloyd's market for personal accident insurance was around $500,000 and this would have been for insurance excluding flying. Where flying had to be added, the amount available was considerably less. He was insured with us, as our files reveal, for accident insurance totaling $262,500. This is the sum we paid the estate."

Will had indeed added to his life insurance. He had policies with the Equitable Life Assurance Society of the United States, the Penn Mutual Life Insurance Company, and the Mutual Life Insurance Company. (He had two policies with Penn Mutual.) His total life insurance ran up to $482,500. But this was not all. He had endowment policies amounting to $200,000. And there were annuities, but I am unable to find how much they totaled. And he had U. S. Savings Bonds.

He had more invested in real estate than in life and accident insurance. He had the Santa Monica place and he owned the Rogers ranch in Oklahoma and he still had the Indian allotments.

When the will was admitted to probate in the Superior Court in Los Angeles, James K. Blake swore that the personal property was as follows:

$30,000 as the value of furnishings on the Santa Monica ranch

$1,920 as the value of fourteen horses

$75 — two mules

$700 — ranch equipment

$200 — office furniture

$860 — two automobiles, a truck and a trailer plus the money and travelers' checks found on the body at the time of the crash (given in the previous chapter).

When everything was counted up his estate amounted to $2,300,000.

How much did he make his last year? The following would seem to be a fair estimate. He made three motion pictures, each at $110,000. (His new contract, as we've seen, was an even more impressive one.) He had annuities which kept throwing down money; now and then he went out and lectured. The year's income would seem to be:

Twentieth Century-Fox	$330,000
McNaught Syndicate	130,000
Radio	60,000
	$520,000

(That year he did not write anything for the *Saturday Evening Post*.)

It is surprising that a man who had made as much money as he had had not been trapped by get-rich-quick talkers. But he hadn't. One, however, had hooked him. When Will was in vaudeville he had bought some lots near Montauk Point, Long Island, New York. It was going to make him rich; when vaudeville played out, he would have him a bit of mother earth. One day, after he had bought it, he went out to see his particular bit of mother earth. It took some searching, but he found it. It was a miserable sandy waste that made anything in the Cookson Hills look as rich as Imperial Valley. He got rid of it as quickly as he could. This unhappy deal may have taught him a lesson, for later none of the vast throng of California promoters ever slipped a hand into his pocket.

His gifts and donations were amazingly liberal. Sometimes he seemed to be giving away money right and left. But when the end came he was a rich man.

It is interesting to compare Will's estate with Al Jolson's. The latter, who died in October 1950, left almost the same amount; to be exact it was $2,366,000. This is the way he had his money invested:

6000 shares of United States Steel

U. S. Treasury notes worth $800,000

Treasury Bonds worth $145,000

Royalties from *The Jolson Story* (up to the time of his death) $95,073

Royalties (up to time of death) from *Jolson Sings Again* $12,727

Decca Records $120,804

Al Jolson had no life insurance and no real estate.

Shortly after the crash, people began to talk about putting up a monument to mark the spot where the crash had taken place. Finally the plan was carried out and the monument was built by Homer F. Kellems, now a colonel in the United States Air Force (and a brother of Vivien Kellems). His home is near Siloam Springs, Arkansas. The following letter pretty well tells the story:

"After our two talks at the Dutch Treat Club, you asked me to repeat what I had said and to put it in a letter to you. You are now holding the letter in your hands. You will want to know where the money came from. We decided to finance the expedition by the sale of First Covers which would commemorate the occasion. The Philatelic Branch of the Post Office approved and 30,000 were sold for twenty-five cents each.

"I'll skip over how we got the cement and the Marker Stone from Claremore to Alaska without having to spend a cent. Finally we arrived at Walakpa Lagoon, where Rogers and Post were killed. There was a high cliff facing the Arctic Ocean and this I selected as the spot to place the Marker. What a job it was to dig that foundation! The ground there never thaws deeper than ten inches, or a foot. About three feet below the surface we ran into a driftwood floor, the cracks of which were filled with seal and walrus bones. Apparently the Eskimos, when they polished off a meal, tossed their bones on this floor to get rid of them. Also there were pieces of walrus hide, still — after all these years — smelling to high heaven. We found an ivory spearhead which was entirely different from any now in use. It may well have been a thousand years old. The spot we happened to hit on for the Memorial Monument was an old Eskimo igloo which was used, probably, a thousand years ago.

"We used sand and gravel from the seashore — and what a job it was to lug it up the cliff! I wisht you'd been there . . . as water boy. One day half a dozen Eskimo boys came along and helped to get it up cliffside. The cement we had brought in bags from the grand old state of Oklahoma. We sank a hole four feet deep and seven feet square, all done with picks and shovels in the hardest ground known on the face of this planet. Water to mix the concrete was taken from nearby pools on the tundra.

"My daughter — Vivienne LaFerne Kellems (now Proctor) — composed the words for the stone: 'Will Rogers and Wiley Post ended life's flight here, August 15, 1935.' Then there is a statement that the stone was taken from a quarry near Clare- more. At last we were ready for the dedication services. There was an Eskimo choir under the direction of Mrs. Nan Klere- koper, a missionary at Barrow; her husband Fred offered the dedication prayers. The dedication was exactly three years to an hour after the crash. The singing of the Eskimos amid the bleak, wild surroundings was a touching sound.

"We put a piece of conduit from the bottom of the monument to the top so that the monument can be used as a beacon for the ships at sea and planes in the sky.

"Now I'll add a word about the cause of the accident, for I do not follow Dr. Greist's theory. The plain matter of fact (as I see it) is that Wiley Post *ran out of gasoline*. Stanley Morgan told me that there was not a drop of gasoline in the tanks and none on the surface of the lagoon. Here are two theories that are held in this northland section:

"*Theory 1.* Wiley had been flying for hours and was about out of gasoline. He came down, when he saw the white tent, through a rift in the overcast and did not stop his engine as he and Will talked to the Eskimos. When they found out where Barrow was they decided it was better to try to make it by air than to walk over the tundra and the pebbly beach. It is believed that as Wiley took off and banked to the right, he ran out of gas and side- slipped to the crash.

"*Theory 2.* He made the mistake of taxiing down the lagoon for the take-off and his pontoons hit a submerged sandbar. This catapulted the plane into the air and caused it to crash. I was told that the pilot who flew the bodies out examined the site and found imprints of both pontoons on such a sandbar."

And so it would seem there are four theories as to what caused the crash:

1. The one given the Accident Board of the Bureau of Air Commerce (outlined in the Sources for a preceding chapter).

2. Dr. Greist's theory.

3. and 4. Outlined above by Colonel Kellems.

It's doubtful if the cause of the crash will ever be satisfactorily explained. Too many unknown factors. But here's the opinion of the author for what it's worth (nothing on a declining market and no prospect for the future): Wiley simply ran out of gas. The plane was doomed from the time, in Seattle, when he put on the pontoons without an inspection.

A movement was started to have a bronze statue of Will; Jo Davidson was in America and was selected. He returned to Paris and two of Will's movies were sent over; a projection machine was rigged up in the studio and the pictures run off and there Jo studied him afresh. Betty sent over some of Will's clothes. A model was engaged; he put on Will's clothes and the statue was made. It was eight feet high; there are two copies, one in the Claremore Memorial, the other in Statuary Hall, Washington, D. C. The state of Oklahoma paid Davidson $35,000. On the base of each statue are the words: "I never met a man I didn't like."

CHAPTER 29

Myths and Legends. An Analysis of His Humor

THERE WERE MYTHS about Will even while he was still living. Probably the best known was the Edward L. Doheny story. According to this pleasant fabrication, Doheny called up to say that he was giving a party and would Will come? Will went and during the party was called on to "say a few words." He said them and the next day sent the oil man a bill for a thousand dollars.

The oil man called up in considerable agitation and explained that he had invited Will as a guest and that he should not be expected to pay the bill.

"I was there as an entertainer," said Will. "If I had been there as a guest you would have invited my wife."

Will and Betty suffered much embarrassment from this impossible story and both went to extremes to deny it, for in it there was no word of truth.

Another fireside tale was that he was much better educated than he pretended and that, as a matter of fact, he had gone to school at Oxford. The one who thought up this bright idea was Arthur Brisbane, the journalist. He and Will used to take flings at each other in their columns. One day Brisbane said, in what he considered a rare burst of humor, that Will was a well-educated man and had gone to school at Oxford. Brisbane's humor was never very robust; in fact sometimes it was barely able to drag itself around. He was at his best when asking in his column if a prizefighter could lick a gorilla.

Will was amazed at the number of people who accepted the

statement as true. It put him in the position of faking — something that was as alien to Will as a bathrobe to a cowboy. He always denied it, a bit at a loss to understand why anyone would believe such a preposterous tale, and a bit hurt. Sometimes he would take the opposite tack. "Well, this old Oxford grad has got to git to work. Just because you got a good education don't mean you can set around and do nothin'."

Another was that he never wore a dinner jacket. Not quite true, either. At different times he owned two. He had his first when he and Dick Paris set out to see the world; he wore it, as we have seen, to the dining room on the ship — that is, he wore it as long as he could crawl to the dining room. Later, when he became an entertainer, he had a dinner jacket. But as he grew older and became more and more a personality, he tossed the semiformal attire aside altogether and substituted a suit which would do in a pinch; it was a blue double-breasted suit which he wore with a white shirt and black tie. At a quick glance it would pass as a dinner jacket. Even if it hadn't, he wouldn't have worried too much. In his early days he had been the best-dressed boy in the Cooweescoowee District; in fact, a dandy. But as he grew older and fame and fortune became his companions, he grew more and more clothes careless. He wore rough-and-ready things that he would not have been seen in in his early days. As he advanced in age, he became more and more a "character" and less sensitive to what people thought as to how he dressed. Also, as a master showman, he knew the value of his knockabout attire and, as a result, wore clothes that any other man wouldn't have been seen in outside the woodshed. When foreign diplomats and visiting nobility came to the studio (they always wanted to see Will) he liked to meet 'em in something that looked as if it had come out of a missionary barrel. The publicity department loved him.

Another persistent folk tale was the valet story. Once the studio hired a valet to help him dress when he was getting ready for a picture. One day the studio manager came to Will's dressing room and asked where the valet was. Then the studio manager found that Will was paying the valet five dollars a day to stay away. This, too, was the flowering of a press agent's mind. In all his days in show business, Will never had a valet. However, for a time Will "dressed" with Fred Stone. Fred had to have one because of the quick and elaborate changes he had to make. Will may have called on the valet to hand him a rope, certainly never anything more. No one was ever more independent than Will. He wanted to do everything for himself. And he just about did, too. As a matter of fact, much of the time he used his car as a dressing room and made his changes by dodging in and out of the car, like a small boy in and out of a swimming hole.

An amusing story is told how Will would forget to go around to see the studio and collect his weekly pay check. One story had it that he let eleven checks accumulate before he bothered to pick them up. Not quite true. He was not paid by the week but by the picture. Usually the shooting schedule lasted thirty-two or, at most, forty days. As a matter of fact he was always eager to get the money; however, after he had it he took little interest in it. Once, in the early days when he was getting ready to make a silent picture, he said to the producer, "If my check don't come the day it should, the next morning you're goin' to find yourself a hand short."

Another is that he tried out his newspaper pieces on anybody he could find and that if the person didn't like it, he would change what he had written. This is not quite true. When he had time he read his daily dispatches to grips, cameramen and electricians; if he didn't have time he sent the message without anyone seeing it. Many of the daily dispatches were written on planes when he was alone, or sometimes he would go to a telegraph station, sit down at the little table and write it there. Or at a chili heaven. His Sunday pieces were far too long for off-hand reading. His pieces for the *Saturday Evening Post* were even longer; he read few of them even to Betty, for often they were written when he was miles from her.

A tale that millions have enjoyed has to do with his roping proclivities at Kemper. According to this story Will liked to hide in the halls at night, waiting for the unwary. When a schoolmate came along, Will would swish his rope and have him ignominiously his prisoner. One night Colonel Johnston, the head of the school, came along. Will sent out his rope, gave a yank and sent him sprawling. He was flabbergasted when he saw whom he had roped. Good Colonel Johnston was flabbergasted, too; in fact, he was so thoroughly and completely flabbergasted that he fired poor Will. It is a fine story — very amusing — but, unfortunately, it is not true. Will did, as we have seen, rope his fellow students, but he never made the mistake of roping the commandant. Seems almost too bad.

One of the popular bar stories is that Will in his radio broadcasts did not really have an alarm clock, but an electrically operated bell which he touched off himself. This will hardly stand up. He was on the air several times and several times he ran over; so one day he turned up at the studio with an alarm clock that must have seen the Cherokee Run, and said he was going to use it so he'd know when to stop. The production manager smiled agreeably, not believing that Will was serious; but serious he was. He set the alarm, put the ancient alarm clock on a table, and tore into his broadcast. When the clock went off, so did Will.

An aspect of Will's humor is that he never told a "funny" story in his life. He never put on ridiculous clothes to make people laugh. He was funny only with ideas. And his humor always dealt with *now*. He made a living off the headlines. He wrote his syndicate squibs from the front page; in his lectures and on the radio he talked about the subjects the newspapers were dealing with. For this reason his humor was evanescent. Things that were tremendously funny at the time no longer have any interest: prohibition, Congressmen drinking wet and voting dry, Queen Marie's visit to America, the Prince of Wales falling off his horse. Ford jokes, Coolidge jokes, "Peaches" Browning, La Follette, Senator Borah . . . the present generation knows them not.

But he did have the way of putting an editorial into a sentence. He could do that and do it superbly. He had the ability to crystallize the unspoken thoughts of the common man. When a person heard Will say something of a humorous-philosophical nature he would nod and say, "That's right; that's exactly what I think."

Will knew this and liked to talk to audiences where people didn't guffaw but nodded approval.

One night he had to speak in Symphony Hall, Boston; it was filled with the aristocracy of Boston. Will stood in the wings for a moment, trying to think of something that would fit the audience. When he came out he said that he was pleased to meet the descendants of the Mayflower. He hesitated — always just the right length of time — and then said that his ancestors hadn't come over on the Mayflower — but they had met the boat. This became one of his most successful quips. He used it endlessly; it finally went into one of his movies.

The hold Will had on the affection of the American people was tremendous. Not only on America but every country in the world, except, possibly, Russia. When he would arrive at a small airport in Guatemala, for example, the people would rush to see him, their eyes dancing, their mouths set to laugh. And it must be said that the great showman rarely disappointed them. Sometimes they understood what he said; sometimes they didn't. It was all the same. Here was a jolly person with a warm, friendly, smiling manner who completely won them over.

For American audiences he epitomized something that had been in our nation for a hundred and fifty years: the simple country boy making a place for himself in the world. He had risen to where he could walk with presidents and kings, and yet still be one of the common people. One of us. That was the way America felt; and, for that matter, still feels. He represented the best, the most wholesome aspects of American life. He was honest, he was a devoted family man, he was generous, he was kindly. But most of all, he made people laugh.

Probably the deepest appeal of all was that he could criticize the government — "cuss it out," in the words of the plain, street-corner citizen — and go right on believing in it. He thought it was the greatest form of government in the world; meantime, now and then, he could give it a piece of his mind . . . and what citizen doesn't want to do that? The average man could more nearly see himself in the mirror as Will Rogers than as any other person on the American scene.

One great, one tremendous, asset for Will was that he was always himself. In his movies the people saw Will rather than the character he was playing. In his humor they thought of him as having said it. The same quip could have been tossed off by somebody else and it would not have been considered especially noteworthy, but coming from a man they could visualize and one they loved, it took on added luster.

His philosophy was not very profound. It was what the average person was thinking but Will stated it in terms of entertainment. He would fly into a foreign country, stop at an airport, then tell what was wrong or right with the country. It satisfied the average reader. And it must be said he was right much of the time.

What was the secret of Will's humor? He always said, to people working with him, "Give me the truth. I'll exaggerate it and make it funny." And that, simple as it is, is about as good an explanation as there is. He was a truth revealer.

Also he projected his humor beyond what it immediately was; he hooked it up with something big and important. Examples:

"Every time Congress makes a joke it's a law. And every time they make a law it's a joke."

"It is much easier for America to whip a Nation than to collect a dollar from them."

"The United States never lost a war, or won a conference."

"We are the only nation in the world that waits till we get into a war before we start getting ready for it."

"We hold the distinction of being the only nation that is goin' to the poorhouse in an automobile."

"We are all igerant, only on different Subjects."

"One thing we got to be thankful for, our Soldiers can win wars faster than our Diplomats can talk us into them."

"There's one thing no nation can accuse us of — that is secret diplomacy. Our foreign dealings are an open book — a checkbook."

But this was not all, for he had a way of whipsawing between exaggerating and deflating a subject. He would enlarge a subject. Or he would deflate it. As an example of deflating a subject he would say, "About the time we were having that Set Too with Germany." Maybe his next sentence, or thought, would be the exaggeration of a simple truth beyond its ordinary proportions.

A matter that appealed to the public was the offhand way he dealt with the biggest and most important people in America, or, for that matter, in the world. He spoke of a congressman as if he were something a boy had thrown on the front porch. He spoke of a statesman as something we had to make up our minds to live with whether we liked it or not. He called a senator a "guy," he called the President by his first name; sometimes he would say "ol' Cal," or "Herb" Hoover, as if they were renters on Brush Creek. He said that the Prince of Wales was "a great little guy." He called the King of England "the Prince of Wales's old man." These impertinences delighted people. They could visualize themselves as treating these dignitaries the same way.

He always said, to his friends, that he used a joke seven times. One of his jokes was: "England has the best statesmen and the worst coffee in the world." He first used it at the Palace Theater, in London. (One of the British papers hopped on him about it.) When he came back to America and went on a lecture tour, he used it night after night. He used it in his daily newspaper feature and on his radio program and he put it into *So This Is London*.

I am often asked: "Was he the same off stage as on?" The answer is both Yes and No. When he was talking to one in person, he was serious. "Alfalfa Bill" Murray said that he once talked to Will two hours in his office and that during all this time Will did not say even one amusing thing. That night Murray went to a banquet where Will spoke. He talked about the same things that he and Murray had spoken of that day; to Murray's astonishment they were funny. Murray could hardly believe it was the same person. The explanation is that when Will was gathering material — interviewing people — he let them do the talking; he wanted to get the facts; he would exaggerate them into comedy. When Will had a crowd around him, he was always the showman.

He can be thought of as the typical American; in reality he was not this person at all. He was born of a prosperous family; he was important in his community; his parents were respected and looked up to. He never caught a fish in his life; he never carried a gun; he never killed an animal; he never played golf; he never indulged in cards; he never told funny stories; he was not a "joiner."

But in other ways he was a typical American. He was close to the grass roots, he was restless, he wanted always to be on the go, he was democratic, he liked all sorts and kinds of people, he was exceedingly generous, he believed in new things rather than in the old. He himself put his view and philosophy about as well as anybody ever did for him: "I'm just an old country boy in a Big Town tryin' to get along. I been eatin' pretty regular, and the reason I have been is because I've stayed an old country boy."

What would be his position if he had lived? It is a fascinating speculation. Several things must be taken into consideration. One is that he went down at the very peak of his career — to a martyr end. America has never been as touched by the death of a private citizen as it was by his. But if he had lived? His following would certainly have lessened; he would have become an elder states-man whom interviewers, from time to time, would have seen to get a good-natured "story." He might even have been considered a garrulous old man. The younger generation would have thought he was out of step with the times and would have looked on him as a genial curiosity. But he did go at his zenith and has become one of the brightest symbols America has ever known. He will increase in stature rather than diminish. And justly so, for he was truly a great, a magnificent American.

Note: The Rogers family as of today.

The family is quite outstanding and has always been a credit to Will.

Betty Rogers died in June 1944.

James W. Blake ("Sandy"), her brother, who was important in Will's life, died November 27, 1952. He had been in ill health.

"Aunt Dick" (Miss Theda Blake) lives in Los Angeles, California. She helped rear the children.

Will Rogers, Jr., was elected to Congress on the Democratic ticket from California. Later he ran for U. S. Senator but failed of election. He is, as I write, following his father's footsteps in the entertainment world. Will and his wife Collier have three boys. They adopted a Navajo boy whom they call Clem. Randy is not legally adopted but has lived with them as long as Clem has; he is the son of a teacher on the Navajo reservation. (Will has done a great deal of work for the Navajos.) The third is, as I write, a baby — Carlos, adopted. For several years Will owned and published the weekly *Beverly Hills Citizen*, but he sold the paper in February 1953, with the announced intention of giving all his time to acting.

Jimmie is a ranchman near Bakersfield, California. He married Astrea Kemmler and they have three children: Kem (James Kemmler Rogers), Charles, and Betty (the latter named for Betty Rogers, Jimmie's mother.)

Mary Rogers was divorced in March 1952, from Walter Brooks, stepson of General Douglas MacArthur.

Will, Senior, owned the Oologah ranch at the time of his crash; the children now own it. The ranch has never passed out of the hands of the family.

Mrs. Paula McSpadden Love (Will's niece) is curator of the Memorial, in Claremore. Her husband Robert M. Love is manager. And right now I want to thank them for the great help they were to me when I was working in the Memorial. The back room (not open to the public) is piled with scrapbooks and crates of unpublished material; the two took me by the hand and spread light to a bewildered and nonplussed soul.

Sources

CHAPTER I

The genealogical tracing of the Rogers-Schrimsher families is based chiefly on Emmett Starr's remarkable book, *History of the Cherokee Indians*, published in 1921. He traveled highways and back roads interviewing old Indian families and early settlers. The book is full of typographical errors and gold. And also on Carolyn Thomas Foreman's article on Mrs. William Penn Adair in *Chronicles of Oklahoma* for September 1943 (Vol. 21, No. 3). And on an article on "William Penn Adair" in *Chronicles of Oklahoma* for 1951 (Vol. 28, No. 1) by Mrs. Cherrie Adair Moore, a descendant of the Adair family. She is now Mrs. Junius B. Moore and lives at 631 South Bois D'Arc, Tyler, Texas. And also on studies made by Noel Kaho, Claremore, Oklahoma. And thanks to Mrs. Rella Looney, archivist for the Oklahoma State Historical Society, from whom no item of history can long hide itself.

Showing how casually the Cherokee Rolls were kept, the name Adair doesn't appear in the authenticated Indian Rolls for 1880, but "Col. W. P." does, which of course stands for Colonel William Penn.

Colonel William Penn Adair died in Washington, D. C., when Will was less than a year old. He never saw his distinguished namesake. He is buried in the Indian cemetery at Tahlequah. When he died three prominent Indians were chosen to draw up resolutions of sympathy for his services to the Cherokees. Clem Rogers's is the first name on the list.

The *Southern Literary Messenger*, May 1940, has a study by Mittie Owen McDavid of the Irish-Indian blood of Will Rogers.

The names of the two men richer than Will's father, as shown in the 1890 census, were: William E. Roberts, worth $25,000; William C. Patton, worth $20,000.

Noel Kaho, in his book *The Will Rogers Country*, tells this story about the company that Clem Rogers had joined. The names of some of the Indian volunteers were a bit unusual. The sergeant liked to call the roll slightly out of order, ending thus: "Kickup, Turnover, and Roundabout." They were all members of the company.

In the 1890 census record Clem Rogers is listed as married, but in reality his wife had died. I asked Rella Looney, my port in a storm, and she said, "I think Will's mother had died before the census taker got around to listing the family. As to the exact dates, there is, here, a Register of Warrants issued to pay Census Takers $3000, dated April 22, 1890. Also a warrant in the sum of $2823 to pay the claims of census takers for 1890 for extra services performed; this was approved by the Principal Chief, December 24, 1890."

CHEROKEE TRIBAL ROLL OF 1902
The enrollment of the Rogers family reads:

NUMBER	NAME	AGE	SEX	BLOOD
11,383	Clem V. Rogers	63	M	1–4
11,384	William P. Rogers	22	M	1–4
11,696	May Stine (died 1909)	29	F	1–4
11,697	John V. Yocum (died 1952)	9	M	1–8
11,698	Edward J. Stine, Jr.	2	M	1–8
13,071	Sallie C. McSpadden	38	F	1–16
13,072	Clem McSpadden	15	M	1–32

13,073	May McSpadden (Mrs. Walton C. Poole)	11	F	1–32
13,074	Herbert T. McSpadden (Oologah, Will Rogers Ranch, Okla.)	9	M	1–32
13,075	Maude I. McSpadden	6	F	1–32
13,076	Helen McSpadden (Mrs. Lucian A. Eaton)	31	F	1–32
13,077	Pauline McSpadden (Paula M. Love)	1	F	1–32
13,515	Maude Lane (Will's sister — died 1925)	33	F	1–16
13,516	Estella Lane (Mrs. James T. Neal, Tulsa)	10	F	1–16
13,517	Ethel Lane (Mrs. E. E. Hedges, Wichita, Kansas)	8	F	1–32
13,518	James G. Lane (Denney, Okla.)	5	M	1–32

BIRTHS AND DEATHS OF THE ROGERS CHILDREN

Elizabeth died before she was three years old.

Sallie Clementine born at Bonham, Texas, December 16, 1862. Died August 25, 1943.

Maude born near Fort Gibson, Nevember 28, 1869. (She became Mrs. Cap L. Lane.) Died 1925.

Robert born in 1866. Died at the age of seventeen, while a student at Worcester Academy in Vinita, Oklahoma.

Homer died at the age of three months.

May was born in 1873 on the Rogers ranch. (She became Mrs. Matt Yocum, later Mrs. Frank Stine.) She died in her sister Sallie's home in 1909.

Zoe died in infancy.

Will born on Rogers ranch, November 4, 1879. (He was, as can be seen, the eighth child.)

CHAPTER 2

A glimpse into pioneer conditions is given me by Bill Hoge, Skiatook, Oklahoma: "You can tell 'em in your book that Oologah was plenty tough at this time. Many outlaws had come into the Territory to escape the United States laws and many of them had married Cherokee women and raised a bunch of half outlaws that were about as tough as you'd want to come across. They couldn't keep a teacher at the Oologah school, as the big boys would run them off. In 1904 the United States Government sent D. M. Battenfield to Oologah to teach our school. He taught it, all right, but he carried a club and wore his gun in the schoolroom."

Note from Mrs. Rella Looney of the Oklahoma Historical Society: "You ask me to double-check on 'Uncle Dan' and 'Aunt Babe' Walker. I find this in the Cooweescoowee District census of 1890: 'Daniel Walker, adopted, colored, 38 years of age, farmer; and Aggie, his wife, colored, adopted, 27 years of age. Neither can read or write. Five children.' I take it these were your Uncle Dan and Aunt Babe Walker."

Rella Looney shames me with the following information: "The correct, the Indian way of spelling 'con-hennie' is *kanahe'na*. In Cherokee this means hominy. *Sofkey* was chiefly a food of the Creeks, but I found, in one case, that the Cherokees ate it. Now as to *canuchi*. It's a delicacy of this day with the Cherokees. It's made by picking the kernels from hickory nuts and pounding them in a mortar till they make a kind of butter.

"I checked our historical library on the Cooweescoowee District for 1890, and found there were seven pianos in this district at that time, so if you said that Clem Rogers had the only piano at that time, in that district, you would be wrong. It is possible he had the only piano at some time, but that time was not 1890."

Will had occasion, in later years, to write about Drumgoole but he never got the name spelled quite right.

Note: For some reason or other, in later years Will was sensitive about the size of his ears and said he had been given the name of "Rabbit" because he could run so fast. (The Indian word, which was the one usually used, was *Chiestu.*)

The Harrell Collegiate Institute stood where the City Hospital is now.

The story of the fire laddie who so gallantly lifted his hat is from an interview with an old-timer published in the *Vinita Daily Journal*, August 26, 1952.

The matter of the second-hand organ is told by Noel Kaho in his *The Will Rogers Country;* he got it in turn from members of the family. The name of the company that sold Sallie the organ was the Carol Hoffman Music Company. "Uncle Ed" Sunday, of Claremore, was a boyhood friend of Will's; he was the repository of much information about Will and Will's early days.

When Scarritt was going full sweep it had about 400 students; many of the Methodist families in the Indian Territory sent their young hopefuls off to Scarritt. The Institute began with the first grade, went through high school and gave the students four years of college, quite a considerable hunk of education for one institution. In 1905 it combined with a Methodist school at Morrisville, Missouri; this promptly failed. This, in turn, combined with Central College in Lexington, Missouri. This combined with Howard Payne College in Fayette, Missouri, which changed its name to Central College; it's still a Methodist College, still going.

A person helpful in reconstructing these early days of Will Rogers is Clu Gulager, a cousin; he lives at 1615 West Okmulgee, Muskogee, Oklahoma. His memory is bright and shining.

And I want to thank Cal Tinney, of Tulsa. In 1932 he interviewed many old-timers and made shorthand notes. He was good enough to turn over a transcript to me. I thank him long and loud.

Will once wrote about his early days at Scarritt, but dealt with them sketchily. He covered his whole scholastic career at Scarritt in three sentences. One of the points he made was that he spent all of his Scarritt days in *McGuffey's Fourth Reader*. This must be looked on as a bit of humorous exaggeration, for he had long ago turned his face on McGuffey. In fact all that he ever wrote about himself was of the most meager nature. He was planning to write his full and complete story but the end came before he could do this.

Will also stayed, for a short time, at the home of Mrs. W. W. Miller. He paid ten dollars a month for board. Will spent much time with his friend Sam Cobb, roping and riding yearling calves. They liked to get them to run across the campus where the boys and girls were innocently walking and talking.

Once, in later years, when they were to have a rodeo at Vinita, Will wired to the *Vinita Daily Journal:* "I was in love with my teacher, Miss McLatchie. I studied elocution, but stopped in time to keep from being a Senator."

The story of Will's music lesson is based, in main, on material in Harold Keith's excellent book, *Boys' Life of Will Rogers*.

Mrs. Garland Price says that "Jess," mentioned in letter, was Jessie Price who, also, was one of Will's girls. She married Gurney Lowe, and lives, as I write, at 2654 Grand Avenue, Huntington Park, California. Mr. Lowe has a business known as "The Scrollmaster."

Mrs. Garland Price writes: "The only thing I ask in connection with the note is that you will make it plain to your readers that Will Rogers didn't drink. I wouldn't create that impression for anything in the world."

CHAPTER 3

In the Claremore Memorial is one of the books that Will studied at Kemper. It is a huge affair with a title that would discourage even the most avid student thirsting for knowledge: *Lyman's Historical Chart, Containing the Prominent Events of the Civil, Religious and Literary History of the World from the Earliest Times to the Present Day*. By Azel S. Lyman. It's a wonder Will stayed as long as he did.

Mac Koontz figured in Will's life. As I write, he has a grocery and market in Boonville. I did not get to interview him, but he did give me information in a letter:

"I am glad you told me about the *Historical Chart*. You said it was in the Claremore Memorial and in safe hands. Will said, in later years, that the way the countries were marked off in different colors fascinated him so much that it almost caused him to study. He said also that the *Historical Chart* contained the names of the seven wise men of Greece and that he memorized the first two.

"No, I am not part Indian. I was a 'home town boy,' and Officer of the Day when Will put in his appearance. The court back of the school, where we had to march guard duty, was paved with brick. We had to march back and forth so much on guard duty that the bricks actually had grooves worn in them. Will's feet went up and down that court many times. We had a Springfield rifle for drilling. The hammer was large and was supposed to be carried, when at right shoulder arms, flat against the shoulder, but by turning the rifle a little, the hammer would rest on top of the shoulder and take the weight off the hand. Will liked to carry it thus, so he drew demerits. Besides there was always a hole worn in the right shoulder of his coat. More demerits. You ask if a Mexican boy named Puente showed Will how to rope. No. When Will arrived, he was already an expert with the elusive rope. Thomas Puente knew nothing about handling a rope. When Will left school he had about one hundred and fifty hours of guard duty to do. He laughed and said, 'That's one debt I'll never have to pay.'"

Will dealt with his Kemper career as sketchily as he did with all matters in his autobiographical writings. Four sentences covered Kemper: "My old daddy — Uncle Clem, they called him — then sent me to a military school at Boonville, Mo., Kemper, thinking the disgrace might tame me. Me and Ben Johnson, down at Chickasha, Oklahoma, were buddies together at Kemper, just a couple of poor ornery Indian boys. But the fact is we were sent to the Missouri State Reformatory which is located near the same town and through somebody's mistake, they enrolled us at the Kemper Military Academy instead. Col. Johnston — the head man — didn't run Kemper in accordance with the standards I thought befitting my growing intellect. I was spending my third year in the fourth grade and wasn't being appreciated, so I not only left them flat during a dark night, but quit the entire school business for life."

Note: This school is often referred to as the Kemper Military Academy. This is wrong. It was the Kemper Military School. Will, in his writings in later years, never got the name of his school quite right.

Contrast: Mark Twain did not go to school after he was eleven years old. Will attended school until he was eighteen.

From Dan Cosgrove, Franklin, Missouri: "I'm afraid I can't help you much re Will Rogers. He was just another boy in school. I remember him no better than I do several others."

Comment by a famous sports writer: "I guess I'm one of the people who spread that Roping the President story. I grew up on it; had heard it since I was a boy. Like all showmen, Will loved publicity, so it could have been that he just thought it was a good story from his standpoint. I was on his radio program two or three times, but didn't get many words in edgewise. Which was another definite trait he had. He was a smart man and he became a great figure in this country, but he was smarter for Rogers than for anybody else. I never saw him, even at a funeral, when he didn't somehow manage to be the 'Main Event.'"

Appendage: Cal Tinney, who went over this chapter for me, asked, "Where did Will get the money to go to Buffalo?" I had not thought of it till he asked; I'll have to answer that I don't know.

CHAPTER 4

The motion picture of Will's life blithely assured us that Will spent two years in Texas; that is the Hollywood touch. The time was four months. But, for that matter, the picture had little that was correct.

Letter from Frank Ewing, Ewing Ranch, Higgins, Texas: "You have quoted me correctly, with the changes I've made. Wish you would make it plain that Will came back several times later to visit us and would stay two or three weeks. I have seen clippings which purported to say that Will was lazy and would not work and that my father kept him just to hear his funny remarks. This is distinctly not true. Will was a good worker. Percy Gassoway was never on our ranch when Will was. I like your thoroughness."

The story about the dogs' names is from Spi M. Trent's book.

Here are some of the boys who came to see Will and Spi in their log-cabin retreat: John Smith and his brother Owen Smith; Charlie Harris, Dal Walker, Conley Speaks, Dick Nicholson, Dick Paris, Owen Journeycake, Charlie Gilbreath (father of Joe Galbreath; Joe changed the spelling of his name), Ed Walford, Kirk Tucker. They even got up a baseball team. Will played first base; and the way he twitted the runners who came down the line! Too bad some of his off-the-cuff remarks couldn't be preserved. Dal Walker still lives in Oologah, and gave me much valuable information, and I want to thank him here and now.

The incident about how Will started out to have a man arrested for killing a steer is, chiefly, from Spi M. Trent's book, *My Cousin Will Rogers*. The book was published by G. P. Putnam's Sons, 1938.

"Uncle Blue" was Blue Starr, close friend of Clem Rogers. He lived south of Claremore.

The Yale movie house is now on the spot where Clem Rogers's livery stable once stood.

About Will's broken arm: A letter from G. H. Scudder, Wann, Oklahoma, says: "As I remember it, the horses at the Tincups' had been turned out and Will had to ride his own to the doctor's. A small point, but I thought I would put it in as some of the old-timers might question it. When Will got to the McSpaddens' he said he wasn't 'feeling very good.' That's the way he took things."

The town of Bluejacket, in Craig county, was named for the Shawnee chief Bluejacket. When he died he left behind him twenty-three children. There are still Bluejackets in the county. This is understandable.

Here are the names of some of the riders who went with Will on his strange adventure to Memphis: Jim Rider, Heber Skinner, Hurt Flippen, Gordon Lane, Leonard Trainer, Jim Hopkins and Dick Paris. (The latter becomes important in our story.) An unusual touch was lent to the affair by the appearance of the first cowgirl in the world — Lucille Mulhall. The *Claremore Progress* reported the trip to Memphis; and in it, for those especially interested, can be read more details than I have put in.

Thanks to Jesse Cunningham, librarian, the Cossitt Library, Memphis, for digging the story out of his ancient files. His letter: "You have no business addressing me 'Unmet Friend,' but of course you had no way of knowing that this old Delta Tau Delta man was librarian here in Memphis. And certainly I had no idea of knowing that you lived over the Dolly Madison Saloon and Dance Hall."

A description of the "tacky party" and Will's notable efforts at doing the cake walk are told in some detail in the *Claremore Progress* for August 19, 1899.

Personal: I was shocked to find that my publishers didn't know what a Johnny Blocker was. It shakes one's faith in Hobart College. Well, here it is: the loop falls across the back of the steer and rolls rearward so as to envelope the creature's hind feet, a trick no publisher in the world could possibly perform. Will was an adept at it.

CHAPTER 5

The direct quotes give the names and addresses of the people I interviewed.

The date that William Jennings Byran traveled on Coin Harvey's railroad was June 12, 1902.

The Woman's Study Club in Rogers, Arkansas, is still going; it is the oldest local organization in the town. The date of *Mrs. Jarley's Wax Works* was May 17, 1904.

Letter from the Missouri Pacific Lines, St. Louis, Missouri, signed by the publicity and advertising director: "A check of payrolls shows that Betty Blake was employed as a clerk for the station agent at Jenny Lind, Arkansas, from June 1, 1904, to April 6, 1905. She was paid $45 a month."

Chester Holland, former mayor of Fort Smith, Arkansas, writes me that I should point out there were two Jenny Linds — the "new" and the "old." "If you say in your book that Betty Blake worked in *old* Jenny Lind, the old-timers will climb you," he writes. I don't like to be climbed by old-timers, so I am calling special attention to the fact that she worked in new Jenny Lind.

Newsreel pictures were made of Coin Harvey's amphitheater and development. He was eighty when he was nominated for President of the United States, something of a record, I believe. He died in February, 1936, eighty-four years old, sick and tired of civilization.

CHAPTER 6

A hard chapter to write, because of the untrustworthiness of the available material. Will, in his Sunday and magazine articles, wrote of these days but briefly; and sometimes he got the dates wrong, for he was writing from memory.

The most dependable sources are the letters to his family and to the *Claremore Progress*.

When Dick Paris got back he told of his adventures, but this Indian drew a long bow, so many of the things he said are not to be written in bronze.

The incident about Dick Paris having to wire to Will's father for money was told by Will's cousin, Clu Gulager.

A great help was the material Cal Tinney gathered in interviews with old-timers during the years 1930 and 1931.

From Bill Hoge, Skiatook, Oklahoma:

"I've checked your chapter on Will's meeting Betty. I think I can add something to it. Kate Ellis was my first school teacher, and Will's first sweetheart. He was quite gone on her. She was the prettiest girl in Oologah. Her father, Jake Ellis, ran the hotel. During the time that Will was going with her, Betty Blake came from Arkansas to visit her sister and brother-in-law, as you tell in your book. As soon as Will spied Betty, he fell in love with her, but she had become a close friend of Kate Ellis and would not accept Will's advances. One night Will brought Kate home later than usual. Old Jake Ellis was laying for Will and the moment Will put his hand on the doorknob, he pounced out at him, gave him a talking up and down, and told Will he was never to see Kate again. Will was set back by the suddenness of the attack and the bitterness of the words. After this he moved his attentions over to Betty, and Betty, feeling that the affair between Will and Kate was over, was willing to accept Will as a suitor. That is how it all came about."

In addition, I have heard Will himself tell of his South American and South African adventures, but I never dreamed at that time they would become important to me, so I did not make notes. I found myself shockingly hazy on many of the things he told me.

What kind of letters did he write home? He wrote many (too many to reproduce here) for he was lonesome; in some of them, he urged not only his relatives but his friends to write to him.

Durban, Natal, South
Africa.
November 17, 1902

DEAR HOME FOLKS:

I will write you a short letter as you will get this about Christmas time and will know that I am "Proceeding magnificiently." I am back at the port where I landed. I shoved off from that big "stiff" I have been with. I have made a long trip up into the interior where the war was the hottest. I was in Ladysmith and passed several English grave yards that showed where there had been a battle and where probably one Boer horse was killed. It is a very pathetic sight to see the Boer families returning to their former homes and finding some all torn down and others occupied by the English. The Boers are as fine lot of people as one would wish to see, peaceful, law abiding and friendly to all. They speak English as well as Dutch.

I am going up to Pretoria in the Transvaal with a lot of stock for a man here and when I return I'll be ready to go home, as I will have seen a large part of the country. You get good pay here but it costs more to live than at home, so you are none ahead. The weather is getting very hot here now and by Christmas will be at its hottest.

I am up against it good and hard now. Coming down the other day my "cargo of merchandise" was misplaced, consisting of clothes, saddle, and in fact my "whole works" except a small grip I had with me. They do not have a system of checking on the railways here; it is "catch as catch can" and I was caught for my roll. I have suspended operations till I hear from it but it has been ten days and no tidings so I have begun to prepare for the worst, which is to adopt the garb of my black neighbors. I have just investigated the contents of the small bag and find that it contains thirteen collars, one shirt — all soiled — one unmarried sock and a clothes brush. The major part was occupied by a Spanish library of four volumes entitled, *How to Learn Spanish in a Day*, by Antonio Pedro Gonzales, one little manual of 975 pages called *Spanish Made Easy*. By remembering these few hints and various others you will readily see I have not yet got next to their learning process. This grip also contained old letters and programs of every theater from New York and London down to a magic lantern show in Zululand. I have gone to work brushing up the soiled linen, reading over the theater bills and thinking what a discouraging scene I have just passed through.

I will close by wishing you a happy Christmas and a cloudy Ground Hog Day.

As ever,
WILL P. ROGERS

The letter was published in the *Chelsea Reporter*, January 2, 1903.

This is just about an average letter written home by a young man off on a lark. Certainly no one reading it would ever guess that later its author would ever become a world figure as a humorist. It has none of the spelling or punctuation that came to be associated with him, but this may be because the editor was pained to see such shortcomings in one of his correspondents.

Cuff note: The year Will wrote this letter was the year Colonel Lindbergh was born.

The strange episode of the gas is attested by Dal Walker, of Oologah, who himself told me about it. He was a boyhood friend of Will's and heard Will describe the event.

A question his old friends like to argue is: Did Will blow out the gas? Many years later, when Will wrote on the subject, he said that he did not blow out the gas. But on his immediate return he told at least two friends that he blew it out. It is possible, for in the old days the Territory was kerosene country. Lamps had always been blown out. That night Will got in, tired, and it is entirely possible that he blew out the gas. One would think, in later years, that Will would have seized on this as a subject for joking. But he never did; he always kept away from it.

My thanks to Izak Johannes Theron, 38 Minni Street, Sunnyside, Pretoria, South Africa, for patiently plodding through the *Pretoria News* until he found Will, to say nothing of Apollo, and Ajax, the Flexible.

One of the disappointments in writing this book is that I have not been able to run down Texas Jack. Who was he? What was his real name? Was he really from Texas? When did he die? Where? I've tried every way I could think of, but have found out nothing at all about this man who was so important in Will's life.

A footnote to a footnote: One of the men at the San Antonio contest was Johnny Blocker who became famous as the inventor of the Blocker Loop. Another was Clay McGonigle. The latter became Will's rope teacher.

CHAPTER 7

The chicken-train story is from the *Claremore Progress*.

The Black Chambers story was given to me by Joe Chambers, Black's brother. Black Chambers appears later in the book also.

Mrs. Will Rogers, in her book, tells about the red velvet suit. And she tells how she met Will at the St. Louis World's Fair. One or two details have been added by Bruce Quisenberry whose mother was Betty's sister and who went along with Betty.

For a brief time, this hectic summer, Charlie Tompkins employed Will in his "Tompkins Famous Riders," which put on exhibitions on the Delmar Race Track. He says that Geronimo was part of the Indian Village, and that Geronimo functioned as a roper. Will would study how Geronimo handled his ropes, but, so far as he knows, Will never talked to him.

Other cowboys who went to New York with the redoubtable Colonel Mulhall: Jim Minnick, Chet Byers and Bill Pickett, the Negro, who soon made riding history. And also went Mulhall's two daughters, Lucille and Mildred, and their brother Charles J. Mulhall. (The latter two, as I write, are still living. I interviewed them.)

In 1930, Jim Minnick gave a twelve-page interview to Cal Tinney, covering the time dealt with in this chapter and the next.

CHAPTER 8

In regard to the steer roping, Jim Minnick, in an interview in 1930, said: "I was one of the ropers and saw the incident. Will got his rope over the steer's horns, but lost control. He never claimed any glory for the event. It was Lucille's steer all the way through."

The quip about the policeman and his billy is also from Jim Minnick.

One of the papers had this item about Charles J. Mulhall, brother of Lucille: "Charles Mulhall fell from his pony and was taken to the New York Hospital. He recovered sufficiently to appear in the performance last night." (Mr. Mulhall lives at 1328 Northwest Third Street, Oklahoma City, Okla.)

A letter from Mrs. Mildred Mulhall Acton, Guthrie, Oklahoma. She is a sister of Lucille Mulhall:

"I was present at the now famous steer-roping. Each day I drove a tally-ho with four horses, coachmen, dogs, and bugles. This was in the Horse Show part and not in competition. I was chosen, I suppose, because of my ability to handle four high-stepping park type, cob-tailed and matched pairs. I was seven years old. My father used a wide strap to fasten me to the seat, for my feet would not touch the floor.

"The steer saw that the foot gate at the end of the arena (below the band shell) was open and started for it as fast as he could travel. He did not jump over any fence, or barrier. He was scared, not mad, and wanted to get away. The steer did not run all over the place, as stated. The people were panic-stricken, but it was their fault; no one was seriously hurt. Jim Minnick, Tom Mix, and Will Rogers ran the steer back into the arena. I think Will was the one who threw the rope over him. When the steer returned to the arena, no horses or cowboys came in with him. Lucille roped him, got off her horse, and tied the steer — no one helped her.

"Please note. There is no such thing as the worst-behaved steer on the American continent. A Mexican bull will fight when tortured. The American steer is either gentle or scared and, if he can, will run away.

"I'm glad you do not say that my sister bull-dogged steers, as most writers do. She never bull-dogged a steer in her life. She was a roper and rider. For years she held the steer-roping record over men — no woman roped in those days. My mother did not approve of Lucille's riding and roping and never went to see her engage in it.

"The statement about my brother and the accident is not correct. Charlie was thrown from his bucking horse and hit his head on a concrete post on the ground floor of the arena and was unconscious about four hours. My father came up, threw his big cowboy hat over Charlie's face and said, 'He's dead, boys. Take him to the morgue.' Charlie promptly woke up. That's what cowboy shows were like in those days. I must add that Charlie came back and drew another horse for the night show."

The explanation of why Tom Mix was entered under the name of "Tom Mixico" is given by David Randolph Milsten in his authoritative book, *An Appreciation of Will Rogers* (the Naylor Company, San Antonio, Texas, 1937). The information came from Tom Mix in an interview. The story:

Colonel Mulhall asked Will and Tom to help him prepare the wording for the program. The two, in a spirit of fun, wrote each other's announcement. Will proclaimed Tom as "Tom Mixico, the Cowrunner from Mexico." Tom set Will down as "Will Rogers, the Cherokee Indian." And thus it was on the program and this was the way it got into the newspapers.

However, this was not quite the end. One afternoon Will saw a dashy-looking girl in an arena box and purposely went over and performed in front of her. She seemed delighted and he thought he had made a new acquaintance.

Immediately after his part of the program, he went up to the box to meet her, but she was cold. He was puzzled and asked why. She showed him the program and said, "I see you are a Cherokee Indian. I think that closes it."

In Oklahoma, people were proud of their Indian blood. And Will was, too. So this came as a shock. According to Tom Mix, Will was moody and depressed the rest of the day. He did not say much about it, for it was not his way to talk of the things that hurt him.

Here is an insight into the relationship between Will and Tom Mix. The two were born the same year; they were both show-men — and there the comparison, for all practical purposes, ends. One of Will's deepest traits was his innate modesty; one of his greatest dislikes was a boaster. The two men had ridden together (as we've seen) at Madison Square Garden; they had roomed to-gether. Two men more different would be hard to enclose in one room. A story attesting this was told me by Zack T. Miller, Jr., of the 101 Ranch, Ponca City, Oklahoma. The story was passed along to him by his father. The story:

Tom Mix was born in John DuBois's stable, in Mix Run, Pennsylvania, where Tom's father was coachman for Mr. Du-Bois. Mr. Miller, senior, found Tom working in a saloon in Guthrie, brought him to the 101 Ranch and gave him a job with the "dude" part of the ranch. This "dude" part was only a side-line to the regular, or working ranch. Tom's duty was to herd the dudes away from the working part of the ranch, where they would be a blamed nuisance. He entertained the dudes with wondrous stories of his adventures.

Will Rogers came to the ranch to help with the work — really to sing for the cowboys, says Mr. Miller, Jr. It happened that while Will was there, a relative of Tom's from the East dropped in and told the story of Tom's life, which was far from glamorous. Especially he told that Tom had been born in a stable.

A few days later, Will happened to come up to where Tom was holding a group of dudes spellbound with the exciting and romantic story of his fabulous life. He had been born on the plains in Texas, Tom said, and had ridden before he could walk.

He told how he had run away from Texas, gone to South Africa and had fought against the Boers. In one of the engagements he had captured a machine gun practically singlehanded.

Will listened to the wild tale, growing more and more disturbed. Finally he stepped into the circle and said, "Tom, you know there's not a word of truth in what you say. You were born in a manger in Pennsylvania, and you know it. Jesus Christ was born in a manger and wasn't ashamed of it and didn't lie about it, so why should you?"

Tom mumbled an excuse and tried to pass it off, but the people knew that Will had spoken the truth.

But, according to Mr. Miller, Jr., it didn't put Tom down. The next day he had a new tale. But the fact that he wouldn't admit his humble birth and dealt in fabrication completely enraged Will, who was always truthful and never tried to make himself anything but what he was.

Fascinating item about Tom Mix turned up by the author in his researches: He was a bartender for Ohio Miller, owner of a saloon in Guthrie. Also he had a physical-education class in the basement of the public library where he taught the youth of Guthrie the joys of outdoor life.

I want to hand a Thank You to Robert A. Hug for digging out the facts concerning the steer. I started to read the ancient files of the New York papers, for no index has even a mention of the steer . . . "by all odds the worst-behaved animal on the American continent" . . . but grew discouraged and heavy of heart. Then Mr. Hug, of the Microfilm Department of the New York Public Library, came along and kept me from running amok, probably trailing a rope.

CHAPTER 9

The original notes for "Gags For Missing the Horses Nose" are in the Will Rogers Memorial, at Claremore.

The lather story appears in an interview with Buck McKee in the *Sacramento Bee*, January 18, 1941, now in the possession of Buck's widow, Mrs. Maude McKee, Route 1, Box 140, Roseville, California.

Buck McKee died in 1947. He had once been sheriff of Pawnee County, Oklahoma.

The material about Mort Shea is from an interview with him conducted by Cal Tinney.

A letter from Fred Tejan, Laguna Seca Ranch, Monterey, California:

"What you say is substantially correct, except I did not laugh for him as long as you seem to indicate. I received no wages. I did it because I liked Will and wanted him to become a success. I wish you would include this in your write-up. Will Rogers once saved my life. We were playing with the 101 Wild West Show and while the performance was in progress, a bull buffalo broke out of the corral, knocked my horse down and was about to gore me when Will roped it. You have chosen a wonderful man for your work. I wish you luck in your endeavor."

CHAPTER 10

Some of the material about the early days of their marriage is from Betty's book, some from conversations with the Gulager family, and some from talks with Bruce Quisenberry, Betty's nephew.

The agent referred to as booking the act for the Mercantile Club is Mort Shea. He acted as Will's agent for almost four years. The material is in an unpublished interview which I have in manuscript form.

The story of Black Chambers was told to me by his brother, Joe Chambers, a well-known attorney of Tulsa, Oklahoma. His address is Ritz Building, Tulsa 3. He said that Black Chambers's first name was Evans, but that he was so dark-complexioned that he was called Black.

Comment by Joe Chambers on Will's father: "I knew Uncle Clem Rogers about as well as anybody ever knew him, and we were close friends. During his last years I played pitch with him frequently. While he was my friend, he was never the kind of fellow you felt you had a feeling of warm friendship for. You respected him and appreciated the many good things he did, and the things he would do for you if you, in his opinion, were deserving. But he never grew mellow enough to inspire children to run 'squealing toward him' as you state. He was kind to children, but he always maintained a certain reserve that did not breed familiarity.

"I wish you would put this in, too: Will told me that Black Chambers was the greatest trick roper who ever lived. And Black told me that Fred Stone was one of the finest gentlemen he had ever met.

"Oh, yes! You ask where Colonel Mulhall got his title. My information is that he got it by appointment as honorary colonel on the staff of one of the Governors of Oklahoma Territory. Colonels were thick, down here. We had Colonel Joe Miller, Colonel George Miller, Colonel Zach Miller — and that just disposed of the Millers. No, I never made it."

Joe Chambers tells this anecdote. He lived on the edge of Claremore. One day when he came home the maid was very much agitated; she said that someone had stolen the riding horse. She said that a man had sneaked into the stable, put the saddle on the horse, and had ridden away. She hadn't told the police because she thought that Mr. Chambers might have given the man permission. No, he hadn't given anyone permission, said Mr. Chambers. Well, he would see about it. Just then — it was about five-thirty — the maid looked out the window and said, "There comes that man now!"

"Hello, Joe!" called the man. "Did you miss your animal? This morning I wanted to spend the day with Rabb, so I borrowed your horse and rode out to see ol' Rabb. I shore had a good dinner."

The bill at Keith's Union Square Theater where Will rode his running horse:

Henry V. Donnelly. . . .   comedy sketch
Egbert Van Alstyne and Miss Louise N. Henry . . . in a sketch
Hoey and Lee . . .   Hebrew impersonators
Miss Emma Francis and her Arabian Whirlwinds
Zazelle and Vernon. . . .   acrobats
Will Rogers, a lasso thrower

CHAPTER 11

People who love stage history may be interested to know that when Will opened in London there was another American on the program — Julian Eltinge, the female impersonator.

Will said little about his failures; this one he barely mentioned, but it was one of his big defeats. Where the information came from is shown in the text itself. Additional information was sent by letter by Mrs. Henry W. Turner, New Hope, Pennsylvania, who was a partner with Charles H. Tompkins in the "Tompkins Wild West Show."

From Guy Weadick, 3401 East Thomas Road, Phoenix, Arizona: "Yes, Flores LaDue was my wife. We both came to New York at Will Rogers's request for her to do Fancy Roping in his big, all-girl

Western act. I was there when the act was rehearsed and presented. It was not suited for vaudeville, as the stage room would not permit Will's ambitious ideas. The show lasted a week. I know many stories about Will Rogers, but I am writing a book dealing with cowhands, in which I have devoted some space to Will Rogers, so I do not feel I care to give out any information until my book has been published."

CHAPTER 12

I interviewed Blanche Ring at Hotel Buckingham, 101 West 57th Street, New York.

Some of the material about Will's crippled arm came from a conversation with Fred Stone; later, details were filled in by correspondence. His present address is: 4321 Clybourn, North Hollywood, California.

The Gene Buck material came from conversations with him.

CHAPTER 13

Will, in his later writings, made frequent mention of these early days in show business. In addition to this, the men in Ziegfeld's publicity department were working like hayhands.

And here's a thank you to Mrs. Norman Collyer, 32 Tennis Place, Forest Hills, New York, for her memories of Will's days in our town.

Mrs. Burns Mantle, widow of the former drama critic, wrote: "We were, as you know, Will's neighbors (yours, too, for that matter). Will said he would teach my daughter Peg to ride. He put her on a horse; the horse wagged its tail and she fell off. But his children could ride like Indians. When Dr. Thompson got his house back, he said he thought that the Rogers children must have ridden their ponies up and down the stairs. Will paid the damages without protest. I wonder, now that the children are grown, if they appreciate how everything was done for their pleasure and advancement?" (Mrs. Mantle's address is: 256 Thomas Drive, Monroe Park, Wilmington, Delaware.)

CHAPTER 14

Inquiry reveals the later history of Charlie Aldridge. He died in a hospital in New Britain, Connecticut, September 22, 1951, two days before his seventy-sixth birthday. He was with Will Rogers off and on for ten years. His specialty was riding bucking horses on the stage. But once one bucked a little too earnestly and Charlie was flung into the orchestra pit, the horse on top of him. It was quite a mess. Charlie's leg was broken. This was at the Fourteenth Street Theater, New York. When Charlie died he owned a saddle which Will Rogers had had made for himself during the St. Louis World's Fair. On the cantle was stamped "W. R." An active-minded reader (I have many of them) may ask, "What was the difference between Buck McKee and Charlie Aldridge?" Buck did not ride bucking horses on the stage; he rode running horses, a wise decision, it would seem.

The anecdote about Will, Fields and Chic Sale is based on Robert Lewis Taylor's life of Fields, and on talks with Chic Sale's widow, who lives in Carmel, California.

(*Note in passing*: Will was as weak about the correct names of people as he was about spelling. He always called Ziegfeld, Ziegfield; and Chic Sale, Chic Sales.)

The Clay McGonigle story is chiefly from the book *W. C. Fields: His Follies and His Fortunes*, by Robert Lewis Taylor. The story also appears in Eddie Cantor's *My Life is in Your Hands*. I sent a carbon of the story to Joe Chambers who wrote me: "The reason you had trouble running Clay McGonigle down was that he was a Texas roper, not an Oklahoma product."

The "Big Bertha" story is from Eddie Cantor's autobiography. Mrs. Rogers, in her book, tells the story of the fateful dressing room. The story has also become a kind of legend of the theater.

The two Rogers books mentioned were published by Harper & Brothers, New York.

I thought I would like to see Will's old dressing room and tell what it is like today, so I wrote to the management of the New Amsterdam Theater. Back came an abrupt letter from the Cinema Circuit Corporation, 214 West 42nd Street, New York: "We can see no point in your writing about Will Roger's dressing room as it is presently being used today." Sorry, readers. No firsthand report on Will's old dressing room.

CHAPTER 15

The story about the colored boy and the ice cream was told to me by Mrs. Mary L. Pruyn, 160 Pinehurst Avenue, New York. Her daughter was in the cast and saw the incident.

Two inconsequential sentences have been left out of the Rogers communication. E. B. Garnett has the original letter in a safe in Kansas City. The letter had no punctuation except periods. I have put in three commas to make the reading easier. The spelling and capitalization are his.

The theater the two attended was the Newman (now the Paramount). Mr. Garnett adds this fascinating item about the old Newman theater: Gus Eyssell, who became general manager of New York's Radio City Music Hall, was an usher in this theater.

Will's telegram to Goldwyn about *Jubilo* has been condensed. Titles of pictures that Will made for Goldwyn:

Jubilo	*Laughing Bill Hyde*
Doubling for Romeo	*Water, Water Everywhere*
Almost a Husband	*The Strange Border*
Jes' Call Me Jim	*Cupid, the Cowpuncher*

Honest Hutch	*Guile of Women*
Boys Will Be Boys	*A Poor Relation*
An Unwilling Hero	*The Headless Horseman*

The Arrowhead Springs story came from the Hal Roach studio.

Merle E. Selecman of the American Bankers Association, 12 East Thirty-sixth Street, New York, writes me that the convention was held in Hotel Astor and that this meeting was an informal smoker. (The story, as it's usually told, has it as the International Bankers' Association. There is no such organization.)

His leading ladies:

Helen Chadwick	Louise Fazenda
Sylvia Beamish	Peggy Wood
Lila Lee	Margaret Livingston
Irene Rich	

The Eminent Authors were: Rex Beach, Rupert Hughes, Mary Roberts Rinehart, Sir Gilbert Parker, Elinor Glyn, Gertrude Atherton, Gouverneur Morris, LeRoy Scott. Seems a long time ago, doesn't it?

CHAPTER 16

The *New York Tribune* said hardly anything about Will Rogers's speech. In fact, this is all: "Will Rogers, making his first political speech, spoke humorously on bootleggers and other campaign topics and concluded with a tribute to Theodore Roosevelt, 'The only man who ever thanked me for saying something nice about his family.' "

Editorial Comment: It will be noticed, in reading his Mills speech, that Will was using more and more the approach of startling his listeners with his opening statement. And it is worth while again to call attention to the fact that the *New York Times* did not pay Will for the telegrams he was sending back; nor, for that matter, did he expect to be paid. It was, in main, a personal promise to Ochs.

To complete the record it should be shown that Will had a previous fling at daily printed comedy. The idea was handled by NEA Service, Cleveland, Ohio. The title of the series was "What's News Today?" It was illustrated by Roy Grove. The drawings showed a cowboy twirling a rope and making killing comments. Will's part was to write the killing comments. The idea lasted just two and a half months (from September 29, 1920 to December 15, 1920). There were no mourners.

"I think," says V. V. McNitt, "Will was more impressed by his success as a writer than by anything else that ever happened to him."

CHAPTER 17

The sources of the material used in this chapter are revealed in the text.

The de Reszke Singers were J. Erwyn Mutch, J. Hardesty Johnson, Floyd Townsley, Howard Kellogg.

Letter from William E. Hayes, executive assistant of the Rock Island Lines, La Salle Street Station, Chicago, Illinois:

"We have checked up on your story of how Will Rogers hired a train from us and, so far as our records show, the story seems to be substantially correct."

The anecdote about Will stopping to do rope tricks for children was told me by Bruce Quisenberry.

A story illustrating how Will threw himself into whatever he was doing was told to me by Eddie Dowling, the New York actor and play producer. Eddie was playing polo with Will at Sands Point, Long Island, where Will tore into the game like an Apache into battle, screaming and yelling and flourishing his mallet like a scalp-stick. But the tides of battle went against him:

one of the players hit Will a whack with his mallet, splitting Will's upper lip wide open. Will didn't want to be taken out of the game, so great was his enthusiasm for what he was doing. He was told that there was a veterinarian at the stables and off to him Will went. The veterinarian sewed up Will's lip and soon Will was back, knocking balls right and left. That night, before Will was to go on the stage for his evening performance, the lip fell apart and Will had to face an audience with a lip that flapped. He sounded, declared Eddie, like somebody talking through a keyhole. He went three days before he would visit a physician and have the lip taken care of professionally. He had, said Eddie, a scar on his upper lip for the rest of his life.

CHAPTER 18

Will wrote about his trip in his *Post* articles, and in her book Betty Rogers recounted some of the incidents that happened after she joined him.

Details of the Rogers-Mussolini meeting are from a speech that Charles Evans Hughes made at the Deerfield Academy, Deerfield, Massachusetts. Hughes gave a letter of introduction to Ambassador Fletcher which started the ball rolling. Hughes's speech was reported in the *Springfield* (Massachusetts) *Republican* in a feature article signed with the initials "H. L. G."

Ivan Dmitri, the color photographer, was on the *Leviathan* — first class. Years later I got acquainted with him and he told me about the speeches and how rich people traveled. I was immensely grateful.

In looking through my diary, I find this for July 19, 1926:

"Went to the Pavilion today to see Will Rogers open in London. He sure 'nuf got away with it. He came out in a striped suit, soft collar, yellow shoes, and was chewing gum. I especially noticed his shoes; I was up where I could see them. He seemed made to order for the English idea of an American. He spoke for twenty minutes, a little too long. He said that during the General Strike in England he went to the House of Commons and they were debating a Boer War bill. He said that England had the greatest statesmen and the poorest coffee in the world. Said he dreaded to see morning come. At the end of his speech he introduced some of the celebrities present. One was Dorothy Gish, who is making a picture with him. He called on Sir Thomas Lipton, Lord Dewar and Irving Berlin. The audience liked it and Will closed in triumph."

In the faithful diary for the next day I find: "The papers are very much shocked that Will Rogers actually called on people in the audience. They never heard of it before, so, of course, are against it. I think that Rogers has more humor than Mark Twain, but of course he can't put it in story form which is the lasting form."

For July 26: "I see by the papers that Will Rogers is going to attend George Bernard Shaw's seventieth birthday party. The world is paying Shaw great honors. I don't think the papers will enthuse much when H. G. Wells reaches his three score and ten. He's not the interest-arousing character Shaw is."

Sunday, July 26: "The entertainers from the first class came down and gave us a concert. Will Rogers said that he would like to see Coolidge a bit lit up; said it would be a wonderful sight. I did not tell the people that I once lived neighbor to Will Rogers. It would sound funny. Charles Evans Hughes made a speech. It was much better than I expected."

CHAPTER 19

The sources not indicated in the text are as follows:

The major incidents were reported by the papers. Will also mentioned the matter in his writings.

Some of the mayor material is from a feature article appearing in a number of papers, Sunday, January 9, 1927, by Mayme Ober Peake.

The Pickfair story was told to me by Mark Larkin who, for years, was publicity director for Douglas Fairbanks and Mary Pickford. He is now connected with the *Traveller*, 119 West 57 Street, New York. He does not remember the second man's name.

The Durham, South Carolina, anecdote was told to the author by Charles L. Wagner, the lecture manager.

The name of the chauffeur who rode for Will was Fred Lacey.

A person Will treated with great respect was Bill Pickett, the first man to leap from a running horse onto the head of a steer. But, for that matter, everybody in the roping and riding world treated him with great respect, for he had contributed more to rodeos than any other one person. One morning Bill Pickett went out to rope a bronc which was part of his everyday work on the 101 Ranch. Suddenly the horse he was riding reared and threw him. He was not able to rise. Other hands saw him, rushed to him and carried him to the bunkhouse and there he died, April 2, 1932; he was buried at White Eagle Monument, Marland, Oklahoma. Everyone was greatly touched by his tragic end. Zack T. Miller, who had been his employer for thirty years, wrote the following poem which has appeared on endless postcards and can be seen stuck up in almost any bunkhouse in Oklahoma or Texas:

BILL PICKETT IS DEAD

Old Bill has died and gone astray,
Over the Great Divide,
Gone to a place where the preachers say
Both saint and sinner will abide.
If they "check his brand" like I think they will

It's a runnin' hoss they'll give to Bill.
And some good wild steers till he gets his fill,
With a great big crowd for him to thrill.
Bill's hide was black but his heart was white.
He'd sit up through the coldest night
To help a dogie in a dyin' fight,
To save a dollar for his boss.
And all Bill wanted was a good fast hoss,
Three square meals and a place to lay
His tired self at the end of the day.
There's one other thing, since I've come to think,
Bill was always willing to take a drink.
If the job was tough, be it hot or cold,
You could get it done, if Bill was told.
He'd fix the fence, or skin a cow,
Or ride a bronc, and even plow,
Or do anything, if you told him how.
Like many men in the old-time West,
On any job, he did his best.
He left a blank that's hard to fill
For there'll never be another Bill.
Both White and Black will mourn the day
That the Biggest Boss took Bill away.

CHAPTER 20

After examining this chapter, Lindbergh made the following notes:

"You might also say, when Will asked about how a pilot could tell which way the wind was blowing, that I also pointed out other indications such as smoke. This impressed him greatly.

"According to my memory, the flight between San Diego and Los Angeles was made preliminary to, or at the start of, a regular passenger service. I'm vague about this. The statement should be checked, if used. As you know, Maddux Airlines did run a

passenger service for some time before it was consolidated with
T. A. T.

"I'm afraid you've overemphasized the roughness of the landing at Mines Field. Mines Field was rough when it was new, but not rough enough to damage a plane in landing; and a plane would probably be rather badly damaged before passengers would run into danger of injury.

"Thanks for sending also the chapter ' Will Becomes a Writer.' I read it with appreciation and interest, and liked its humor."

Thanks, Colonel. I wish everybody would be as helpful. That was a nice lunch, wasn't it?

CHAPTER 21

Some of the information in this chapter came from Will's writings; some from newspaper clippings dealing with the events. The Will Rogers Memorial, at Claremore, has about twenty scrapbooks which also cover some of the matters dealt with here. These scrapbooks are remarkable; they were kept, during Will's lifetime, by admirers and were contributed to the Memorial after the crash. They are a unique tribute to him. Some were kept evidently by elderly ladies; at least it would seem so to judge by the handwriting on the clippings. The strangest and most out-of-the-way clippings turn up in them.

Robert E. Sherwood is the playwright.

CHAPTER 22

Al Lewis is the well-known New York play producer.

The giant story is from Cal Tinney material.

The story about Will and Eddie Cantor was told me by Al Lewis who was present.

The story about Will and Jim Minnick is from dispatches in the newspapers at that time.

A glance back at the cast in *They Had To See Paris:*

Irene Rich, Marguerite Churchill, Owen Davis, Jr., Fifi Dorsay, Ivan Lebedeff, Marcelle Corday, Theodore Lodi, Rex Bell (Clara Bow's husband), Ed Kennedy. The picture was directed by Frank Borzage.

Quips from the picture:

"It's gettin' so if parents can keep their children out of jail they've fulfilled their obligations as parents."

"One consolation about goin' on a spree in Paris is you do wake up."

"What good is a title? It's no more good than a dead battery."

"That oil well was drier than a Congressman's speech."

"I tell you a horse doctor is the smartest kind of doctor there is. He can't ask a horse what is the matter with him; he's got to know."

CHAPTER 23

Most of the sources are shown in the text.

The story of Eli Walker, the problem son of Aunt Babe and Uncle Dan Walker, was an Associated Press dispatch dated April 23, 1933, and appears, among other papers, in the *Tulsa World,* for April 26, 1933. (Aunt Babe's real name is Agnes. She had eleven children, three of whom played with Will.)

Examination of the legal books in Bartlesville has this succinct record:

State of Oklahoma *vs* Eli Walker. Number 2065
In the District Court, Washington County, Okl.
March 24, 1933. Information filed charging the defendant with assault to kill.
April 26, 1933. Dismissed on motion of County Attorney.

William F. Hurt was County Attorney. J. R. Charlton represented Eli Walker. Both are now dead.

CHAPTER 24

The sources are revealed in the text.

My memories were revived by talks with Owen Davis, George Middleton, Al Lewis and Ben Lucien Burman.

Emil Sandmier's address, as I write, is 760 Pacific Palisades, California.

The Fields-Rogers story is based on the account in *W. C. Fields: His Follies and Fortunes*, by Robert Lewis Taylor

The sanitarium credited by Mr. Taylor is Las Encinas Sanitarium, 2900 Blanche Street, Pasadena, California. But the sanitarium has no record of Fields's stay while Will was alive. Dr. C. W. Thompson writes me: "Mr. W. C. Fields was under our care July 5, 1936 to April 22, 1937. He was re-admitted May 17, 1939, and discharged June 26, 1939. He was re-admitted October 29, 1945, and died December 25, 1946. From these dates the answer to your question is that Will Rogers, having died in 1935, did not visit Mr. Fields at Las Encinas Sanitarium as alleged. I never had the pleasure of meeting Will Rogers personally, but Mr. Fields told me many stories of their days in the *Follies*. I wish you success with your book."

CHAPTER 25

Mrs. Daisy Tyler lives at 8219 West Norton Avenue, Hollywood, California.

The anecdote about Will's sensitiveness to his age appears in an interview by Grace Kingsley in the *Los Angeles Times*.

The story of Will's anger at the *San Diego Union* was supplied by Eddy Orcutt who wrote the editorial. He was editor of the *Labor Leader*, 204 Crystal Palace Building, San Diego, California, when he died in January 1953.

The authority for the statement that Will paid Ziegfeld's funeral expenses comes from Cameron Shipp, 1544 Ard Eevin Avenue, Glendale, California. In collaboration with Billie Burke he wrote her memoirs entitled, *With a Feather On My Nose*. She told him in person that Will had done this, and the statement is made in the book, page 241.

Ivar Kreuger died in Paris, March 12, 1932.

The Reverend A. Raymond Grant is now Bishop of the M. E. Church, Portland Area, and can be reached at its headquarters 806 SW Broadway, Portland, Oregon.

Here's an example of Will's generosity to funds and organizations. It's a letter from Charles S. Nicolai, of the Salvation Army, 120 West 14th Street, New York, dated March 4, 1953: "I find that in 1933 Will Rogers made a gift to us of about $30,000. I can't tell you exactly, because all of our records were transferred to London when Evangeline Booth became international leader, and were lost during the war period. It may interest you to know that the Central Territory used its part of the money to help erect a camp at Camp Lake, Wisconsin, which bears the name 'The Will Rogers Shagbark Camp' and is used for youth work."

CHAPTER 26

The anecdote about the lawyer epitaphs came from Judge George T. McDermott, of the United States Circuit Court of Appeals. He died January 19, 1937.

The first time that Will applied the famous phrase without its being attached to an epitaph was in July 1926, in an article in the *Saturday Evening Post*. He had tried to see Trotsky in Russia, but an official had denied him the interview. Will was miffed but finally wrote: "I bet if I met Trotzky and had a chat with him, I would have found him an interesting and human fellow, for I never met a man that I dident like." It was a passing comment and aroused no special interest.

CHAPTER 27

The material in this chapter was pretty well covered by the press associations. Additional information has been gathered by correspondence with Lawrence B. Williams, principal of the Barrow Day School, Barrow, Alaska, and with Frank J. Daugherty who is mentioned in the chapter. He is, as I write, principal of the Navajo Mission School, Holbrook, Arizona. (He asks in one of his letters to be sure to put in that the much-heralded grief of the Eskimos was "pure baloney.")

The crash is pretty well covered by Charles D. Brower in his book *Fifty Years Below Zero*.

In a letter to the author approving of the chapter, Dr. Greist wrote: "You might add this point. When I talked to her, Mrs. Rogers said, 'Will looked very natural. The children and I stood at his open casket until it was finally closed.' "

A reader may ask why Will had such a frog sticker of a knife. It was because he liked, at the studio, to play "drop knife." It is a kind of sight-unseen swap. The two players drop their knives on the ground, and each picks up another's knife. It was a favorite game of his. When he came out on top, he would laugh loudly and delightedly; when he got a poor knife he would be cast down about it, for he played the game as seriously as some men play poker.

Rex Beach wrote two articles for the Associated Press dealing with the Juneau and Fairbanks experiences.

Stanley R. Morgan is now a captain in the U. S. Army; his home address is 1707 North 185 Street, Seattle, Washington.

This chapter was read in manuscript form by Colonel Charles A. Lindbergh.

The information about how Betty Rogers got the news is based on talks with Grant Mills, Mr. and Mrs. Owen Davis and Humphrey Bogart. Humphrey Bogart said that when Betty Rogers was told the news she cried, "I did not want him to go on that trip."

A point in passing: on word of Will's death the Fox Film stock fell from 16¾ to 15½.

An official investigation was made as to the cause of the accident. This is what the Accident Board of the Bureau of Air Commerce reported, September 21, that year:

"The airplane, at the time of purchase by Wiley Post, was a Lockheed Orion, model 9–E, and bore a Department of Commerce license. The plane was completely rebuilt and several major changes incorporated which changed it from its original model. The engine, propeller, wings and fuel tank were completely changed. The remodeling was inspected and approved for workmanship by the Department of Commerce and Restricted License Number NR–12283 was issued. Mr. Post held a Department of Commerce temporary pilot license. At Seattle pontoons were substituted. No inspection was requested.

"A study of the various changes made indicated that the plane was decidedly nose-heavy and must have been extremely difficult, if not impossible, to control properly without the aid of the engine.

"The temperature was about 40 degrees. The failure could have been due to the engine having become cool while standing on the lagoon, or to ice water condensate forming in the carburetor.

"It is the opinion of the Accident Board that the probable cause of the accident was loss of control after sudden engine failure, due to the extreme nose-heaviness of the aircraft."

One of Will's watches stopped at 3:15. (It has a St. Regis trademark.)

The other stopped at 6:24. (This has a Pocket Ben-Westclox trademark.)

Both watches are in a showcase in the Memorial at Claremore. A few years ago a woman rushed in great excitement to Mrs. Paula M. Love (Will's niece and in charge of the exhibit) and said that she had been standing in front of the showcase looking at the watches when suddenly one of them had started to run. This was impossible. But when Mrs. Love went to the showcase, there, sure enough! one of the watches was eerily ticking away. This strange phenomenon, it was discovered, had been caused by the jarring of a power lawn mower just outside the window.

The fascinating figures about the tonnage reception accorded different returning heroes were furnished by the Department of Sanitation, 125 Worth Street, New York.

The Memorial broadcast was over the Blue Network, August 16, 1935, at night from ten until eleven, New York time. Those on the Hollywood part were, Will Hayes, Darryl F. Zanuck, Ruth Etting, Roscoe Turner, Fred Stone.

The poem by Ada Jackson originally appeared in *This Week,* September 29, 1935; it is reprinted here by permission of the author.

CHAPTER 28

The sources are shown in the material.

The statue of "brave" Balto still stands in Central Park, New York. Every day admiring children come to see it.

At the time of the crash, Will was getting $110,000 for each picture. The new contract called for more, as shown elsewhere.

CHAPTER 29

The story of Will's paying a valet to stay away was carried by the Associated Press, February 20, 1935.

The production manager who passed along the information about the alarm clock was Paul La Porte, now with the Maxon Advertising Agency, 12 East 53 Street, New York.

Personal to all who helped me: you number a hundred, I'm sure; to you a thousand thanks (a small down payment on my vast indebtedness) and a heart bursting with gratitude.

Index

* * *

Now that I am at the final, the absolute, the unchangeable end, I feel a sense of inadequacy. I think of many things I didn't do; for one, I had an appointment to interview Dorothy Gish, but didn't bring it about. I think of other people I should have seen, but didn't. I think of phases of Will's life that I dealt with sketchily and of some that I'm sure, now, that I dealt with in too much detail. But under the circumstances I've done the best I could. That is my rock and there I must build my house.

H. C.

* * *